OLAF GEORG KLEIN

SUDDENLY EVERYTHING
WAS DIFFERENT

GERMAN LIVES IN UPHEAVAL

Translated by
Ann McGlashan

Edited with an Introduction and Annotations by
Dwight D. Allman

CAMDEN HOUSE
Rochester, New York

First published 2007 by Camden House

Camden House is an imprint of Boydell & Brewer Inc.
668 Mt. Hope Avenue, Rochester, NY 14620, USA
www.camden-house.com
and of Boydell & Brewer Limited
PO Box 9, Woodbridge, Suffolk IP12 3DF, UK
www.boydellandbrewer.com

ISBN-13: 978–1–57113–369–4
ISBN-10: 1–57113–369–0

Originally published as *Plötzlich war alles ganz anders: Deutsche
Lebenswege im Umbruch,* © Kiepenheuer & Witsch, Cologne, 1994

Library of Congress Cataloging-in-Publication Data

Klein, Olaf G., 1955–
    [Plötzlich war alles ganz anders. English]
    Suddenly everything was different: German lives in upheaval / Olaf
Georg Klein; translated by Ann McGlashan; edited with an introduction
and annotations by Dwight D. Allman.
        p. cm.
    Includes bibliographical references and index.
    ISBN-13: 978–1–57113–369–4 (pbk.: alk. paper)
    ISBN-10: 1–57113–369–0 (pbk.: alk. paper)
        1. Germany—Social conditions—1990—Public opinion.
    2. Germany—Economic conditions—1990—Public opinion.
    3. Germany—History—Unification, 1990—Public opinion.   4. Public
opinion—Germany.   5. Interviews—Germany.   I. Allman, Dwight
David, 1957–   II. Title.
HN445.5.K53413 2007
306.0943'109049—dc22
                                                        2007003494

A catalogue record for this title is available from the British Library.

This publication is printed on acid-free paper.
Printed in the United States of America.

CONTENTS

INTRODUCTION

Dwight D. Allman

History and German Identity

NO NATION HAS BEEN more consumed with, if not also by, the problem of history than has Germany. On the one hand, the historical saga of the German nation-state confronts contemporary Germans with a particularly grim experience of the modern world. Conceived strictly as a theoretical matter, however, the problem of history spoke German before it spoke any other language. In the nineteenth century, German scholars tutored European civilization in how "to think historically." In philosophy, philology, literary criticism, sociology, and theology, for example, German thinkers introduced new categories, frameworks, and modes of approach that recast the study of humanity and society in ways that gave special prominence to the question of history. And with its pioneering inquiries into the unfolding secrets of history, nineteenth-century German thought and scholarship held out to the world the prospect of a fully modern vantage point. Not only other Europeans, but Americans too trekked dutifully to the centers of German learning to sample the waters of high modernity. Speaking as much for his generation as for himself, Henry Adams rightly observed, "All serious scholars were obliged to become German, for German thought was revolutionizing criticism."[1]

Early in the twentieth century, however, the dawning promise of the German modernity seemed to turn suddenly into that dark night of which Nietzsche's "madman" warns when he appears in the town square searching frenziedly for a sun that no longer shines.[2] It is German expressionism, in turn, with its lurid colors, cinematic shadows, and leering focus, that perhaps best documents the disenchantment that the Great War imprinted upon European consciousness. The turbulent years of the Weimar Republic (1919–33) would see a war-ravaged Germany become the avant-garde home of almost every form of anti-modernism. With the catastrophe of Hitler, which underscored among other things the monumental failure of the German nation-state founded in 1871 to achieve a viable modern politics for itself, an entirely new historical sensibility was born — history as inexpressible and collective moral burden. In particular, West

Germans who came of age after the war found the question of citizenship in the Federal Republic (FRG) inextricably entangled in the problem of negotiating the Nazi past. No other European polity has experienced a public life so dominated by anguished memory, not to mention the abiding sense that every humane aspiration directing its contemporary statecraft was already mortgaged to the genocidal horrors of the past. This consciousness of historical burden always remained in the foreground of the West German self-understanding, anchored perhaps in a collective embrace of the idea that the Nazi era represented an undeniably German event. It continues, moreover, to shape the politics and policies of a united Germany today, and by extension every common approach to the question of what it means to be German. And thus have the sins of the fathers been visited manifold upon the children, not least in the form of a historical legacy that still serves as the index of evil for a postmodern world.

In the East, history was also a perpetual concern. But the communist regime in the Soviet zone sought to establish itself, in effect, as the realization of the best elements of the German tradition. Leapfrogging the problem of a post-Nazi political and cultural identity, it traced fascism, on the one hand, to sources that were not essentially German, and equated socialism, on the other, with the international march of the working class and the modern forces propelling German history. German communists had, after all, opposed the Nazis in the name both of the universal interests of workers worldwide and, perhaps more meaningfully, of an authentic German identity, culture, and nation. In the German Democratic Republic (GDR), in turn, Hitler's Reich was officially written off as imperialistic capitalism at its most raw, while the governors of the regime represented their own reign as the vindicating *telos* towards which German history had long stumbled. One consequence was that East Germans found it possible to evolve a much less conflicted version of German identity than West Germans. In fact, a *völkisch*[3] attachment to the *Vaterland* remained very much alive in the East, even though Marxist-Leninist ideology officially relegated nationalism to an earlier stage of the historical struggle for the universal society. In the West, by contrast, the quest for identity led away from the notion of a peculiar German *Volk* in the direction of a cosmopolitanism animated by the ideal of "the good European." When the walls enclosing the GDR finally crumbled, however, both *Ossis* (East Germans) and *Wessis* (West Germans) found themselves confronted by the realization that the workers' utopia had somehow become another version of the nightmare that haunts modern German history.

Nevertheless, in the first decade of the twenty-first century, Germany is once again a unified state, a dominant presence in the heart of Europe, and seemingly on its way to becoming a stable, modern, constitutional republic, finally bringing to fruition hopes stretching back almost two centuries. Challenges, however, abound. And chief among them is the melding together of East and West into a cohesive entity whose political, economic, and cultural seams do not merely trace the outlines of the former division. Recent public-opinion research indicates that support for the idea of democracy is in decline among former citizens of the GDR, many of whom now hold a negative view of German unification.[4] At stake may be not only the question of whether a united Germany will fully realize itself as a vibrant society, but also the hopes for a genuine integration of East and West within the new constellation of post-cold-war Europe. For the present, it seems, the future of Germany as a fully functional nation-state remains ransomed to its past, especially to forty years of German history bifurcated between East and West.

It is therefore likely that the future will be shaped in large part by the extent to which, and the ways in which, present generations undertake to negotiate the past, to explore the question of who they really are as a prelude to inquiring who they might become. These broad, albeit urgent, questions underlie the framework within which Olaf Georg Klein sets the concrete reflections of *Suddenly Everything Was Different*. Klein encircles the reader with twelve discrete accounts of the experience of life in the GDR, the simultaneously exhilarating and traumatic prospect of its dissolution, and the tangle of aspirations, hopes, and disappointments resulting from its absorption into West Germany's Federal Republic. The overlapping reflections of these different voices suggest a dialogue that the reader is invited to mediate, one animated in a central way by a desire to comprehend the full historical import of the East German (if not also, the Eastern European) experiment in communism. The significance of that past and its possible relation to the future marks the circumference within which the dialogue that Klein has captured takes place. Klein, it must be said, understands himself not as a historian, social theorist, or philosopher but as an artist who conceives of his book as a work of literature. The book stands, as such, well enough on its own merits, an unmistakable and possibly unrivaled example of *Dokumentarliteratur*. As the eminent scholar of East German literature Wolfgang Emmerich has noted in his acclaimed compendium, *Kleine Literaturgeschichte der DDR,* Klein's book ranks as one of the best in the genre of *Wendeliteratur*.[5]

It would be a mistake, however, to segregate Klein in his achievements as writer and artist from the field of practical affairs, where active men and women who would improve upon the past roll up their sleeves and apply themselves to present challenges. A hallmark of the artistic life as pursued by many in that bloc of states tethered to the former Soviet Union was the depth of its political seriousness. It is in Eastern Europe that the classical connection between art and the quest for a truly just and humane life has been perhaps most fully preserved. It is certainly from the

East that the image of the artist-statesman has been made visible again for western eyes. Václav Havel, the first president of the Czech Republic, whose own artistic labors have consistently expressed a civic spiritedness animated by a deep acquaintance with the problem of justice, is only the most well-known example. Consider the terms in which Havel has summed up the wisdom of his very serious and political life: "I daresay that the basic political lesson taught to us by life under communism is the recognition that the only kind of politics that makes sense is a politics that grows out of the imperative, and the need, to live as everyone ought to live and therefore — to put it somewhat dramatically — to bear responsibility for the entire world."[6]

A kindred seriousness is evident in Klein's own preface to this book, when he speaks of the reasons behind its writing, including an encompassing concern with certain questions: "How was living a fulfilled, humane life made difficult, if not impossible, back then, and is it still the same today? How aware of this are we? And how does each individual deal with such things? What promises and hopes spur us on? In the final analysis, what will remain when we look back on it all?"[7] Here we confront a version of the question that has prompted political-philosophical reflection on the right ordering of human society at least since Socrates; a question that springs, it would seem, from the conviction that our humanity has essential dimensions, involving more than the material requisites of bodily existence, by which we take the measure of a truly *good* politics. It is an orientation rooted in what Czeslaw Milosz, another artist whose moral seriousness derives from a confrontation with the pervasive soulcraft exercised by the state in the former Soviet system, describes as the hard-won "discovery" for which "the suffering of millions of human beings terrorized by totalitarian governments" paid the ransom, namely, that there is "a clear line dividing good from evil, truth from lie."[8]

Growing Up with the GDR

Born in 1955, Olaf Georg Klein grew up in communist East Berlin. His biography encompasses most of the history of the German Democratic Republic, which came into existence just six years before him in October 1949. A review of Klein's life and times can therefore serve also to introduce readers to the important events that serve as the backdrop for his documentary-literary account of the uncertainty, disorientation, and self-revelation precipitated by the dissolution of one nation and the inception of another.

A particularly important event that occurred in Klein's homeland prior to his birth was a 1953 strike initiated by Berlin construction workers against low wages and a government-mandated increase in work norms. Demonstrations in Berlin spawned similar protests by industrial workers across the GDR. Although spurred on by matters of economic policy, workers also called for the release of political prisoners, free elections, and the ousting of Walter Ulbricht — a Soviet-trained German communist who became the unrivaled leader of the ruling Socialist Unity Party (SED) with his election as First Secretary of the Party in 1950. The "June Uprising," as the strike came to be called, quickly grew into a nation-wide event involving hundreds of thousands of protesters. By 17 June, the second day of the uprising, a crisis threatening to bring down the fledgling regime had fully evolved. Some three hundred thousand East German workers were in revolt against the "workers' state." Perplexed and desperate, East German officials responded with a declaration of martial law, and with Soviet tank patrols to impose and to enforce it.

A second crisis for the regime came to a head in 1961. The status of Berlin, the former German capital that had been carved up by the occupying powers after the war, remained an unsettled and divisive question throughout the 1950s. In 1958, Soviet leader Nikita Khrushchev therefore decided to present the Western powers with an ultimatum: Berlin, now divided into an eastern sector under Soviet control, which functioned as the capital of the GDR, and a self-standing western sector under the protection of the Western allies, was to become a unified, but neutral and demilitarized city. Access to this independent city, however, would be left in the hands of the GDR, and thus under the ultimate control of the Soviet Union. Khrushchev threatened, moreover, to impose this arrangement unilaterally if the Western powers did not proceed within six months. In the end, Khrushchev backed away from his threat to resolve in single-handed fashion the question of Berlin. Tensions between East and West, however, had been considerably heightened, exacerbating in turn the internal situation of the GDR, especially as social and economic conditions deteriorated over the next few years.

Emigration from the GDR to West Germany rose significantly in 1960, and even more precipitously in the first months of 1961, as the campaign to collectivize industry and agriculture, and to centralize economic power in the ruling government, resulted in a deterioration of economic infra-structure as well as severe shortages of consumer goods. So-called "re-cruitment teams" (*Werbetrupps*) sent out by the government in 1958–59 to persuade farmers of the advantages of transferring control of their properties to state-run collective farms subjected reluctant individuals to blackmail, coercion, and the threat of imprisonment. And Khrushchev's reiteration in June 1961 of his determination to settle the Berlin question on Soviet terms roused new fears that access to West Berlin might be suddenly cut off. As more and more East Germans packed up for the West, a sense of panic began to spread among those left behind. By early summer, emigration totals approached fifty thousand a month, which included a disproportionate number of young, technically skilled workers, whose flight promised to make only more critical the already serious labor shortage. Officials in the GDR had to confront the possibility that mass emigration on this scale would lead to economic collapse. Erich Honecker, the official who oversaw the closing of the border, would later justify the regime's action by characterizing it as a necessary response to "an unprecedented economic war" launched by the imperialist powers of capitalism in an attempt "to bleed our republic to death."[9] Olaf Klein was six years old in August 1961 when the world he inhabited was abruptly sealed off and confined behind the Berlin Wall — a structure that would come to symbolize, of course, the extent to which Soviet-bloc governments sought to exercise a totalitarian control over their citizens.

In that same year, Klein began his formal education. He excelled at his studies and was afforded the opportunity to extend his schooling beyond the mandatory ten-year "polytechnical school" for several years of additional course work followed by the *Abitur*, a diploma awarded on the basis of comprehensive exams certifying an individual's suitability for higher education. Despite this achievement, Klein would face opposition from the state in pursuing his ambition to enroll at university. In August 1968, as Klein was in his thirteenth year, Warsaw Pact forces, including two divisions from the GDR, entered Czechoslovakia to suppress the indigenous reform movement that had blossomed during what came to be called "Prague Spring." The invasion of Czechoslovakia would play a formative role in Klein's political development. In 1971, Erich Honecker replaced Walter Ulbricht as First Secretary (a position later retitled General Secretary) of the governing Socialist Unity Party, followed in 1976 by his formal designation as head of state. Honecker would occupy this position of preeminent authority for almost 20 years, until the final days of the regime, his somber visage becoming for the world the public face of the GDR. Upon receipt of the *Abitur* in 1974, Klein was conscripted into the military. Since 1962 the GDR had required all males between eighteen and twenty-six to serve a term in its National People's Army. Long conversations with a soldier who had been deployed to Czechoslovakia, however, had convinced Klein that he could not allow himself to be co-opted into a military force that was more likely to be used against student protesters in other Warsaw Pact states, or even his fellow citizens, than in any legitimate defensive action.

Klein's refusal to do military service cost him his chance at a university degree in anything but theology, where the Church retained its historical control over curriculum and admission. He was consigned, moreover, to a period of internment as a "construction soldier" (*Bausoldat*). Branded an "enemy of the state" (*Staatsfeind*), Klein was issued a clownish uniform with shovels on the epaulettes to stigmatize his status and required to carry out the most revolting assignments military officials could dream up. It was at this point in his life that he began to devote himself seriously to writing. The exercise of his literary skills became, as he has expressed it, a kind of "survival-training" (*Überlebenstraining*) in coping with the torments inflicted upon him by the regime he had come to oppose. While Klein was serving out his time as *Bausoldat,* the Honecker government found itself besieged by criticism arising from its expatriation of a notable intellectual and cultural figure. Wolf Biermann immigrated to East Germany in 1953 out of sympathy for its socialist aims, studied philosophy at Humboldt University in East Berlin, and rapidly became culturally prominent as a balladeer whose satirical and politically charged songs were often critical of the regime. Banned from singing in public for eleven years, Biermann was allowed finally to perform again at a Protestant religious service in 1976. In that same year, he was invited by a West German labor union to take part in a concert tour that the union was sponsoring. He sought and received permission from East German authorities to travel to West Germany in order to participate in the event. Once he had departed the country, however, East German officials announced that Biermann would not be allowed to return to the GDR. The expulsion of Biermann provoked an unprecedented reaction from the nation's intelligentsia. Twelve of East Germany's most celebrated writers composed an open letter to the Honecker government in protest of its actions. Some of these individuals held leading positions within the officially sanctioned Writer's Union, through which the GDR sought to cultivate the literary arts. Copies of the letter were eventually signed by hundreds of individuals, including many of the most important intellectuals and artists in the GDR. The regime retaliated with significant disciplinary action against more than a hundred people, placing some under house arrest, while expelling others from the SED and the Writer's Union or forcing them to emigrate. The "Biermann Affair" marked a low point in relations between political authorities and the cultural elite of the GDR, stoking at the same time the fires of protest and opposition that would flare up in unprecedented ways over the next decade.

After an eighteen-month stint as *Bausoldat,* Klein was allowed to return to civilian life, where he again risked legal sanction by attending lectures at Humboldt University without being enrolled. During these years, he also made the acquaintance of Robert Havemann, a physicist at Humboldt, who had been expelled from the University in 1964 for a series of lectures proffering a Marxist critique of the GDR regime. One of the most prominent dissidents and critics of social and political life in the GDR, Havemann had been placed under house arrest in 1976 for his forceful condemnation of the expulsion of Biermann. Contact with Havemann led

Klein to sharpen his own critique of the political order. In 1978, the Honecker government announced that a course of practical and theoretical training in military science would hereafter be compulsory for all students between the ages of 14 and 16. The new policy confirmed the apprehensions of many that life in the GDR was undergoing an increasing militarization, a development that became a catalyst for the emergence of an autonomous peace movement. And Klein, who had long held the view that the military forces of the GDR represented more menace to than security for its citizenry, was quick to associate himself with the fledgling peace movement.

In 1979, the peace movement picked up steam as debates in West Germany prompted by NATO's plan to deploy 108 Pershing II nuclear missiles within its territory captured public attention in the GDR as well. There were only a few places in East Germany from which one could not receive broadcasts of West German television with a conventional antenna. That year the Soviet Union also sent troops into Afghanistan to shore up a pro-Soviet government beset by a fundamentalist Muslim insurgency. The move rekindled cold-war tensions between the NATO allies and Warsaw Pact nations, derailing the détente of the 1970s. Meanwhile, Klein began a course of study in Protestant theology at a Humboldt University, concentrating on the works of the existentialist theologian Paul Tillich. He likewise became increasingly productive as a writer, composing numerous short stories, several of which found their way into publication.

The first year of the 1980s witnessed the emergence of *Solidariność* (Solidarity), the independent Polish labor movement that challenged the monolithic economic and political powers of the communist government in Poland. Officials in the GDR responded with vehement denunciations of the movement, which seemed to betray considerable anxiety that it might ignite a similar revolt within their own borders. Around this time, Klein undertook to deliver a series of lectures to groups of peace activists and fellow dissidents on the methods of non-violent resistance. His activities drew the unwelcome notice of the Stasi, East Germany's State Security Service, which began continuous surveillance of his movements and affairs. Thereafter, frequent reminders of the encompassing powers of the East German state punctuated his life. The GDR maintained a secret police force of some fifty thousand full-time agents, who assembled, in turn, a vast network of "unofficial co-workers," or informants. The regime sought to use this massive intelligence-gathering apparatus to pervade every corner of East German society in an effort to insure its unfettered control. Klein, to whom the Stasi assigned the codename *Querulant* (malcontent), regularly had his mail confiscated and was periodically ushered into custody for interrogation and intimidation sessions. The Stasi, however, carried out many other, more sinister assignments, including torture of political prisoners, attempted sabotage of West German nuclear power plants, and even the facilitating of terrorist enterprises in Western Europe by the Red Army faction.[10]

Completing his theological studies at Humboldt University in 1984, Klein became an assistant to the seminary faculty at the *Evangelische Akademie Berlin-Brandenburg*. In this capacity, he organized the first public conference in the GDR devoted to Sigmund Freud. Klein also began to devote himself more intensively to his writing. In 1985, he composed a radio drama entitled *Freiheit und Abschied des Herrn von Kleist* (*Freedom and Farewell of Mr. von Kleist*) concerned with the final days in the life of the acclaimed nineteenth-century playwright and novella writer Heinrich von Kleist. In the wreck of Kleist's life upon the feudalistic shoals of nineteenth-century Prussia, Klein found an allegorical way to illuminate the brutalizing character of social life in the GDR. The program was broadcast in 1986. Klein's use of a historical setting and a major figure from the canon of German literature as devices for exploring a subject matter that he knew government censors would not permit him to tackle directly illustrates the rhetorical texture that necessarily characterizes the serious literature from the former communist states.[11] The fact that the literary arts flourished in Soviet-bloc countries like the GDR sheds perhaps a complex light on the institutional guarantees of free speech, which Americans rightly prize so highly. It appears that such guarantees are not, as we often seem to believe, a sufficient condition of a politically serious and morally engaged life. Surely one of the lessons for the West arising from the history of Eastern Europe is that a rich public culture develops as much from substantive ideals, commitments, and traditions as from formal structures and institutional arrangements. Perhaps, at the same time, this history should highlight for us the dangers posed to public culture and vitality by a marketplace that relentlessly commercializes every common space and activity.

The rupture of a nuclear reactor at the Chernobyl power plant near Kiev in April 1986 made suddenly tangible the fear of many Europeans that this technology posed dangers international in their scope and genocidal in their potential. The disaster led Klein to apply his creative energies to issues the affair brought poignantly into focus. For the next two years, he labored to produce his first novel, *Nachzeit,* now translated and published in English as *Aftertime* (1999).[12] Set against one of the technological nightmares of our nuclear age, the novel concerns itself most immediately with the personal tragedy of a young German woman who is studying in Kiev when the nuclear reactor at a nearby plant explodes. She must subsequently come to terms with the consequences of her exposure to the fallout from this disaster, including her inability to bear children and the prospect of wasting slowly and painfully away. On another level, however, the novel suggests an allegorical treatment of the entanglement of East

Germany with the descending industrial and environmental course of the Soviet Union and its bloc of states. Small but independent groups concerned with ecological issues proliferated in the GDR over the first half of the 1980s, prompted by a growing recognition of the acute state of environmental degradation in certain regions of the country. And in response to the Chernobyl disaster, more than ten thousand citizens were emboldened to sign a petition that called for a referendum on the use of nuclear power in the GDR.[13] By 1988, however, as Klein was finishing work on *Nachzeit,* the course of events had advanced along a path all but unimaginable a few years earlier.

The Revolution of 1989

The introduction by Mikhail Gorbachev of the term *perestroika* into the active vocabularies of Eastern Europeans in 1986 laid the groundwork for a breathtaking series of political events, the most dramatic of which would include the dismantling of the Berlin Wall and the peaceful unification of the two Germanys. Almost immediately upon assuming the leadership of the USSR in 1985, Gorbachev set about to reform its laggard economy with a radical set of strategies packaged together around the idea of *perestroika* — a comprehensive "restructuring" of the political and economic spheres of the communist system in the interest of accelerating material progress and finally actualizing the promise of the Bolshevik Revolution. One of the strategies, or reforms, encompassed by Gorbachev's concept of *perestroika* was that of "public criticism," what Gorbachev termed *glasnost,* which promised an openness of government officials to the criticisms of individual citizens and interest groups.[14]

This campaign for a restructuring of the Soviet system posed a direct threat to the old-guard communist leadership of Eastern Europe, since the authority of those leaders based itself on rigid state and party structures and on their hierarchies of patronage, which were a principal object of Gorbachev's strategy for reform. At the same time, the call for *glasnost* emboldened reformers within the different Soviet-bloc states in their determination to challenge existing configurations of power. Officials in the GDR were among the most resistant to Gorbachev's campaign for change. They had good reason to fear that the end of one-party authoritarian rule, in perpetual ideological opposition to the Federal Republic, would imperil the very idea of an independent East German state. The GDR represented, after all, a unique political order within the Soviet bloc in that its boundaries in no way corresponded to traditional linguistic-cultural or ethnic cleavages. The FRG, moreover, had emphasized at its inception that it was merely a provisional arrangement, in lieu of an encompassing resolution and unified nation-state, and had always extended its citizenship to every resident within the territory of the former German Reich, making West German citizenship immediately available to the citizens of the GDR.[15]

The wave of reform, however, swept quickly through neighboring Poland and Hungary. In January 1989, the Polish government agreed to negotiate with leaders of the outlawed Solidarity organization in an effort to ameliorate political and economic problems linked to the government's 1981 imposition of martial law. By the end of June, a Solidarity member had been elected prime minister. Hungary, in the meantime, gave a green light to the formation of opposition parties and opened its western border with Austria.[16] East Germans soon discovered that they could enter Hungary, a fellow Warsaw Pact country to which travel was unimpeded, slip across the border into Austria, and make their way to West Germany. Unlike their East German counterparts, Hungarian border guards did not operate under orders to shoot-to-kill anyone trying to flee the country. They did, however, attempt to turn East Germans back in accordance with a longstanding official agreement; increasing numbers nevertheless found their way out. When Hungary staged a pan-European festival in late August to celebrate the opening of its border with Austria, some seven hundred East Germans showed up uninvited, taking advantage of the occasion to scurry into Austria. By the end of August, more than four thousand East Germans had made their way through Hungary to the West. In September, a frustrated government in Budapest suspended its agreement with the GDR to deter its citizens from escaping across Hungary's borders. East Germans began pouring by the thousands into Austria. When officials in the GDR, desperate to stop the flow, announced an end to travel permits for Hungary, East Germans began flooding into Czechoslovakia and then Poland, where they scaled the fences around the West German embassies in Prague and Warsaw. When overcrowding at the West German embassy in Prague created a sanitation crisis, East German officials finally agreed to allow the seven thousand refugees to emigrate, but only after traveling in locked trains through East German territory so that the regime could properly claim to have "expelled" them.

The evident weakness of the regime also emboldened those within the GDR more intent on reform of the existing state than on its dissolution. In mid-September, a collection of such activists organized "New Forum" and became the first opposition group to apply for formal recognition. A principal spokesperson for the group was the artist-activist Bärbel Bohley. Soon thereafter, she was summoned to the Ministry of the Interior, where authorities explained that New Forum could not register as an opposition party because there was no social necessity for such a party in the GDR. But Bohley and her colleagues would not be deterred. Having set up branches of New Forum in eleven of the fifteen governmental districts in the GDR, they courageously pressed ahead with plans for a first congress, which convened on 24 September in Leipzig.[17] Other critics and opponents of the regime followed suit, as a jumble of new political parties such as the "Democratic Awakening" (*Demokratischer Aufbruch*) and the SDP (*Sozialdemokratische Partei*) organized themselves over the next few weeks. For his part, Olaf Georg Klein joined forces early on with New Forum and played a leading role on the governing council of the branch established in Berlin.

On the day after New Forum staged its first congress, a demonstration involving more than five thousand people took place in Leipzig. Small demonstrations growing out of a traditional Monday-night vespers service and peace vigil at St. Nicholas Church (*Nikolaikirche*) had occurred earlier. On 25 September, however, peace activists were reinforced by those protesting the denial of official recognition to New Forum. Ever larger protest marches against the Honecker regime became weekly events in Leipzig, connected to the Monday services at the *Nikolaikirche*. Dresden, another center of the opposition movement, also saw regular demonstrations, but it was in Leipzig that these events first coalesced into a full-fledged popular revolt.

Gorbachev himself showed up in the first week of October, invited to help celebrate the fortieth anniversary of the GDR. He urged Honecker to set a course of reform, drawing on a Russian proverb to warn his East German counterpart: "Life punishes those who arrive too late." On 7 October, Gorbachev and other foreign dignitaries stood by Honecker on the review stand to witness the traditional parade of military equipment and goose-stepping soldiers. Afterwards they gathered at a government building adjacent to the Alexanderplatz, a central square in East Berlin, for a reception. Opposition groups, however, staged their own parade to commemorate the anniversary. Despite a heavy police presence, several thousand protesters marched from the Alexanderplatz towards the Palace of the Republic, where the reception for foreign leaders was being held. Hundreds of policemen in riot gear were summoned to form a human wall blocking the marchers' progress towards the reception. Once dignitaries had been shuttled off to the airport, police moved in, forcing the crowd to disperse and arresting some of the protesters.

A third protest march was slated for 9 October in Leipzig, even though local SED leaders had publicized their intentions "to restore law and order," with force if necessary. On everyone's lips was the question: "Will it happen like it did in China?,"[18] where communist authorities had quashed demonstrations in Tiananmen Square just months before with a show of force that left hundreds dead. By the time of the evening vespers service, over seventy thousand people had massed in and around the *Nikolaikirche*. Extra police units, backed up by SED militia units (*Kampfgruppen*) had also been strategically deployed. The stage had been set for a showdown that promised to have a decisive influence on how the unfolding challenge to the regime would proceed: with bloody conflict, escalating violence, perhaps civil war, or with unprecedented calm, constructive dialogue, and nonviolent transition. Looking to history (1989 also marked the two-hundredth anniversary of the original modern revolution in Europe, which had culminated in a bloody Reign of Terror), could lead one only to despair, since in its light a peaceful outcome seemed almost too much to hope for.

On to this stage, at the decisive moment, stepped one of East Germany's most prominent citizens: the internationally renowned conductor of Leipzig's *Gewandhaus Orchestra,* Kurt Masur. Over the weeks during which the showdown between protesters and representatives of the regime had been building to a climax, Masur and his orchestra had been rehearsing in another corner of the city's main square for a recording of Beethoven's third symphony — the *Eroica.* Their production of this symphony, inspired by the great composer's attachment to the ideals of 1789, had been complicated by the distraction that events at the *Nikolaikirche* posed. At the same time, Masur and his fellow musicians felt increasingly burdened by the historical and moral weight of the *Eroica* in light of what was unfolding before them. On Monday afternoon, as crowds began to gather for the evening vesper service, Masur used his influence to bring the local leadership of the SED together with the pastor of the *Nikolaikirche* to sign a document promising not to use violence if the demonstration remained peaceful. The document was read to the mass of protesters and police during the evening service and the subsequent demonstration transpired without incident. Masur's heroics were later credited with having defused the situation and with paving the way for the opening of dialogue between government officials and reform activists.[19] While these events offered perhaps the most inspiring example of the initiative exercised by individual citizens in hopes of avoiding the blood and violence with which history has usually framed political upheaval, they were hardly unique. Repeated instances of mass events that defied historical expectations marked the German Revolution of 1989.

Facing an outbreak of large protests and an on-going exodus to West Germany, government officials felt pressured at the same time by their Soviet sponsor to take seriously the demands for reform. Demonstrations continued to spread and to strengthen as more and more individuals filled the streets chanting, "*Wir* sind das Volk!" (*We* are the people!). With their intonation protestors gave particular emphasis to *wir* (we), thereby drawing implicit attention to the opposing *ihr* (you) of the ruling party, which had long presumed to speak in the name of the *Volk.* By mid-October a full-scale grassroots revolution was plainly underway. On 18 October,

Honecker was forced out as General Secretary and replaced by a younger protégé, Egon Krenz. Momentum behind the broad-based uprising, however, would not be quelled by a simple shuffling of chairs within the ruling SED, especially as it became ever more evident that the Soviet Union would not intervene in the situation. Increasing divisions within and defections from the SED (between October and December over a million members left the party) likewise suggested that authorities would be hard pressed to find subordinates willing to carry out any orders that risked violence.

On 4 November, the largest demonstration in GDR history convened on the Alexanderplatz in East Berlin. At least half a million people turned out to hear an eclectic gathering of critics voice their discontent with the regime and call for reforms — in particular, a liberalization of restrictions on travel. Unlike previous protest rallies, this demonstration had received official approval from an increasingly compliant Krenz regime, which had also authorized live television and radio coverage of the event to demonstrate its seriousness about reform. On Monday, 6 November, two days after the demonstration, the government announced a new travel law; the next day the forty-four-member politburo, the governing body of the SED, resigned en masse. The way had been cleared for Krenz to begin piecing together a new, reform-minded government composed of the party members most closely identified with the cause of *perestroika*. At the same time came an invitation to leaders of New Forum to begin registering their organization. On Thursday evening, 9 November, SED media chief Günter Schabowski somewhat prematurely declared that the government had decided to open its borders with West Germany, including the Berlin Wall. What followed will no doubt forever stand as one of the most poignant scenes in German history: East Berliners, some giddy with excitement, others undone by a complex of unfamiliar emotions, poured into West Berlin; friends and families fell into each other's arms after years of division; and jubilant youths danced on top of the Wall.

Despite frantic efforts to win the confidence of the East German people, Krenz was unable to keep his government floating atop a cresting wave of new expectations, criticisms, and demands. Reports that party officials used public money to finance comfortable villas and private hunting reserves for themselves created irresistible pressure for the party to relinquish its hold on the state. On 6 December Krenz resigned "in the interest of stability," marking the end of communist rule in Germany, if not also of the GDR itself. Hans Modrow, a reformist member of the SED installed by Krenz, remained as prime minister, but the regime that controlled the GDR for forty years had collapsed. For the next several months a skeleton government headed up by Modrow administered the powers of state, as SED officials, dissident intellectuals, and opposition party leaders debated the immediate course and future configuration of East Germany in round-table discussions. Having played a key role in the Berlin chapter of New Forum from its institution, Klein also took part in these discussions. Mounting economic problems and threats of unrest convinced officials and opposition leaders that free elections should take place as soon as possible. On 18 March the GDR held its first (and last) genuine parliamentary elections. Results made it clear that an overwhelming majority of East Germans desired unification with the Federal Republic. A coalition of parties linked to the Christian Democratic Union (CDU) and Social Democratic Party of Germany (SPD), the dominant parties of West Germany, received better than three-quarters of the vote and formed a coalition government that served until formal unification in October 1990.[20]

Suddenly Everything Was Different

Olaf Klein's literary treatment of what Germans call the *Wende,* the protracted collapse of the GDR under the press of a popular revolution followed by the eventual unification of the two Germanys, grew out of a research project in which he became involved not long after formal unification occurred. A group of scholars and social scientists organized a team to interview East Germans in an effort to document their views and emerging self-understanding in the wake of these events. When the undertaking bogged down in methodological disputes, Klein took his leave of the scholars and set to work on a novel, using the interviews he had conducted as a painter might use a photograph to help orient him in crafting a work that is at once more comprehensive and comprehending than the image in the photograph.

The book has the aspect of a documentary film (the enterprise after which *Dokumentarliteratur* self-consciously styles itself) in which a series of representative types narrate their experiences and views to an interviewer never seen or heard. Through his art, however, Klein silently makes his presence known. The language by which each voice reveals itself unfolds a dynamic understanding that shifts, turns, deepens, and expands before us on the page. At the same time, Klein has different characters recollect many of the same events, providing competing perspectives that call on us as readers to mediate the implicit dialogue suggested by these interlocking monologues. These recollections, of course, all take place at a specific moment in time, shortly after East Germans became a part of a unified Germany in October 1990. Klein would thus compel his readers to wrestle with this history, believing that through this activity memory can be made to serve a future that overcomes the past rather than one perpetually overcome by it.

The various accounts that make up Klein's portrait of life in and after the GDR are intimately concerned with a history and a social-political order that may not be well known to many in the English-speaking world. In keeping with the educational spirit of documentary film, we have thus tried to make the text as accessible as possible with the adjoining apparatus. Detailed annotations contained at the back of the volume, in addition to this historical overview, should help the reader gain entry into the world of the former East Germany. Words, concepts, events, and challenges of translation explained in the annotations are organized by chapter and page number in the section that follows the text (see page 159, below). Each annotation is preceded by the page number and a brief quotation from the text to signal what passage the annotation concerns. The task of annotating each chapter has likewise been approached on the assumption that some may choose to read only select chapters from the book. Relevant annotations that occur in the treatment of previous chapters are therefore noted so that readers can easily find them.

It is appropriate that I conclude this introduction to Olaf Georg Klein's book with a statement of my appreciation for the assistance, support, and encouragement of those individuals without whom this production of an annotated translation would not have been possible. Dean Lee Nordt of Baylor's College of Arts and Sciences has been a model of administrative support and assistance as my colleague, Dr. Ann McGlashan, and I struggled to find the time and resources we required in order to produce an English version of this work suited to its merits. In this same vein, I would like also to acknowledge the aid and encouragement of my department chair, Mary P. Nichols. The capable staff of Baylor's Department of Political Science — and, in particular, Jenice Langston and Cynara Butler — proved, as always, indispensable to meeting publication deadlines and to an efficient exchange of materials with editors at Camden House. It has been a considerable pleasure to work with Jim Walker, editorial director at Camden House, who deftly steered this project through every encounter with rough waters. Our work has been much improved by both his critical and editorial assistance. A special note of affection must likewise go to Wendy, Anthony, and Sebastian for their patience and devotion, especially when familial duties had to be postponed and sometimes neglected in order to complete different parts of this project. Finally, I want to thank Olaf Klein for agreeing to work with us, and for helping us at every stage to improve upon our attempts to render his book into a new language and to convey its meaning to readers largely unfamiliar with the culture from which it springs and the history it concerns.

Dwight D. Allman
Baylor University
March 2007

Notes

[1] Henry Adams, *The Education of Henry Adams* (Boston: Houghton Mifflin Co., 1961), 62.

[2] See Nietzsche's *Die fröhliche Wissenschaft*, #125.

[3] Although the adjective völkisch has a philological equivalent in English (folkish), it is impossible to make proper sense of this word without reference to the cultural and political significance of the concept of das Volk (the people) in German history. That history extends back much further than 1871, the year in which a modern state called Germany came formally into existence under the leadership of Prussia. Political unification was anticipated and to an important extent prepared by the evolution of a romantic German nationalism that had at its core the idea of a German people or Volk — the historical, cultural, and racial ground of individual nobility and achievement as well as of collective political action and identity.

[4] Detlef Pollack, "Wie ist es um die innere Einheit Deutschlands bestellt?" *Aus Politik und Zeitgeschichte* 30–31 (24 July 2006): 4–7.

[5] Wolfgang Emmerich, *Kleine Literatur Geschichte der DDR*, 2nd ed. (Berlin: Aufbau Taschenbuch Verlag, 2000), 498–99.

[6] Václav Havel, "Paying Back the West," *New York Review of Books* 46, no. 14 (23 September 1999): 54.

[7] See below, author's preface, page xxvii.

[8] See Czeslaw Milosz, "The Telltale Scar," as quoted in Thomas L. Pangle, *The Ennobling of Democracy: The Challenge of the Postmodern Age* (Baltimore: Johns Hopkins UP, 1992), 87.

[9] Quotation cited in Mike Dennis, *German Democratic Republic: Politics, Economics and Society* (London: Pinter, 1988), 31.

[10] See David P. Conradt, *The German Polity*, 8th ed. (White Plains, NY: Longman, 1996), 20–21.

[11] Klein's work here builds on a tradition of East German literature that includes Christa Wolf's *Kassandra* and Stefan Heym's *Der König David Bericht*.

[12] *Aftertime* (Evanston, IL: Northwestern UP, 1999).

[13] See Dennis, *German Democratic Republic*, 179–83.

[14] See David Lane, *Soviet Society under Perestroika*, 2nd ed. (London: Routledge, 1991), 10–17.

[15] See Article 116 of The Basic Law of the Federal Republic, in Conradt, *The German Polity*, 313; also 13–16; and Russell J. Dalton, *Politics in Germany*, 2nd ed. (New York: Harper Collins, 1993), 40–45.

[16] See William R. Keylor, *The Twentieth Century World*, 4th ed. (Oxford: Oxford UP, 2001), 451–55.

[17] See reports in the *Manchester Guardian Weekly*, "Leipzig Marchers Protest at Ban on Reform Group," 1 Oct. 1989; and *Sunday Telegraph*, "Dissidents' Party Upsets Honecker Anniversary Bash," 1 Oct. 1989; as well as the account in Conradt,

The German Polity, 25–29, and in Charles S. Maier, *Dissolution: The Crisis of Communism and the End of East Germany* (Princeton: Princeton UP, 1997), 174–75.

[18] See below, chapter 3, page 33.

[19] An extended account of the 9 October showdown can be found in Maier, *Dissolution,* 142–45.

[20] See reports in the *Christian Science Monitor,* "East German Public Protest Sets Pace for Reform," 5 Dec. 1989; the *Los Angeles Times,* "East Germany Picks a Non-Communist," 7 Dec. 1989; and *The Boston Globe,* "East German Center-Right Triumphs in a Vote for Unity," 19 Mar. 1990; as well as the account in Conradt, *The German Polity,* 29–35.

TRANSLATOR'S PREFACE

Ann McGlashan

IT IS MY GREAT PLEASURE AND HONOR to be able to present to English-speaking readers a translation of Olaf Georg Klein's book on East German lives caught in the turmoil of reunification, *Plötzlich war alles ganz anders*. I have tried to be as respectful as I could of the variety of voices within the work and of the particular situations in which these voices found expression, while at the same time making them accessible to readers from a very different background.

There were many challenges in translating this work, but I would like here to touch on two in particular. First, although it is becoming more and more the norm to retain the German noun *Wende* (from the verb *wenden*, to turn) to denote the circumstances surrounding the fall of the Berlin Wall and Germany's subsequent reunification, in no small part because of the many nuances of meaning inherent in the term, I made the decision to translate it here. Due to the frequency with which *Wende* appears in the German text, I felt the inclusion of the term would have been too distracting to the English-speaking reader. Throughout the text I have translated *Wende* as "changeover": this term seemed to me to be a more neutral choice than other possibilities (such as "turnaround" or "turning point" or even "revolution") and as such to better encapsulate the variety of responses to the *Wende* presented in Klein's book, both positive and negative.

A second translation challenge was presented by the designation *Inoffizieller Mitarbeiter* or *IM*, the term used for an East German citizen who worked secretly with the *Stasi* (State Security), either willingly or unwillingly. Now that the vast network of neighbor passing on information about neighbor has come to light, one can readily understand why this term is most often translated as "informer." However, again because of the varied nature of the responses to the changeover presented in Klein's book, a term carrying less moral freight was needed. I made the decision to render the term more literally, as "unofficial co-worker" or UC. Of course, whenever a protagonist uses a different term, such as *Spion* ("spy"), I have used a more value-laden translation.

Discussions of other translation challenges can be found in the annotations, and I thank my colleague, Dr. Dwight Allman, for allowing my input in that particular venue, and for his invaluable help at all stages of the translation. I would also like to thank Baylor University, especially Dr. Manuel Ortuño and Dr. Michael Long of the Department of Modern Foreign Languages, as well as Dean Wallace Daniel and Dean Lee Nordt of the College of Arts and Sciences, for their help in making this English edition a reality. At Camden House my thanks go to Susan Innes and Jane Best for their attention to detail, and especially to our editor Jim Walker for his faith in the project and his unflagging energy on our behalf. But most of all I have to thank the author, Olaf Georg Klein, for the trust he has placed in me in giving me the chance to translate his work, and for working closely with me on problem passages. I hope this English version lives up to his expectations.

Ann McGlashan
Waco, Texas
March 2007

AUTHOR'S PREFACE

Olaf Georg Klein

THESE LITERARY MONOLOGUES can be read as a "book of histories," or as a "book of upheaval"; they show how party-liners and dissidents, victims or fellow travelers deal with themselves and the world when the "system" they have fought for, tolerated, or fled from disappears.

But there was another reason why writing this book was so important to me. More than anything else, I was interested in certain questions: How was living a fulfilled, humane life made difficult, if not impossible, back then, and is it still the same today? How aware of this are we? And how does each individual deal with such things? What promises and hopes spur us on? In the final analysis, what will remain when we look back on it all?

Perhaps what happened to people when the country known as the German Democratic Republic disappeared can best be compared to a kind of collective heart attack that brought with it the chance of a new orientation, not only in the political and economic arenas, but even more in the areas of attitude and behavior. Which values and orientations that will not become useless overnight can and should determine my life? What meaning does my existence have for other people? To what do I devote my strengths, my energies, even my life?

The question of what remains of life and what that life means when the coordinates by which we have oriented ourselves or the antagonists against whom we have fought suddenly disappear is certainly justified at any time or place, but we are more likely to pose such a question in times of upheaval rather than in times of stagnation.

In this book we are dealing with nuances and shadings rather than superficial assessments. Perhaps the unspoken can crystallize behind the spoken, as can the various levels at which someone perceives, assesses, or makes decisions. At times, these were kept separate from one another; at others they clashed in an unexpectedly harsh manner. I saw it as my job to present the cracks, the inconsistencies, and the contradictions in the characters in such a way that any judgment on the part of the reader would not become too self-righteous — in such a way that he or she would be led towards a (perhaps even critical) self-examination.

While working on this book I tentatively felt my way towards questions that have intrigued me for a long time: Can someone be an informer for years and yet be free of feelings of guilt? Can someone be a cog in a murderous machine without feeling pity, without anything weighing on his or her conscience? And how does it happen that someone from a very narrow, bourgeois background can not only develop an incorruptible sense of what is true and just but also act upon it? Can it be that the "perceptive frameworks" that are shaped in early life irreparably distort the reality of our lives so badly that we can no longer speak of "perception" in any real sense of the word?

Wherever possible, I have taken on the task of a chronicler, so that those who have experienced the situations described here from various perspectives might understand the respective "other side," and those who are not familiar with such situations might gain insight into the contradictions and many-faceted processes that belong to the past, yet are also ongoing.

At the very first public reading from the manuscript of what has now become this book I was asked whether these texts should be seen as documents in the sense of mere transcripts of recorded interviews: whether they dealt with fictitious characters, or were retellings of stories. Behind these comments lurked the unspoken question of how "true" or "real" the twelve characters were.

That's a difficult question to answer. While writing the texts, the image of a translator would come to me. A translator, too, must transfer the "content" of a work as exactly and as faithfully as possible. But at the same time, the translator must always make decisions about how to transfer the reality that an author from another cultural milieu wishes to describe with his or her poetic images in such a way that it will be not only understood in the translator's own cultural milieu but also appreciated for its difference and uniqueness.

Do we not all express our own life in images, parables, examples? Is not each person his or her own "cosmos"; do we not all have our own values and interpretations; do we not present ourselves today in one way, tomorrow in another; do we not try to hide; are we not narrow and forgetful; and do we not "color" our experiences and memories differently depending on the situation? Whether an "event" becomes the greatest defeat of our lives or a mere meaningless episode chiefly depends on what we have "decided" for our lives, what is "important" for us, and what we think makes life worth living. But this is exactly what can change rapidly in times of upheaval. Victories suddenly become defeats and vice versa; what was the center of our lives years ago suddenly becomes unimportant, and an almost accidental honesty suddenly becomes a symbol. And who has not experienced using standards to judge the behavior of others that he or she is not prepared to extend to his or her own life, at least not in so strict a fashion. So the chronicler and translator must not only set down *what* was said, claimed, or contended, but above all *how*, when, and in what context it was done or not done.

Therefore readers must decide for themselves who these fictitious characters are "in reality," just as judges put together their own images from clues, the prosecution, and the defense in order to condemn or acquit according to agreed-upon principles, while never wholly losing sight of themselves as judges.

Olaf Georg Klein
September 1993

I thank all who have encouraged me in my work, be it through conversations, pointers, criticism, suggestions, or work opportunities. I would like to give my express thanks to those who allowed my often probing questioning and those who were by my side with patience and understanding during the work on this book.

Suddenly Everything Was Different

Was Different

German Lives in Upheaval

I THINK IT COMES FROM KEEPING EVERYTHING BOTTLED UP INSIDE AND NEVER OPENING YOUR MOUTH . . .

— Klara D., artist, emigrated to the West in 1984

I DON'T THINK I'M A "wild child," now, at thirty-seven. I'm all grown-up. But it depends on what you understand by that. Being grown-up doesn't mean giving in to all the pressures that crowd in on you from outside. Sure, you have to accept certain ground rules that make it possible to live along-side other people. For me that includes, for example, a willingness to help. But ground rules that people think up just so they can trample on others because they themselves want to get ahead — I don't hold with that at all.

When someone tells me they find such and such disgusting but some-times you just have to compromise — well, not me. I'm no one's psychia-trist. And there aren't any fixed ground rules that you have to keep to. You yourself help make the ground rules by accepting certain things and not others. I can't wear a mask either: acting cool when I'm excited, in-terested when I'm bored. There's an advantage to this: I don't need to say certain things, because people can read it in my face.

* * *

I still remember getting up in the dark, very early in the morning, when-ever we went on a trip. My knee socks were lying over the chair, and my dress; everything was ready, and I wasn't tired at all. But then it became a nightmare, every time. My father had reserved seats months in advance, and of course other people would be sitting in our seats, and my father would make a huge fuss; he'd roar and wave his arms about and couldn't calm down till we were halfway there.

Sure, I don't let anyone get away with anything either, but you can protect your rights in a different way. I don't scream at anyone, not even during an argument, and I don't need to keep myself under control. I'm much quieter, use gestures more — it's simply a different kind of lan-guage, not one expressed so much through words.

* * *

My father has a violent temper, but what's actually even worse is that he isn't capable of communicating. There's no real exchange. He speaks, but then when you ask him something he simply doesn't answer. As if he hasn't heard a word. What's more, he has no wit, no humor; he can't look critically at himself at all. As long as I can remember, one of us kids always had to massage his bald spot. When I think of the disgusting smell of the birch hair lotion that was supposed to encourage hair growth . . . Didn't though, not one iota. But still, we had to do the massage.

I have five siblings: three brothers and two sisters. I'm the fourth. The Catholic upbringing worked for them; not so much for me. If they ever went out, I guarantee it was to some function organized by the church. My mother was submissive and in poor health, and I was beaten by my father. With a rubber hose! For coming home late, for being impudent — actually any old reason was enough. I spoke to him about it recently.

He said if I was slapped now and then, I probably deserved it.

I can remember in detail times when I sat under the table and he stood in front of it with the rubber hose. I did defend myself, sure. Once, when my older brother had punched me in the stomach, I shoved his plum-jam sandwich in his face. He came after me, was going to beat me, and I threw a flowerpot at him. It hit the built-in cupboard.

When my father got home, of course he was told at once what Klara had gone and done now. He didn't ask how it happened, he only said, "If you had hit Peter, I would have killed you."

Later I developed a trick. When he was going to beat me, I'd go to the window and say, "If you touch me, I'll scream really loud that you're a murderer."

True, I've been a bit reckless. But I don't have these problems with my son. He's now thirteen, and I think it's wonderful to have a child. I don't feel overwhelmed, either, but I'm growing up along with him. Sure, I have one child and not six. But do you have to have six? Well, if you're Catholic and can't take the pill, that's bad, of course. But the three children before me were well behaved, you know. Real "fellow travelers." I have no idea how it happened that I was so different.

For years I thought, "That's not my *real* father." Not that my mother cheated on him. For God's sake, no! But there was a deep longing within me: One day, someone completely different would come along and finally say, "That's my daughter!" Like in a fairy tale, where they're always waiting for their fathers or their husbands.

This feeling of alienation also came from outside our family, of course. School friends of my older sister and brothers would say, "You're the sister? Can't be!" Or my father's pupils: "What a nice daughter you have. We would never have expected that." Of course, I secretly went to the dance club on Saturdays with the worst hooligans in his class. Eighth grade, lowest level. My father blew his top. He taught physical education at the vocational school.

As a young girl, my mother had been a servant in someone's house. She came from Silesia. My father met her after the war, at the Catholic youth group. He had just returned from being a prisoner of war, and he always went to pick her up. Even back then he got furious if she was a few minutes late. That continued throughout her life. After the older children left home, my mother worked as a sales assistant. She was very well liked because she would do any job; nothing was beneath her.

We were all in the Pioneers. That was taken for granted. We could get West German TV at home, but the children had to watch East German programs. My father didn't want to draw attention to himself. That's why he didn't go public with his religious faith. He didn't say, "We're Catholic, so my kids are not going to the Pioneers." No. This "don't draw any attention" was really his faith, or the unspoken motto of his life. Of course, we went to church on Sundays. Thank God they came up with the idea, whenever it was, that we could go to church on Saturday nights, too. So my parents always went in the evenings — so that my mother could see to the roast on Sunday mornings. I used to say, "I'm going on Sunday," and then I'd just hang out somewhere else during that time.

I officially left the Catholic Church a year ago. But I felt it was a farce even as a child. I always liked the Protestants in my class better. They didn't need to go to confession, either. Catholicism only meant one thing to me: taking all the joy out of life. I knew this from pure intuition. For confession, I would write myself a note with a few standard sins on it: I fought with my brothers and sisters; I ate sweets; and finally, I lied. That way, if I'd said anything wrong, it would be immediately absolved.

The only interesting thing was that the boys stood in line at the other confessionals. That's what made confession bearable. And afterwards, when you had received your orders to go and say a few "Our Fathers," I would sit in a pew and think, "So, enough time for an 'Our Father' has gone by, now I could probably stand up." But then I would think, "What if there really is a God? Who knows . . . Okay, you can pray one, just in case."

We were never told about the history, the meaning of Christianity, about the symbols or such like. Apart from a lectionary, a Bible, and a cookbook, perhaps also a dictionary, there were no books for us in the entire house. Perhaps my father had some in his desk, but that was out of bounds for us.

We were all in the FDJ. But my older sister and brothers didn't take part in the initiation. I was the first. You see, some bishop decreed that Catholic youth could take part in the initiation ceremony without it being a contradiction. And so my parents decided I should take part. Of course, there was no celebration at home, nor did I get gifts like all the rest, but I had to take part in the official celebration at school. "Whatever you do, don't draw attention to yourself. Even the Church is allowing it now, so why should we make it unnecessarily hard on ourselves. That's that!" I was never raised to be a rebel. But in spite of this my report card always contained the words: "Klara does not take a clear stand on issues of class." At that time, this sentence meant as much as if a report card in the West were to say "She is a terrorist sympathizer." For all intents and purposes, you were washed up.

* * *

Well, everything really started when I met this nice guy at the dance hall. I was fifteen at the time. I hitchhiked to Leipzig with him. I told my mother I was going to the town of D. to see a girlfriend. In Leipzig, we sat on the rim of some fountain making out until the police came and wanted to see my I.D., which I had left in a locker at the train station.

"You'll have to come with us, then."

"Why?"

There had been an official complaint about a "public nuisance." So I had to go along with them, and while I was hanging around at the police station, my parents got a call on their "sacred Saturday afternoon." Did they know where their daughter was? She had been picked up in Leipzig. All hell broke loose, massive trouble. I sat in the police station and the cops watched soccer. Now and again one of them would come in to take a look at me and make some stupid remark. At that time, I had just prepared for a drama exam and so I had learned various texts by heart. Like *Kabale und Liebe* and so on. Eventually I found all the gawking just so stupid that whenever a cop came in I began to quote the most explicit parts. That confused them quite a bit; they probably thought, "the girl's completely crazy."

Actually, apart from that, they left me in peace and took me to the train station the same evening. I had to take my stuff out of the locker, buy myself a ticket, and get on the train for home. The guy I was in Leipzig with wrote to me for a while after that, but we didn't see each other any more.

Perhaps a year and a half later, I come home and there's someone sitting in the yard. I go inside, and he follows. Inside, my father says: "The police have been here!" So, this smart-looking, plainclothes cop comes inside and immediately makes a good impression on my parents. It's about a criminal matter, he says; he has a few questions and would like to take me with him. My parents thought this was quite okay. "If the police come, well then, there must be a good reason."

I thought this was absolutely wrong. If something like this were to happen to my son, I would go with him, at least until he's of age. Unless he himself said he didn't want me to.

So I had to go with him, wait for hours, and then I was questioned about the guy from back then. What kind of a relationship did I have with him? There were letters, they said, and so on. I already had the feeling that he'd pushed off to the West. I only said, "Sorry, I can't answer your questions." When they realized that I wasn't going to say anything, they wanted to question me about my friends.

We were a threesome, were together all the time, went to school dressed completely in black, which was pure provocation in those days, sometimes talked back to the teachers. Really small stuff, actually. Nevertheless, after that the cops or the Stasi looked up the parents individually, and made clear to each of them that their daughter was to be forbidden to hang out with the other girls, since they were "a bad influence."

Anyway, I came home and caught hell from my father. Didn't interest him in the slightest what the cops wanted. "All we get from you is trouble. None of the other kids have ever had anything to do with the police!" And so on and so forth.

Perhaps this was why my Catholic upbringing seemed so hypocritical to me: no trace of what you could perhaps call "love your neighbor." It was always just running to church and presenting a good image in public. But when my sister, who was three years older than me, got engaged, I had to tag along and make sure they didn't "do anything" while they were out. I always said: "I'm going for a little walk," sat behind a tree, and watched. "So do something already," I thought, but all they did was sit beside each other on the blanket for hours and didn't even kiss.

At age sixteen, I met this great woman. She had a child, and lived the life that we, in our small town, had always wanted to live. Free, independent, and in her own apartment. And she was only three years older than we were. She said to us: "You can come back any time and stay overnight if you want." So our team of three dropped in quite often, and it turned out that there was a real circle of friends there. Of course, the word had gotten around that three young girls had settled in. When the entire troupe went off to N. for the Whitsun holiday, we were asked if we wanted to come along. We cajoled our parents into allowing it: "After all, the others are getting to go."

So we hitchhiked to N. and found a note there: "Gone to the cathedral for an organ concert." So off we went. When the concert was over and we were waiting in front of the cathedral, I suddenly saw this guy come out. I thought: That's the one for me. And it was. Sebastian.

We were sitting afterwards in a bar, he across from me, my girlfriend beside me. We whispered to each other:

"I think he's looking at me."

"No, I think he's looking at me."

Then I thought: Shit, you're going to have to think of something. Later, when it came time to decide where we were going to sleep, the other two girls found a space and shouted: "Hey, Klara, are you coming over here with us?" By chance I was standing near Sebastian; he looked at me out of the corner of his eye, so I said: "No, I'll stay over here, with him." So that decided it. He wrote to me after that; I turned up in Berlin where he'd moved in the meantime, and he came to visit me quite often. I mean, we met at our friend's house in D. Anyway, just as before, I had to show myself at home on Sundays and go to church.

So I spent the night with Sebastian — my first time in bed with a man — and then went to church the next day. I thought: "If only you all knew." And, "Thank you, God!" Something like that.

* * *

After I finished school, all I knew was that I wanted to do something in the craft or artistic line. I did not get an apprenticeship as an interior decorator because I had my diploma. However, the people in D. introduced me to a theater designer. I thought her work was fantastic, but in order to study this field you had to have at least two years experience in the theater. So I moved to Berlin, to Sebastian, who lived at that time in a big apartment with several other people, and I moved scenery around at the State Opera. But I had only been in Berlin a couple of months when Sebastian had to go into the army.

Then someone suggested that I interview at a theater in Berlin. As soon as I got there, it was all very clear: the good-looking girls who worked there were all scantily dressed, and the boss showed an immediate interest in my starting work there. But when I refused to go and have coffee with him, he became a bit chillier, and the next time he no longer knew who I was.

So I took odd jobs. As a sales assistant; in the library; always as an unskilled worker. For a time I was a teacher in after-school care. Only twenty-six hours a week, not bad, and I found the work fun, too. But the boss was an old Stalinist. One Monday, I get to work and she says to me: "Miss Klara, where were *we* on Sunday?"

"We? On Sunday? Well, *I* was at home. Why?"

"So, she was at home on Sunday? 'Our' Karl and 'our' Rosa were taken to their graves, and there she is at home." She meant the usual obligatory demonstration. I laughed myself silly, and she totally flipped out.

It was even worse when the Russians marched into Afghanistan and they were gathering signatures to say how great you thought it was. "I'm not going to sign." Of course, that was another entry in my personal file.

Even when I would march through the stairwell singing songs with the children, she would come out and just have to tell me that I was singing the "wrong" songs. It was my job, she said, "to anchor" the tradition of workers' songs "in the hearts of the children" rather than to warble songs from the *Zupfgeigenhansl*.

The problem with the West had already begun when I was a child, when the packages came at Christmas. Although I was not quite sure why they sent us margarine, of all things — I thought that was really strange — sometimes there was also some chocolate in the packages. This was then divided into eight pieces.

But then there was this secretiveness. First of all, the package was kept under the bed; then my mother looked in the package by herself; and only then came the sharing. It was all so terribly exaggerated. My friends and I constantly talked about whether to go to the West or not. Especially after I met Sebastian.

Perhaps I projected the narrowness of my family home onto the country as a whole. Anyway, in Berlin I was happy to be able to enjoy my personal life far away from my parents. Sebastian made a completely different life possible for me. Through him, I got to know people who were only two or three years older than me but had read much more, could express themselves, and discussed political and existential topics. It was only at work that I continued to get into arguments, because I simply said what I thought. Once a colleague said: "You're dumb! We think just like you do, but you mustn't say it out loud. Keep your mouth shut; you're only hurting yourself."

That made me extremely angry. "Why should I be quiet? I don't agree with that at all."

So I found the narrowness I knew from my parents' house everywhere. The people who kept their mouths shut, who were quiet and joined in, always got on better. But — and this was the bad thing, or perhaps the just thing — I didn't have the feeling that they were really happy doing it.

For me, it was not about changing the system, but about the small things, everyday life, the atmosphere. Somehow my unruliness always surfaced. One evening in a bar in Berlin we thought about staging a spontaneous demonstration on bicycles, more for fun than anything. We told forty people, on the snowball principle, and so the first "bike demo" in East Berlin took place. And the Stasi went searching for a big organization, when really it was more a joke than anything.

Often there were very concrete injustices I had to protect myself against. I didn't give myself much time to think; it came more from the pit of my stomach. Like signing the Biermann petition. Or, when martial law was declared in Poland, we printed flyers on the anniversary of the founding of "Solidarity." We had been in Poland a lot, we felt freer there, more relaxed, we experienced a different artistic richness, and besides, the Poles, with this hint of anarchy in their being, simply appealed to us. . .

We talked with a friend and his girlfriend, always out in the open, of course; we bought up masses of non-incriminating coffee filters and printed *Solidariność* on them with stencils cut into raw potatoes. We wanted to leave the piles in the shopping arcade on the Alexanderplatz the next day, and let the wind blow them around. Nice idea.

Sebastian and I had dressed in true GDR style: I had on a pleated skirt and lipstick, and had twisted my long hair into an orderly bun; Sebastian wore a shirt and "Präsent 20" pants with creases. We felt like we were dressing for Carnival. Even in the subway I had the feeling that everyone was looking at us. But today we were actually looking "normal." Anyway, we met our friend and his girlfriend and they'd dressed up as tourists from the West: sunglasses, big plastic bags, and a West German map of Berlin peeping out of a pocket. First of all we nearly killed ourselves laughing, then we went to the Alex. It was already crowded. Lots of young, well-dressed, inconspicuous men with walkie-talkies were standing around. So we turned back at once, because it would have been sheer suicide to walk around there.

We met up again that evening. That's when we got the first intimation of success: at a large crossroads, where the subway is elevated and runs in the open, our friend had thrown a few hundred of the printed coffee filters out of the last car. He had gotten out at the next station and ridden back by bike. The crossroads had already been barricaded, and the cops were busy gathering up the whole lot.

First Sebastian and I made love one more time, and then we left with the printed coffee filters and glue, and stuck the things up everywhere. We met up again at the Hackescher Markt. By the time we got to Linienstrasse we noticed that someone was behind us; he looked at the things and then walked faster. We walked faster too, and so did he. Then we separated, one left and one right, up to the streetcar platform, into the streetcar and away.

Only later did I realize how dangerous it had really been. Especially to start off together, with no one staying with the child. But we were simply enthusiastic and aggressive. Our goal was not to shake up the masses: no one could have awakened that herd of sheep any more anyway. But at least you didn't want to stay silent and do nothing.

Sometimes we found flyers in our mailbox. Then we knew that others were also doing something: we weren't alone. Years later, I met one of the people who just happened to have stuffed flyers in our mailbox. He had been in prison for eight years. When I met him, he was completely confused and totally broken. He had never actually wanted to go to the West, but they had bought his freedom. Somehow he had had the idea that he could change something in the East. I never had such illusions. I also couldn't understand how people could say: "We feel betrayed when people go to the West. We have to stay and change things here." My own life was too important for that.

* * *

The external reason for applying for permission to leave the country was that Sebastian was going to be drafted into the reserves. The army had been a trauma for him, and he had told himself that he would rather go to jail than do that again.

We were called to the Department of Internal Affairs and were treated like dirt. We were told: "Socialism is great, and to apply for an exit permit is criminal and illegal." We would be committing an offense, they said, and we should retract the application, if you please. It always ended in a threat. But we didn't let them intimidate us, and whenever we received a denial, we immediately sent off another application.

Of course, they harassed us in other ways, too. Late at night, the cops would drag Sebastian from his bike, twist his arms behind his back, and he would have to show them what was in his briefcase. Things like that were always happening.

One evening we wanted to throw a big party. I made all the arrangements; everyone was there, only Sebastian didn't come. First of all I'm thinking, he's just late. After two hours I'm thinking, perhaps another woman? But he wouldn't do that. After three hours: Perhaps he's trying to tell me something? Got mad about something? But that's not like him. Anyway, the party winds down, and he just doesn't come home. And like a flash it hits me: "There's no other woman or anything, it's the Stasi." I called his father at once, because we weren't married, you see. I was sure that if I called the cops they'd only say: "And who are you, anyway?"

Sebastian came back twenty-four hours later. They'd picked him up directly from work. At the same time they had also interrogated friends of ours near Wittenberge, on the border with West Germany. They accused them of having moved there merely to set up a "flight headquarters." See, we had visited them quite often. In any case, they wanted to hang an accusation of "illegal emigration" on them and us that would bring with it a sentence of a few years in jail.

Afterwards, Sebastian grumbled endlessly about it, but I was really glad to have him back. I was already picturing him in jail and was figuring out how I could spring him. I was ready to move heaven and earth. After all, I knew enough people who had done time in the East, simply because they owned music albums from the West or had passed along books from the West. That was seen as "subversive agitation." Yet most people weren't "dissidents" at all, in the true sense of the word. They were just non-conformist. But the Stasi and the state authorities suffered from paranoia; they suspected a "strictly organized opposition" everywhere, although in reality many people only wanted to expand their personal freedom a little.

* * *

Anyway, we had heard in the meantime of various cases where they allowed one partner and the child to emigrate first, and the other only two years later. Out of spite! So we got scared and married. The people at the registry office wanted to make it all terribly solemn: with "socialist marriage" and all that shit. So we just said: "We would be grateful if you'd keep this whole circus to a minimum." The registrar was knocked for a loop.

* * *

In 1984, everything suddenly happened very quickly. We got an appointment and all of a sudden we were not criminal subjects anymore. They tried to treat us a bit more politely and we were told that our application was being processed. We could count on an answer in about six weeks. We said: "It's very nice of you to finally deal with this after four years."

A telegram came a week later: Appointment in four days. When we got there, the situation was truly Kafkaesque: the door to the room where we were supposed to go did not exist. I mean, the door existed, but no name, no number, no one there. Three doors down sat a fat automaton of a woman, surrounded by huge piles of files, and she asked sharply: "Where do you want to go?"

"We have an appointment."

"Name?" She looks it up. "You're out tomorrow."

I say: "Wait a minute, what do you mean, tomorrow?"

"Yes, yes, yes. Tomorrow, it's off to West Berlin."

I say: "What do you mean? How long do we have?"

Then she says with obvious relish: "Well, let's say . . . till 10:00 P.M."

I say: "How'd you think we can do that? I've got a household to pack up. How am I to do that in one day?"

But she only hissed: "Well, don't stand around here so long! Go! Go!"

We called up all the friends we could find, divided up the most urgent errands, gave away all the clothes we could. The next day we packed two suitcases. We had a drink with friends, called my parents, went out to eat with Sebastian's father, and in between kept calming our son down. At the border crossing, our eyes were really swollen from crying.

Suddenly, all your friends are there, and you have the feeling you're giving something up. You don't know where you're going, and whether you will ever see these people again. Leon didn't know what was happening. In the morning, he'd still been in kindergarten, and suddenly it's a case of: We're moving away. That's the way it was for him; there was no time to prepare him for it. A friend was waiting for us on the other side, and we were able to stay with him for a while. That very evening he took us to the Kurfürstendamm, wanted to do something nice for us. But it made me want to throw up. Much too crowded, much too much, and then all those panhandlers sitting around, and I was afraid that I could end up like that.

* * *

During the next days and weeks I had to comfort Leon, who wanted to go back and didn't know what was happening. I wanted so much to cry with him, because I missed my friends and the surroundings I was used to. I was so lonely.

A feeling of freedom can only come about when one sees possibilities and opportunities. But we had to endure the whole bureaucratic shit. And then there was also the sordid apartment of this friend of ours — it was all one big shock.

Even when we'd go to a concert at the Quasimodo, I would fall asleep right away. Because I couldn't cope with all these impressions. It was just too much. Later, when I slowly began to find things that I liked and that I would have liked to tell my friends in the East about by phone, I realized that it would be better if I didn't talk about them. Somehow, a true exchange was no longer possible. They were only amazed that we traveled to Italy while living on aid from the state. But I couldn't really convey to them my life experience.

* * *

It was great to make our first friends here and to gradually come to see the possibilities. I got to know people who owned a ceramics workshop and store. They liked me as soon as I first walked in, and they asked if I'd like to work with them. Since I had been apprenticed to a pottery maker in the East, I started right away and worked there a few hours every day.

After a while, Leon got into a really good preschool. But the first one was just awful, and he went there for only a week. Instead of taking care of the children, the teachers mostly sat around drinking coffee, and everything was "easy and laid-back." There was a parents' meeting in the second week: one of the teachers came an hour late, the other didn't come at all. In the meantime, the parents traded gossip: Who was doing it with whom, why, and for what reason . . . At first I didn't say anything, because I was still new. But when I wanted to leave at twelve thirty at night, they said: "What? You're going already? Tell us how you like it here with us."

I said: "To be honest, not at all." They were totally taken aback, of course. "For example, I don't understand why you chat about everything under the sun, instead of setting to work and getting things going in this playgroup, which, by the way, looks like a pigsty." Boy, did I hit a nerve!

"God, the same old thing again. It's obvious you come from the East. The overanxious mother. You have no idea. We've been discussing that for years. You'll wake up to it too. When it gets to be too much for the children, they'll clean up by themselves all right. We go through it once a week and clear away the apple cores. You've just got that stuff about order in your head still. The children know all by themselves what's good for them."

I said: "I don't want to listen to this. I'm a bit sloppy, too, but this is just disgusting." They were quite horrified at that. I called up the next day and said: "I'll bring the food, like I said I would, but Leon's not coming any more. I can't do that to my child."

* * *

I find it a great advantage to have known two systems. That's an amazingly intense experience, one that you're not constantly aware of, but you quite suddenly realize the differences. For instance, I've noticed that many people here in the West don't have any friends. They have acquaintances or "contacts." Even when they talk about their "friends," they still don't talk to them about personal things. They do things together, but they don't let others get close to them. Sure, I don't let anyone get close to me either if I don't want to. But that isn't generally the case.

When I was thirty-two and had been in the West for a year, I applied for a place at the College of Art, to study ceramics. They rejected me, although I felt intuitively that I had passed my test really well. I saw exactly how the professors reacted when I presented my pieces.

I knew something wasn't right, but I had no idea where I should begin. So I stayed an extra day in this town, and decided to speak to a professor, although I really didn't know what about. But I had such a feeling of injustice and anger inside me.

The professor I went to see was standing in his underwear in his studio. He was on the phone and said: "Come in, girl."

When he was finished, I said: "I don't know if you remember me?"

"Of course! We discussed your case for a long time and couldn't agree on whether we should take you or not."

"And why was that?"

"Well, your test grades were fine, and we were also pleased with the drawings, and that's not always the case with ceramics students. But you come from the GDR, you see, and we already have enough hardship cases here." It came out that I had more points than were necessary and that I had actually passed. I wrote to the president of the college. He tried to pacify me: I shouldn't make this public, and anyway, about the "hardship case," well, I had misunderstood that completely. The professors were on vacation, he said, and they would discuss it one more time. In any case, the vacation was hardly over before I received my registration papers in the mail, with no comment.

*　*　*

In 1989 I had finished my studies and was back in West Berlin. On the evening of the ninth of November I saw by accident on television: the Wall is open. "Shit," I thought, "now they'll all come over here." I didn't go to the Wall. Not until weeks later. Leon went and hacked off pieces of the Wall. I wasn't interested. I saw them on TV, sitting on top of the Wall and roaring and falling into each other's arms in tears: "At last, brothers and sisters, you are free."

I could have puked. To me, it seemed like affected wallowing on both sides. On the one hand those dreary stories: how long they'd had to save for their Trabi, how bad their lives were . . . But in the final analysis most people's lives weren't all that bad. Many people were hardly touched by the system. If you were nice and well behaved, like my parents for instance, then it made almost no difference whether you lived here in the West or over there in the East. The people here also have requirements and have to fit in, at least at work. They have "the rules of the game" they have to follow, and most of the time they like to follow them because they need a handrail they can pull themselves along with, because they don't have any stability within themselves.

And the West Germans have also been hypocritical: the same people who were totally euphoric pass by bums in the street without a thought. Doesn't disturb them at all. And for years they couldn't have cared less how their "brothers and sisters" lived "over there" in the East. Most people never even went there. "It was all too complicated . . ."

I often got a ride in someone else's car from West Berlin "through the East zone." "They don't even seem like real people," I'd hear. "Do they even have butter yet?" I'm asked these kinds of things almost every time I let it slip that I, too, once came from the "East zone."

And all this freedom!? What were the East Germans freed from all of a sudden? They stood in long lines in front of the banks, with their nylon jackets and their coffee thermoses, but they had really only come from a different part of the city. Not one of them stood up straight. Not one of them walked upright, and they looked so shabby and worn-out. Yes, you can say: hard work, bad food. But I think it comes from keeping everything bottled up inside and never opening your mouth. But all at once they all realized where they had lived all these years. "My God, there was even a secret police! We didn't know anything about that." But *everyone* had been against it. From the start. Pure intuition. All of them resistance fighters.

I feel a sort of hatred, not for the GDR but for this subservient, wretched attitude: we have nothing, we can do nothing, we are nothing. I really don't care *where* these people come from. Perhaps I just couldn't look at those plastic bags any more, filled with all the shit they'd let themselves be turned on to. These happy, foolish faces in front of the camera. As if it meant a renewal of their life, just because they could now buy their junk in the West.

Of course, there were also people in the East who believed in ideals and so remained human, who tried to change things. But far too often I encountered the "concentration-camp-guard" type of woman. When I think back to this one teacher . . . It was a crime to let someone like that loose on children.

And I also expect that if you're over twenty you shouldn't believe everything blindly. There were enough points at which you could have felt doubt. Even if nothing actually happened to you personally. Everyone had experiences where he or she could have felt the injustices. But they simply closed their eyes, so that no doubt could arise. I don't believe in the "fear motive" either. A "comfort motive" was more likely. When I hear, "We would have liked things to be different, but we couldn't do anything. We tried but . . ." my hair stands on end. Most of them simply made it easy on themselves, and the greatest personal humiliation was that they had to wait ten years for their Trabi. My God! But now, after two years, to be whining again because they don't know what to do with their freedom. Okay, when I hear certain individual stories, I do feel sorry for the people. It's also obvious that you can't come of age overnight. But, still, even the individual has a certain power. The rulers weren't scared for nothing: even if only a single person had opened his mouth, that person could well have changed something, after all.

But this "We've been deceived, first by the East, now by the West." They were lying to themselves! Damn it, taking responsibility for what you do is part of growing up.

I can well imagine that many people now want the GDR back. After all, it was only really terrible for those who wanted something different, who thought for themselves, and who knew that there was more to life than gobbling down pork and saving for a Trabi. For everyone else it was the ideal state.

When I look at my parents: what has changed for them? They can buy products from the West themselves and don't have to have things sent to them any longer. But otherwise? My father can now look at newspapers with a couple of naked women in them. But really, everything could just as well have stayed the way it was, apart from maybe being able to buy products from the West for GDR money, if possible. But no, Western money is important because otherwise you're a second-class human being. And Western money is useful when you travel abroad, especially eastward; then you too are suddenly a kind of superior person.

It's true that I'm sarcastic and cynical . . . But I've experienced the people in the subway who say to the Turks: "You can leave! We're here now!" Probably with no idea of what they've said. Because they certainly wouldn't want to be seen as second-class human beings and treated as such — as the Turks are in the West. But it's probably like this: when you're oppressed, you need someone to take it out on.

I have little hope for the future. I think that the problems of this West German society will simply be transferred to the East. Whether it's the garbage that they dump there, or whether it's the atomic power stations — they'll all be wiped out in the end. Never mind about the Two-Thirds World. But all the unsolved and postponed problems will return to this society with a vengeance. And then it will affect everyone here, and it won't go away with taxing our incomes a few measly percentage points.

More and more refugees will come over. Millions. A city like Berlin is tolerant, and will cope with it, but when I think about them building refugee housing in the small town I come from . . . there will be hell to pay.

What I can do is limited to the area of human relations. I don't believe in organizations and structures. Sure, I give to appeals by Greenpeace or Amnesty International. I also take part in certain demonstrations. But otherwise I try to live each day in a truly aware and intense way and to look forward to what is perhaps still to come. If I were to die tomorrow, I could say I'd had a nice life. I don't know what I "haven't done" or still have "to work on. . ." It's important to me to spend my life in a meaningful way, not just to hang out — not just to drug myself with conversations or some activity or other, just because I don't want to be alone.

I think my manner shocks people a little bit at first. I'm too direct, too clear, or too self-assured. In short, I am an acquired taste. But when people get to know me better, most of them say I'm quite social and sensitive.

I don't know where certain things come from. Life leaves its mark on you. You just have to be empathetic and open to many things. It's hard for me to talk about this. Perhaps that's why we have body language, and perhaps that's also why I work with clay. To express things that can't be said. I'm more of an active person and it's quite normal for me to be doing something with my hands.

Happiness is not a state of being for me. At most, there can be "happy moments," I think. And even for these moments of happiness, there have to be a few basic principles. You have to meet the right people and have a feeling for what is good for you and what isn't, so that you can simply avoid certain things and attract certain others. . .

When you are at your lowest point, you think you will never rise again, but somehow life goes on, and when you are up there again, well, that's really quite wonderful. I totally enjoy those moments. . . .

CHAPTER TWO

SO MUCH OF THE REALLY GOOD LIFE WAS LOST TO US. . .

— Petra B., 41, case worker for exit permits

O
N THE BASIS OF THE UPBRINGING I received from my parents, it was a foregone conclusion that I would join the Party. Actually, it's criminal to say something like that when you look at the machinations of the Party today. But at that point in time, it seemed to me that the Party represented very worthy aims.

In school, I was always an organized and reliable student, and of course I was a member of the Pioneer organization.

I also remember very well the circumstances surrounding the building of the "antifascist protective barrier." I thought it was a logical step to take. My parents explained that the Eastern part of Berlin would be ruined, that there was spying going on anyway, that food was cheap here and was being illegally exported by West Germany, that doctors and scientists were being lured away. The protective barrier was necessary so that this country could be rebuilt in peace. Everyone was still marked by the war and we all had the same bases on which to begin a new life in this, our country. We wanted to live together without exploitation. That was also the reason I later joined the Party.

Throughout my entire childhood I was especially influenced by movies, by the content and messages that were transmitted through them. These were movies about the war, about the time before 1945, movies that portrayed fascism. I said to myself: "Something like that must never happen again."

My dad wasn't a soldier. He was too young for that. Born in 1929. I know he almost starved during the war, because the town of M. took heavy bombing. After the war, he trained as a carpenter, then studied at a college of state administration and law, and later became a professor at the same college, teaching people to be mayors. I am trained as a preschool teacher. I found working with children a lot of fun back then. Of course, we had an educational plan. And there was some kind of contact with the army. Every year on the "Day of the National People's Army," our preschool would be in touch with one soldier. The children would send pictures, and he would answer us with a very nice letter. He would report on his work. Of course, the children were very interested in how the soldiers lived, how they spent their free time, where they slept, and so on.

Back then, I had many discussions about "war toys." Discussions with myself, with the parents of the children, and also with friends. But after all, the children were only imitating life in the barracks, playing with the watchtowers and vehicles. I did not have any actual tanks at my preschool. I certainly understood, even in those days, that it would be better not to have to send one's son to the army or to war. But the world was not so perfect that we could do without an army, a defensive army. There was to be no offensive war, just a defense. We wanted to protect ourselves, as I understood it. That's why I had great respect for every soldier in the National People's Army.

It's also good that the 1989 revolution was carried out so peacefully. They might well have sent in the reserve units again, and then there would no doubt have been many daddies to be mourned. That was almost the case, let me tell you.

Of course, there was always the border. But in those days I wasn't aware of information that has now emerged. About all those marksmen at the Wall. Of course, when I went dancing, I talked to the boys, even about the order to shoot. That was a complex topic for everyone. And we all made sure we didn't go near the border. But for me, in the GDR, a soldier wasn't someone who was evil and killed others. They were really marksmen for peace.

Another reason why I ignored the problem of the border was that my brother didn't have to go there. Certainly, he spent a voluntary three years in the "Felix Dzierzynski" watch regiment. But he is still a very sensitive person. He has often told me what kind of thoughts come into your mind when you're standing alone in a forest, because of this order to shoot that the watch has too. No one wants to shoot another human being. Although where he was posted, in Wandlitz, it's clear that nothing happened. What could happen?

* * *

Of course I joined the FDJ. There was no one in my class who wasn't in the FDJ, and I never had any contact at all with people from the church. In 1973, I went to the World Festival of Youth in Berlin. I cannot corroborate what has recently emerged, what's being said about the big anniversary celebrations. I thought it was fantastic to travel to the Festival. No one can take that away from me. I got to know Berlin for the first time! We were terribly hungry to experience everything. In the evening, we almost broke down, we were so tired from walking around, from dancing and so on. Those were amazing experiences. I was twenty-one years old back then.

During that time, there was also a demonstration; an organized march-past, of course, not a protest demonstration. The foreign youth marched one day, and the GDR youth the next day. I can still remember marching past the podium where our Politburo and foreign guests were standing: it was so amazingly uplifting! I don't know how I can explain. It was simply wonderful. To march with the youth of our country, past Erich Honecker, past our FDJ leaders. That was truly a great honor for me. And then some young people from Angola hung a chain around my neck, just like that, on the street. Amazing connections were made, very honest connections. Yes, I think exactly the same now as I did then. I won't let anyone ruin those experiences for me by talking them to death. No one.

A short time after that, I went to the FDJ Youth College. That's the "cadre forge" of the FDJ. If you graduate from this youth college, it's clear that you'll step into a full-time position within the FDJ. I was to become the Secretary of Culture in the district office of the FDJ. In 1975, I also met my husband at the youth college; that would have been when I was twenty-three. It was a very intense time for me. Our professors came from the Party University, and we also had very good training in philosophy. I didn't study just Lenin, but Marx too. Of course, we weren't introduced to any other philosophers. Nevertheless, I had a lot of positive experiences at this youth college. After all, there were many young foreigners there too, from Czechoslovakia and Poland, and also from Western countries; they were there for a year, just like us.

But I also had a negative experience that I will never forget, because it upset me very much. At that time, the "FDJ-Initiative Berlin" was taking place. A meeting was held in a large plenary hall, where many "exemplary young people" gave their statements: They would go to Berlin to support the construction of the capital city. After that, lists were handed out:

Are you willing to take part in the FDJ initiative in Berlin?
Are you absolutely willing?
Are you unwilling?
Are you absolutely unwilling?

You had to mark one. That shocked me a bit, because I thought that everyone should be able to make his own decisions about his life.

But since I had already met my husband, who was from Berlin, and because it was definite that we would stay together, I signed that I was willing to go to Berlin. Others, who had their families at home, had a house or something like that, marked that they weren't willing to go to Berlin. That had immediate consequences. Later, they weren't employed as secretaries, but only as very minor, insignificant workers. That was very upsetting for me.

* * *

It's true that unconditional obedience was expected. But still, I wouldn't want to make any comparison between our youth college and one of those Hitler Youth schools. That's ludicrous. After all, we didn't go along with that kind of "unconditional obedience" any longer. Not entirely, anyway.

There was a pleasant atmosphere there. We didn't have to drill. Absolutely not. A comparison to Hitler gives me real palpitations, because it's so superficial. But perhaps you can't understand it, if you didn't experience it yourself.

Of course, today I judge my time at the youth college differently. But we were always together on weekends, picking lingonberries and blueberries, going out to eat and for walks and . . . It was a lovely time! Hitler made an industry out of killing people, and to talk about that in the same sentence, in the same breath as the SED, well, I'm extremely sensitive about that.

Anyway, after I graduated they wanted me in the Central Council of the FDJ, the highest division of the youth organization, in the department of "International Relations." I thought that was wonderful. But in the meantime my circumstances had changed: my daughter had been born, and my husband had become a full-time FDJ secretary. A very good one, I might add.

After I had been at home with my daughter for a year, I really wanted to go back to work. But not in the Central Council of the FDJ, since my husband was working around the clock, and the Central Council would not have shown any consideration for me or my family. I would have been traveling around the GDR with international delegations, and that's not possible when you have a family.

In accordance with the rules, we informed the cadre department of the Central Council about our thoughts on the matter. We had to show up there twice. That was pure discrimination. I was accused of not having the proper, socialist, consciousness. I had received the assignment and I was also to carry it out. What kind of an upbringing had I had? They meant at home, from my parents. I had a definite allergic reaction to that.

I simply didn't understand it. There was such an inhumane tone to that conversation. And I had thought that the Party was there for the people and paid attention to the individual.

Then, for the first time in my life, I said "no." I'm definitely very naive. I'll have to admit that. Because I still trusted the Party and went to the second district secretary of the SED. My husband and I wanted to complain about how we had been treated by the Central Council. But he didn't take our side. I had to do the job since I'd gone through the training. But then he suddenly offered me the position of full-time FDJ secretary in a large factory together with my husband. That would have meant we would both have been working around the clock.

"You can't be serious," I said. "I've got a child. That child needs security. The family is the smallest cell of society, and when it doesn't function properly, the other doesn't function properly either. I'm not the kind of mother who leaves her child alone all day, and makes a latch-key kid out of her."

Then the district secretary suggested I board my child all week in a home. At first I thought I hadn't heard him correctly. I totally rejected that!

Again my consciousness was called into question, again my upbringing was thrown in my face. All because I put my child first and didn't do what was demanded of me.

That was shattering. I became very heated and told them what an impertinence it was to tell me such things. "When you're a young mother, you cannot devote all your strength to society. Certainly, you can go about your daily work. But no more than that. There comes a time when the children are grown, and then you can be completely available again." In the end, I took up the profession of day-care worker, and experienced the problems that arise when you leave children to their own devices.

★ ★ ★

In my own childhood, I experienced a lot of love and caring, in spite of my parents' high degree of commitment to society. Today, both of them are very dispirited. Mostly because their ideals, their dreams, were not fulfilled. Yet there had been such favorable circumstances after the war. In principle, everyone had the same chances. You could build up a country together, a feeling of togetherness emerged, and my dad was not just a dumb teacher who drew his pay at the end of the month.

All right, it was also the case that my dad had to quit the work he had come to love so much, because of problems in his, or our, party, the SED. He was a man who set much store by discipline — discipline in the workplace. One day the students informed him — at that time my dad was acting director — that one of the teachers at the college drank alcohol during break. That gave rise to arguments. But the man in question had a good relationship with the SED district leaders. After much back and forth, the differences in opinion finally led to my father's quitting. That brought on a heart attack, because this work was his life. Later, he became a professor at an institute for teacher training. Our doorbell was always ringing. Students would come by to ask his advice in person, although he taught Marxism-Leninism, which was not exactly a very popular subject.

My mom was department head in a production plant. She was the practical one, my father the theorist. There were quite lively encounters when we had breakfast together on weekends. And the vacation we took every year with our parents was also wonderful.

We never watched West German TV at our house. Reasoning that "our life" was even reflected in our TV network. The other one wasn't "our life," and it was hard for us to identify with it. There was always the "Black Channel" with Karl Eduard von Schnitzler, when we wanted to see what the West was like. It was certainly a very one-sided upbringing I got at home. But at that time I didn't miss West German TV at all.

Of course, there were always arguments and issues on which we disagreed. But Dad's attitude was always: one can make things better. When I had concrete problems with a Party leader, his argument was: "He is a comrade, but not the Party. You have to understand that, my girl! The Party as such pursues entirely different fundamental goals. This person behaved wrongly. But he's not the Party, my girl!"

You see, at the time that the problem with the district secretary was happening, my world view, my image of the party, was beginning to waver quite a bit.

* * *

It had always been my wish to work with people, so that's why I applied for, and got, a position at city hall when my daughter was two years old. I didn't go back to preschool work, because I wanted to do a little more with my life. First I worked in the department that dealt with council decisions and their implementation. But this work didn't satisfy me very much. In 1984 I received an offer from the Deputy for Internal Affairs, who needed an employee to deal with marriages between GDR citizens and foreigners. West Germany was of course a foreign country. Totally, for our purposes. This work sounded very attractive by my standards. I imagined I would be able to deal with real people and make all the necessary preparations. Real citizenship problems, I mean. In the department, there was a card index and "cases" that had to be dealt with on an ongoing basis. A team met every Thursday, and I had to prepare the preliminary decisions for these sessions.

This group comprised the departmental director for approvals, a director of the registration office of the People's Police, a director of the Office of Criminal Investigation, and a representative of the Ministry for State Security. The latter always made a big deal of not being a "member" of the team, but just an "observer."

The citizens who came to our office hours on Tuesdays knew nothing about this team, of course. I was the one they talked to. Only when the citizens did not agree with me and said: "I want to speak to your superior" did they get to see the departmental director. During my office hours, I took down particulars: When did you meet? Where? How often have you seen each other? They had to prove how often their meetings had actually taken place.

* * *

Perhaps I should explain that at first it was only a matter of asking for permission to make an application. It was only after this approval had gone through that the actual application could be made. This meant that, according to the statistics, very few applications were turned down. It was just "approval not granted."

The preliminary decision that I had to put together was passed on to this team. They had to agree and sign it. Only then could the application go ahead. Of course, it was important that I could document the suggestions I submitted, whether positive or negative. It was bad for there to be too many discrepancies.

Before the case went to the team, however, the applicant had to fill out a form. All family members had to sign it to confirm that they had no more claims on the person who wanted to marry and emigrate.

The purpose of this form was to play on the disagreements within the families. It was often the case that the parents didn't want their daughter, who, let's say, had met a citizen of West Berlin, to marry the man and emigrate to the West. Mostly because the political situation was such that their child would be gone forever. Perhaps they would never see her again. These disagreements were of course useful.

It happened once that the parents of a girl who wanted to marry came to see me in my office hours. They said things like: "I can't sign this statement. She's my only child, and I might never see her again."

I always argued that they should talk their child into staying here. That was my honest conviction. Because I tried to understand how I would feel if my daughter got to know a West German citizen and I were never to see my child again. It would have broken my heart. And so I laid it out for them from this perspective.

So the purely legal basis for being able to marry a foreigner did exist. But if the parents didn't sign, the case was for all intents and purposes null and void. It was not passed on and not approved.

* * *

Of course there were also cases where people had emigrated or fled and then wanted to bring out their girlfriend or wife. In these cases, tragedies sometimes played themselves out. First of all, the team would give me a negative answer on all of them. But then the wheels would begin to grind all over again. The person says he's not satisfied. The person comes back again and again and *I* have to talk to him. I was always the person who had contact with the applicants, who had to find new arguments over and over again to appease them, to calm them down. That's how I'd like to see it today. At that time, I tried to convince them so they would stay here.

I'd say: "You can continue to reside in the GDR, and your partner can come here." Most of them just smiled at that. Actually, I had a very good relationship with these people. Very often they'd say to me: "Too bad about you, but we know you have to act this way." I often said the same thing, from the other perspective. For it wasn't the worst people who wanted to leave us.

So in principle I always answered marriage cases in the affirmative. Unless I couldn't prove the "authenticity of the relationship." However, I often asked myself how that could really be done, since I wasn't actually standing there holding the candles.

Of course, I did sometimes make a negative decision. If I realized that the partner had forced his emigration to the West through the embassy and was trying to get his wife out. Various other factors also played a role. If the applicant were to tell us that her husband in West Germany had turned to public institutions or to the media, then that would be treated as a special case. In a case like this, I always tried to speak to the woman, so that she could prevent her partner from doing such a thing. But if she was stubborn, the matter was dealt with very quickly. This kind of case was not rare.

Over and above this information, of course, the team had the inquiry reports of the People's Police. Some old woman in the apartment building would be asked when the person came home, who came to visit, and so on. This would be added to the papers. I didn't get to see the inquiries carried out by State Security. These were only mentioned now and then during consultations, by the man from the Ministry for State Security. When an application was denied, the meeting to discuss the denial was held by the head of department. I only sat in on it. But even that was often bad.

Once, it was an actor who had a relationship with a teacher who had moved to the West to look after her mother who needed nursing care. He put in an application immediately. I felt that there was a real relationship between the two of them. The award he'd received for his last movie was taken away from him, just because he had put in a marriage application. But that didn't matter to him. This woman was his life.

So I approved the marriage, although the concrete facts spoke against it. But on a purely human level, one had to say that this was a real relationship. The decision of the team was negative. Main reason: his partner had emigrated first. If her love had been that great, she would have stayed here.

Then the first meeting to discuss the denial was held. I was very anxious, because I knew how this person would feel. I had invited him to the meeting by telephone and I felt in no uncertain terms that he thought he would now be granted his approval, after six months of processing time.

My hands were very cold, and I knew that this decision was wrong from a humane standpoint. The head of department expressed it very formally: "I have to inform you, with regard to the decree of such and such a date, that your petition to be allowed to marry has been denied."

At the word "denied," the man had an absolute short-circuit. I saw it in his face. He was a man, of course, but the tears began to flow. You felt that he really was at the end of his rope. The head of department left the room and I said: "Mr. So and so, let me make you a cup of tea. I can't let you leave like this."

So I went into the next room, where my other colleagues were sitting around, and made him a cup of tea. He gulped down the tea and said: "I will take my own life." I believed him. Just for this reason it was important for me to devote five personal minutes to him after the denial.

I was an employee of the State apparatus, and really shouldn't have done that. But I always saw my work intuitively as being there for the people.

He left then, and continued to fight, called up again, made another petition. I indicated to the team that I feared a suicide attempt. That was one point on which they were careful. They accused me of being too sensitive; he was an actor, and something like this could be a performance.

He held out for a few months, made petitions and follow-up inquiries and was finally allowed to emigrate because his wife in the West was about to turn to the media.

* * *

I also found it difficult to hand over the emigration papers with the children of the applicants sitting across from me. I couldn't imagine how a child would make it over there. That made me afraid, and my fear was real. "The poor children who enter that capitalist state," I thought, "and have to suffer that capitalist education system."

After a while, however, I was harassed more and more often. The files were sent back to me because of some minor point or other. They weren't prepared thoroughly enough, they said. There were more and more discrepancies between my suggestions and the decisions of the team. As I found out later, the Ministry for State Security considered me unsuitable for marriage petitions. I was given a stern talking-to: I was unfit for this work and was to work with the ordinary emigration applications.

That was an attempt to break me. The work there was much harder, and they had noticed, you see, that I took a very emotional approach to the matter. I had the feeling they wanted me out of the way. That was in 1986. Now I had to tell the people: "There is no legal basis for your application." At first I took the work very seriously. I entered into conversations with the people, took time to explain. But the bottom line was always: "There is no legal basis."

* * *

In the meantime, the situation had become so overwhelming that a "reclamation plan" had to be worked out for each person. This work demanded great sacrifices. We had to go into all the problems that were formulated in regard to any particular emigration application, problems with their living situation or with work, everything.

But in spite of this, the rate of success was almost zero. The people had considered all the consequences beforehand, and in their thoughts they were already living in the other country. They had the hope that they would be able to start a new life there. I knew nothing about the West. I was not allowed to have contact with West German citizens. That was something I had to deal with in my own life. The brothers and sisters of my mom and dad left before the Wall was built. My dad had quite consciously avoided contact for all these years. His reason was that his brother had, after all, abandoned his home and his mother.

But there's one thing that I have never been able to forgive myself for. I was not present at the eightieth birthday of my grandma. And I was her favorite grandchild. I wasn't there, because I would have had contact with Westerners. And shortly after that, she died.

This upbringing we received was too one-sided. So much of the really good life was lost to us. There was always some sort of pressure or other, even in the family. Pressure due to work, but not only that. And still we bore it in full awareness. And what could my dad have done? If he had met with his brother, he would have lost his job. Today, he too sees that the best years of brotherhood were spent in separation.

In the meantime, they have already had several meetings, and my dad appreciates the fact that his brother has forgiven him, and also that he was accepted politely and hospitably by my mom's sister and her husband, without any reproaches.

* * *

Anyway, the conflicts at work were gradually coming to a head. We stood right in front of the citizen and fought to the bitter end. The people got more and more aggressive. That was understandable. Some of them had been waiting for years. It was really difficult to hold them back so long. Soon I could hardly stand it any more. I went to work every day with this inner pressure. I became less and less confident in my speech; I was no longer a human being. I wasn't even fully there for my family, for the children.

I went to a spa resort once during this period. When I got back and sat in my chair again for the first time, I burst into tears. While I was at the resort, I could be so relaxed, so free, just as I really am. And then this indefinable pressure again. And I wasn't even a dissident.

In any case, the discrepancies got worse, and I wanted to quit like a martyr, simply pound on the table and throw in the towel. What did I have to lose? But my husband said: "Be smart. You can only do it for health reasons. That's the only acceptable way."

Today, when I look at the memo . . . it's really just a scribble. "I hereby inform you that, for physical and psychological reasons, I am no longer able to perform my present job. Because of my husband's new position, which will mean that more family tasks will fall to me, I ask to be released from my employment contract."

This of course was quite something. They couldn't understand why I now "wished to leave them in the lurch." I was called before a meeting of the entire collective. My nerves were completely shot. I cried and tried to put it all down to health problems. But they just didn't want to let me go.

Then my husband spoke to the district secretary of the SED in our municipal district. "I will only begin my new job if my wife is allowed to leave the council."

Then strings were pulled and from that moment on, everything went well. That was in spring 1988, eighteen months before the changeover. You could already sense quite a bit going on.

I had long wished for a travel law like the one that was passed shortly before the opening of the border. We would have saved ourselves such a lot of trouble and could have let a lot of things happen without a fight if we had given people the chance to fulfill their wish to travel within the law. I mean, at the very latest as soon as all that stuff in Hungary started, you could see that there was going to be no stopping it.

In the meantime, we were watching West German TV at home as well, but not in front of the children, because my view was that "our life" was presented in our TV and that's why they should be watching our channels.

When Egon Krenz was elected, I was pleased at first and agreed with the choice. It all looked very honest and above board. A little while ago, I watched again the television address he gave at the time. It was unbearable.

From spring 1988 onwards, I worked in the personnel department of a large industrial plant. After the currency union, I was one of the first to be let go. Right now I have a position in the ABM, but it is uncertain what will happen after that.

I did a lot of thinking during the changeover. I found it all very humiliating. Especially when those revelations about the privileges held by the party leadership gradually began to emerge. I said to myself: "You strengthened the backs of those people. Through your work, in the state apparatus, you ensured peace and order. You held the whole thing together. And those people couldn't have cared less about it." As we can see now, with hindsight.

I was ashamed of myself, as well. It's true that I felt that I had often acted correctly, that my attitude towards the marriage petitions was often correct, from a humane point of view, but, with hindsight, I found it terrible that the state had interfered in such family matters. I had felt the same thing intuitively at the time.

I remember how we once had to read the "Human Rights Convention." At that time, I had the feeling that in reality we were the ones violating human rights; we didn't allow people to be able to choose their own place of residence. But I didn't dare say anything at the meeting. Two people from State Security gave the introduction. They gave us a lot of examples of human rights violations in the capitalist countries, and that was that.

A society molds its careers. My job was a product of this society of the past. It is with grief that I remember that I gave it everything I had. Or had to give it everything. I did it for a long time out of total conviction. Up to a certain point. I intruded upon a very human, private sphere that was really none of my business. That was nobody's business. But I also did a lot for people. I have to take pride in that. I advocated for apartments, I was a conversation partner for many people in complicated circumstances. Also, I learned a lot in this work; I was able to gather a lot of experiences, dealing with people, with dissidents.

My daughter had her coming-of-age ceremony this year. I had been looking forward to that celebration. Then when I go into the city council boardroom, there's a man sitting in my row, the man from State Security who had harassed me so much. It was because of him that I was finally moved to general emigration petitions. In those minutes, as my daughter stood up front and the man's name was read out in relation to his son, many things went through my head.

I said to myself: "At least I had the strength to break out honestly, and you just used your power to oppress others." This is what became clear to me at that moment. I was also a little proud that I had left back then under my own steam.

* * *

In the midst of the revolutionary situation I too said it couldn't go on like that. But I didn't run to the Wall in a euphoric mood. It wasn't until a month or two later that I went to West Berlin. I just couldn't grasp it and I also anticipated it with a lot of fear. In the first place, I was thinking about the children, about what would bombard us after the opening of the Wall. Not immediately, of course, but gradually.

Our isolated life had many negative aspects. Our horizons were very limited. But as far as caring for the children and one's life was concerned, it was actually very positive. We had that under control. I think. Better than now.

I would like to pass on to my children that they should take everything that education has to offer. They shouldn't get to know only one philosopher, like we did. They should develop their own worldview. And I would like to work for my family's sake. So that they can afford a certain standard of living. And I would like to take a look at the world, the part of the world that was kept from me for all those years. I didn't miss it before, but now I'd find it very difficult if I were no longer able to travel.

I also have to learn to deal with this freedom we now have. In this society, we can accomplish a lot of things, and I want to pass that on to the children, because they can make of their lives whatever they want to. But this society will also leave you behind if you can't make it any more.

If you have money, you can enjoy your life. But I think you can have a good life even if you live very modestly. I would like to communicate that to my children, because they often do not see boundaries. They have so many wishes, generated by these unbelievable choices we have. I would like to make them aware of the true values in life, which are not only material values. Honesty, commitment, thoughtfulness, justice. Actually, these are all values that I also saw in my . . . in the former Party.

Back then, I really couldn't imagine that Marx and Lenin could not have been right. There were after all so many clever people, so many scholars, who studied it back then, who lived it and made it accessible to us. It all seemed so logical to me. An alternative to capitalism. I did sense the differences between theory and practice, but that the entire theory was wrong, well, that was just inconceivable. . . .

CHAPTER THREE

YOU SHOULD KNOW I WON'T BE BLACKMAILED . . .

— Protestant country pastor, born 1925

THERE ARE DAYS YOU NEVER FORGET. For instance, March 9, 1960; that was a Wednesday. I remember it to this day. Because it's unusual to have funerals on a Sunday, but on Sunday March 6, in K., I buried an old farmer. Back then funeral services were still held in the home, with an open coffin. Only after everything was over was the coffin closed and carried out. Afterwards, there was the usual coffee drinking, and the atmosphere was very subdued. Normally, you see, gatherings after funerals were quite lighthearted affairs. But the undercurrent was: "Today we buried the last free farmer." Because these "recruitment teams" would come from Rostock and on Wednesday they were ensconced here in our town. They consisted of three or four men who went from farm to farm and, first in a friendly fashion then later by force, made people sign. Some signed immediately. Those who held out were taken to the offices of the local authority. The council chairman at the time turned up as well and gave the recalcitrants a good talking to. They said to Farmer Linkshofen, who stood firm until the end: "If you don't sign — and you don't have to — then we'll fence in your land, we'll brick up your chimney, and then you can see how you get on." That's the kind of tactics they used. In the end, they all signed.

There was a church service again the next Sunday. What an uproar! What had I said? That we had had a very emotional week, something like that, and I also talked about injustice.

"As far as I'm concerned, large-scale agriculture might make sense. But not the way it's happening here."

But it only became really bad when, a little later, all the animals were driven out of their stalls. The horses, the cows, the animals the farmer depends on, you know. And how the animals were treated on the collective farms! The food they got! The horses disappeared right away, the good milk cows were ruined in a very short time. And the farmers had to watch all this happen.

* * *

I wasn't afraid. Of course, sometimes there were people in the church who went and gave a report afterwards, especially when the bishops had ordered a certain pulpit reading. Thirty years I was on the district church council, and deputy superintendent for many of those years. I remember, one Sunday there was to be another pulpit reading, and the Saturday before, three gentlemen suddenly came and asked me whether I already had the "thing." I knew the text was coming — it was always sent by courier — but I really didn't have it yet. "No, I've only heard it's coming," I say.

That wasn't a secret, since they already knew that.

"So . . . well . . . then it'll come, won't it," they say.

"Yes, I'm sure it will come."

Then they say I should instruct the pastors not to read it out.

Then I say: "But that would be overstepping my authority. I'm sorry, gentlemen."

"But you're the superintendent."

"That's true," I say. "But if you were to receive an order from your region, can you then say you're just not going to carry it out in the district of B.?"

"No."

"You see, I can't either. When an order comes from the consistory or the bishop, every pastor has to make the decision for himself. I have no authority over that."

"So, will you be reading it from the pulpit?"

"Yes, of course I'll be reading it."

"Thank you."

And they were gone. Then statistics were gathered. Mondays in B. they worked out which pastor read it and which didn't.

Some pastors were amazed: "How do they know that? Surely our people wouldn't squeal on us?"

"I imagine it's quite simple," I'd say. "Granny was at church, and it's the job of the grandchild or the son-in-law to ask: 'Well, Granny, did the pastor read something from the pulpit?'

And she says, 'Yes.' Quite simple."

* * *

Well, it was relatively quiet here in the village in 1989. The services of intercession were being held in B., the county seat. They began as early as February. And when the migrations started in the summer, through the embassies and through Hungary, more and more people drove to B. from the villages.

Around five thousand people were there during the critical days. They even stood in the church square, because the church couldn't hold all the people who had gathered. So everything was transmitted to the square by loudspeakers.

We didn't hold any services of intercession here in R. It's not usual in the country, you know. But quite a few people had been at the Monday services and demonstrations in B. So many things had been building up over such a long period of time.

I remember one particular meeting. It was October 5, 1989, two days before the fortieth anniversary of the GDR. The former Council Chairman of the district — who would now be called the *Landrat* — had a long tradition of inviting the pastors to a meeting two or three times a year. Of course, there were always some of the SED district leaders present, as well as several from the block parties. The meetings were pretty outspoken. Otherwise, the pastors wouldn't have gone. So, on that particular October 5, the "State Secretary for Church Matters" was invited as a guest, the final one. And he gave us a lecture that must have been an hour and a half long: forty years of the GDR. And everything was wonderful.

We, I mean the pastors, looked at each other and thought: "Where does this man actually live?" So far from any sense of reality. Afterwards, there was a discussion, questions were asked, and he was confronted with a lot of things. It was pretty hard. At first he didn't want to get into it — kept avoiding the subject. But after coffee, he became noticeably quiet. In the end, a pastor accompanied him to his official car and then the State Secretary said: "Well, there are some things one just has to think about."

Then the pastor said to him: "Mr. State Secretary — if I may — it's already too late for that."

At that he completely crumpled. You could see it on his face, clear as day.

* * *

On October 7, I watched a bit of the military parade on TV. At that time we had a son in the "People's Army," in Schwerin. I had endured many an anxious moment. He, too, was on alert. And you didn't know: Will it happen like it did in China? Will he be drawn into it too? Fortunately it didn't go beyond the alert. S. was probably a little bit too far from Berlin. But if they had ordered deployment, then he would have been involved too.

In the village, people did not really dare open their mouths. Everyone knew what had happened in China. You only talked to people you trusted. It was obvious to everyone that it would somehow boil over. But what form that would take, of course, no one could guess. No one thought that the Wall would open and that there would be a reunification.

On November 9, on the very evening itself, I learned that the Wall was open. A couple from West Berlin was visiting us. They left late that afternoon and called us from Spandau. They had noticed at the border crossing on Bornholmer Strasse that something was brewing. They had just managed to get through.

That evening we simply couldn't grasp it. There was disbelief and skepticism and joy, but it was now a fact. The following Saturday, many young people from the village, including our youngest son, went to Berlin. They were wined and dined from Saturday afternoon till Sunday evening — without a break! Simply unbelievable!

Then one evening in January I invited a few young men from the village to my home. There were very different types of people present, even some who didn't belong to the church. And I told them: "If things are not to remain the way they are now, you must get yourselves organized. You must announce that you are ready to run for office when the elections begin."

It was not at all easy to convince them. You see, the younger generation had never experienced elections. It was only handing in a ballot. That's why there was hardly anyone who was willing to get involved out here in the country.

Back in those years, almost everyone went to hand in their ballots. Apart from us, that is, and a very few others. Later, we did take part in the local elections. Goes without saying that we didn't vote for the "National Front" candidates! But by simply taking part in the elections you showed that you were absolutely against those people. I said at the time: "The people on the spot here, in the local council, are not those who really bear the responsibility. We know them all well."

Of course, we always stayed away from the elections for the so-called People's Congress. My wife and I, and the children, too.

But at the meeting I was telling you about, there were some who said: "All right, we'll become candidates for the CDU." And others: "Well, then we'll try for the SPD."

I told no one which party to go up for. They made their own decisions on that. Those who were somewhat church-oriented went for the CDU, and those who were not so church-oriented for the SPD. No one became a member of either party, and still isn't, as far as I know, but they became candidates.

* * *

On the evening before Unification Day, which was October 3, 1990, a dance was held in the village; "Dance Unity," it was called. Because the hall had been in disrepair for years, the dance was held in the school gym.

During the preparations, there was an argument within the church: "Should the bells be rung at midnight or not?" The reason given by those in the district parish assembly who opposed this was: "Unification is a secular occasion, so the bells are to keep silent."

Now, I'm a conservative person and yet I said: "New Year's Eve is also a secular occasion, and we ring the bells at twelve o'clock, and this unique event is surely worth as much to us as New Year's Eve."

Each local church council was to decide for its own church. The consistory put it in such a way that no pastor could make the decision under his own steam, so to speak. I told the Elders that they could make the decision according to their own consciences. But they were all fired up — in favor! "Of course the bells will ring — no question about that!"

So that evening I went to the dance. Primarily because I wanted to stand by the new mayor. He didn't have an easy time of it in the beginning, you see. Still so young, still finding his feet, as they say.

So shortly before midnight, I left with the bell-ringers. Since they had all been drinking quite a bit already, I went along so that no one would fall off the church tower. So they rang the bells, and I lit a fire under them: "Get on with it, they're waiting for us, we have to get back right away."

While the bells were ringing, everyone had gathered outside to listen. Afterwards, they went back inside the gym, and when we got there, everyone was already standing in a semicircle around the band, and we joined them. The band struck up "Einigkeit und Recht und Freiheit." We sang at the tops of our voices. But four or five people kept their seats. Those were the "Old Guard." I asked myself: "Why did they come at all?" They didn't stand up and they didn't sing. But everyone else joined in.

Now the excitement's no longer so great. The mood hasn't turned against unity, but it has gone too quickly for some people. Of course, there are some who always spoil everything. There's more crime, they say, more uncertainty, and so on and so on.

Certainly, much has changed in this short time. When I think of the average senior citizen: he was able to pick up his pension at the mayor's office every month. Now everyone has to have a bank account. Some people never had one of those in all their lives. Now they have to go to B. to pick up the money there. All small stuff, but it's something quite new and unusual for simple people. Then there's the paperwork. Unemployment. Uncertainty. We're a place that always made a living by agriculture. And there are no more prospects when it comes to agriculture. The collective farm went bankrupt. The old farmers are either dead or have moved away or are much too old. No one starts from scratch any more. The generation that followed the organization of the collective farms has gone into other professions, you see. And the people they brought in — and I don't want to tread on anyone's toes here — well, they're no agricultural experts. To put it mildly.

* * *

I came to this village in 1953. My home is on the other side of the Oder river; my home church is in Stolpe, in the state of Pomerania. I was a soldier. The usual length of time. First labor detail, then the army. I was wounded on the Western Front as late as February 1945 and was in several army hospitals in West Germany. I also have an artificial lower leg, the right one. I just got a package: on the piece of land where I was wounded — we were there once, two years ago — one of my wife's school friends found a grenade fragment. She sent it to me. The whole field is still full of them, although the farmers have cleared away so much over the years.

I received my training as a pastor in Berlin. I was born in 1925. When the war was over, I was twenty. I came to R. in 1953 and I've stayed here ever since.

At that time, the place was full of individual farms. A few of them formed a small cooperative. This was when it was still voluntary. The initiator was a woman farmer. Emma Weber. She was just as pious as she was political. She came to church services and always kept her eyes closed. But if you asked her about it, she'd say: "I hear everything."

Well, she was very active politically, but still I confirmed a whole series of her children. But one daughter later became a state prosecutor. She was political in a very bad sense.

In any case, the cooperative was quite weak. You see, only those who couldn't survive any other way joined it. After all, this was back when you had to reach a target.

At that time, the beginning of the fifties, the entire GDR nursed the hope that all this was only a transitional phase. That it wouldn't stay like this. The opinion of the majority was that the economy was not at all viable, that it couldn't go on in this fashion. It was only a question of time, they said, and it would collapse. Of course, there were also the "hard liners" and their followers; I mean, those who expected some kind of advantage from going along with it.

* * *

I was still employed in B. around June 17, 1953. We had a flourishing youth group there, at that time still divided up by age and sex. They only came together after age seventeen, but before that they were kept separate.

The traditional high school had become the school for the county, and the director was awful when it came to ideology. Very set against the *Junge Gemeinde* and against the church. But, according to an old tradition, there was still an official chaplaincy at this school.

The assembly hall was used as the sanctuary. Above the stage, you could see Paul on the Areopagus in Athens, and there was an organ, and the religious services were held here. Later, all that came to an end.

Anyway, the school chaplain, with whom I had shared a landlady for a while when I was living in furnished rooms in B., was right-wing; more right-wing couldn't have been possible. But a very clever man, and he stirred up trouble wherever he could.

He held morning prayers for the students in the forest near the school, as a protest, because he had been banned from the school. There were students there every day, because the man really had fascinating charisma. In addition, he always held a service on Saturdays. Basically, it was a political sermon, and the church was filled to the rafters.

He had a different topic each time, with a biblical basis of course, and State Security was constantly there. Sometimes police officers even sat inside, in uniform. Then he'd have tables and chairs brought forward and he would say: "Ladies and Gentlemen of the Ministry for State Security, please come forward, so that you can be more comfortable writing this down." That's what he'd say. Of course, a rumble would go through the church, like the rolling of thunder. Later, the consistory advised him to go to West Berlin; otherwise the man would surely have been taken into custody some day.

Before June 17, the senior students were interrogated about the *Junge Gemeinde*. Individually. In front of twenty-one adults. They were to say that they had been encouraged to commit sabotage. When they came to school the next day, they were told: "You can take your bags and go home. You're out of here." Many of them went to West Berlin. Later, after June 17, they were allowed to go back to school. But only a few took advantage of this. They had gotten the shock of their lives. At night they had bad dreams and even screaming fits.

* * *

I lived in R. from October 1, 1953 onwards. I held my trial sermon on July 5. The church was filled to the rafters. It was quite natural for them to want to see what kind of a man was coming.

I had been offered three positions as pastor. I had ridden my bicycle over from B. with a friend. The position had already been vacant for two years, and the church, the parsonage, and the old school that still belonged to the church were in a dilapidated condition.

After we rode back, we both sat at the side of the road. I said to my friend: "I don't think I need to look at the other jobs. Someone has to take over here."

* * *

Of course, it was very cramped at the beginning. Even though we were on the best of terms with the two families who lived in the house with us. We eventually had seven children, my wife and I. Six of us slept in this room, now my study. It was only later that the other families gradually moved away.

When we arrived, the wallpaper was hanging off the walls and the windows were broken, and so we had to make the house livable before anything else. Then the church had to get a roof. We were paying back the loan until only a few years ago.

We had hardly finished that when I received the neighboring town too, because the pastor there had died suddenly. There was always conflict between that town and ours. When some kind of leisure activity was put on over there, our boys got beaten up, and when we put on an activity, their boys got beaten up. Because of the girls. "Only *we* tread our hens," as the proverb goes. Oh well.

But I never went to these activities. That was out of the question. And as pastor I had a good relationship with the people from the other town. They always held huge family celebrations, and the pastor was to be there if at all possible, for lunch, for coffee, and on into the evening.

* * *

In our village, most of the conflict centered around the school. I had my children in that school for twenty-five years, from the oldest to the youngest; I often went to parent meetings, and of course I was always public enemy number one for them. There were hardly any reprisals taken against me personally. But the children — they didn't get to go to the upper high school, except for the oldest, who managed to graduate.

But our second child was truly gifted. No, I would never have tried to get my children into the upper high school for the sake of prestige. Why should they struggle if it's not right for them? But our second child, he had an A average and was rejected. A student had to fulfill three prerequisites, they said: excellent academic achievement, excellent attitude, and — I don't remember how they put it — but he had to show evidence of something ideological. So I sat down and wrote three full letter-size pages: "My son's academic achievements are very good, and no one has complained about his behavior, but in spite of all this he has been turned down. In this regard, I would like to express the following. While reading your letter, I had to think back to my own school days. I can still remember quite clearly the day when our Jewish classmates were taken out of school. Not because they were low achievers, but because they were 'different.' They were not yet being gassed at that time."

Of course, I received an immediate summons to B. To face the district council and the Stasi. By chance, I had a funeral one day later in B. So I called and said: "I'll be in B. a day later anyway, so we can take that opportunity to speak with each other." They actually agreed to that. So off I went. Head to toe in black. With my cassock and suitcase for the funeral. I said: "I have only so much time. As you can see, I have a funeral today."

Five or six men were sitting there. The council chairman, his deputy for internal affairs, the superintendent of schools, and also two men from the Stasi.

I had compared the GDR to the Third Reich, and I was to take it back.

I say: "No. I did no such thing. I only told you the thoughts that came into my head." And then I say: "I can still give you the names of my Jewish classmates that were banned from school. They had committed no crime." And: "Where is the difference between those who were not allowed to get their diplomas back then because of race, and these banned now because of ideology?"

I did not give a retraction. I took back nothing. I said: "That was my impression. I recorded that impression in my letter to you. I take none of it back."

Nothing happened. Of course, the boy didn't get into the school, but he graduated from a church high school and went on to become a pastor.

* * *

My dealings with the school principal here in the village were just the same as with any other person in the village. "Hello and goodbye." In the beginning, once, we had a conversation together, four hours at his place and then another three hours at mine. From then on each of us knew what to think of the other. He was one of the politically devout, even a member of the People's Congress. There were only two times that I really got into it with him. Primarily about the "youth initiation." In principal, this was voluntary, but actually an unbelievable amount of psychological terrorizing was brought to bear. Mostly on the Youth Initiation Board. The teachers were also exploited, but they went along with it somehow, some with courage, others really just to keep their jobs.

At first there were more who did not take part than did. Of course, for the education office in B., that meant a black mark against the principal. I didn't want to hurt him personally. But I couldn't say just for his sake: "Now why don't you all just go, so that Principal so-and-so can have his one-hundred-percent-attendance record."

So every year there were some who didn't take part. Our own seven children of course, and a few others.

One time there was a parents' meeting I didn't go to, because I didn't have a child in that class. At this parents' meeting, they were to sign their children up for the youth initiation.

I was told later that there was a heated discussion and one woman said: "We've already signed something, and we're not signing anything else!"

She meant the agreement to joint the collective farm. The principal jumped on her and threatened to report her because of her remark. It wasn't as if people had been forced to sign to join the collective farm. Such a thing just couldn't happen . . .

So the principal said he was adjourning the parents' meeting because he realized that the parents and the school were at odds with each other.

Then they all went home, and some were very worried, especially this woman, and so she came to me. So I went to the principal and said: "Mr. Heinrich, you haven't always weighed every word as carefully as you should have either! Let the people alone! They were overwrought. Let's keep this in this room, or else some of the other things that have been said may have to be made public." Actually, he didn't report anything. The woman hasn't been harassed to this very day.

And I intervened one more time when the preparations for the youth initiation were at their height. Principal Heinrich. was doing the recruiting himself, and some boy's father had refused to sign. The principal said: "If you don't sign, you're not for peace." Well. Who doesn't want to be for peace? Anyway, that was the last straw for me. The father spoke to me about it and I told him: "I can only do something if I have permission to use your name."

"Yes, you have my permission."

So I asked the superintendent to get me a meeting with the council chairman. This chairman was also the First Secretary of the district leadership of the SED, a very hard man. Well, we had the meeting. There were five men; the chairman himself, the deputy for internal affairs, the inspector for schools, and one from the Stasi. I was accompanied by the superintendent and another pastor. The council chairman said: "This meeting was your idea, so what do you want?"

Well, they had also invited Principal Heinrich. Of course, they never said a word about this beforehand. It was supposed to be a surprise. As the fifth man, he sat directly opposite me.

I say: "Mr. Chairman, I would like to protest the way in which the recruiting for the youth initiation is being carried out in our village."

"Examples?"

"In one particular case, someone said: 'If you do not sign, then you are not for peace.'"

The council chairman says: "And who is supposed to have said that?"

I say: "The principal of our school."

And the council chairman says: "Well, surely you don't think the principal would use such a primitive method of argumentation."

I say: "One would not like to think so, Mr. Chairman."

Heinrich went completely white and said: "Where is this supposed to have happened?"

I say: "At so-and-so's house."

— Silence. —

Then we went back and forth for another two and a half hours. And it really became easier in our village after that. Let's say, it kept within limits. But you know, the people became so well drilled later that they did what was expected of them completely by themselves.

★ ★ ★

But our principal also did some good things. You have to say that. Delegations came here from all over the GDR. He introduced the all-day school system that dominated the educational literature of the time. He was an "Outstanding Teacher of the People" and we got on quite well with each other on a personal level. Except for certain subjects of course. Now he has left his position, retired and moved away, a few villages over. Sometimes he comes back for a funeral. Then we'll sit and have coffee together. That's happened a few times. The situation with the district council has never been spoken of again. I'm not going to bring it up. If he were to do that, then all well and good, but he has never done so and I don't think he will.

★ ★ ★

So I was never afraid. We always talked very openly, in church, in our men's group, in the youth hour. Of course, always presuming that everything was being overheard. But "they" knew what I thought. Why should I pretend to be something I'm not? I've noticed that the people who showed their fear, or said: "I'll think about it," or: "Come back later," or: "I don't know yet" were always being needled. They were just never left in peace. The more clearly someone stated their opinion, the more he was respected. On all levels.

★ ★ ★

All right. They did try to get rid of me once. At that time, the school was still using a room here in the parsonage. So the mayor at the time picked up the key from the sexton — he's dead now, too — and wrote to invite the elders of the church to a meeting in the room. I was the only one not invited. By chance, I was at the home of one of the elders, on a completely different errand, and he says: "Well, tonight we've got a meeting."

I say: "Meeting?"

"Well, I got a note." So I asked him to show it to me. They were probably going to make a resolution against me saying that I was unbearable or something.

So of course I went to all their homes and said: "You can do what you want. But this is not our meeting, and here's what's behind it. Just so you know what's going on."

Not one of them went. The meeting never happened. That was the only attempt. But apart from that, I must say that I have always had respect.

★ ★ ★

Once — and this is a true story — there was a scandal in our village. Because of Mr. Reck's funeral. He was a real character and his last job had been as a night watchman. The last night watchman we ever had, in fact. Besides this, he was a beadle, and rang a bell whenever the mayor had an announcement to make. He went to a particular spot and rang his bell, and then people came outside and he read the announcement aloud. This happened in many villages, and it went on until he died. This was back in the seventies.

So this Mr. Reck was a member of the SED, but he also belonged to the parish. He had had a hard life. He was widowed early, his two daughters died of typhoid, and he was left alone with two grandsons. He brought them up very faithfully. I confirmed both of them, and one of them I even married later. The other moved away.

So this Mr. Reck was left all alone at the end. But he always paid his church taxes, and he said to me on just such an occasion — although he seldom came to church — "I want a church funeral." We weren't thinking about his death at that moment. But one day he went downhill very quickly.

Now, what usually happens here is that when someone dies, the parting bell is rung on the following day at ten in the morning. In memory of the dead and as a call to intercession. These days we ring it just before twelve, because ten's a bad time where work is concerned.

So the relatives have to come and say: So-and-so is dead, and then the ringing is ordered. But no one came, so the bell wasn't rung. People asked: "Isn't Reck going to be buried? We wanted to order a wreath. But if he's not going to have a church burial, then we're not going to. So should we order one or not?"

"So far no one has come forward."

And then, on the second day, the former mayor came by with the man who was at that time the head of the collective farm. They were two party stalwarts.

"We just want to say that we want a burial plot for Reck, and the party will take care of everything else."

I say: "Just a moment. Mr. Reck doesn't have any relatives left. If they were to say that, I'd have to accept it. But he told me he wanted a church funeral."

But no; they insisted.

So I say: "You are violating him after death, and he cannot protect himself. I'm not over-keen on funerals. But this goes completely against his wishes." But they just wanted to know whether they could hang up their Communist flag in the hall.

I say: "You can do whatever you want to with your flag, lay it on the coffin or hang it on the door or on the wall. I don't care. But I won't let you hang it in front of the crucifix!"

They wanted to throw the crucifix in the bushes!

I say: "That's out of the question. The crucifix means at least as much to us as your flag does to you."

The mayor says: "Then others will be back to speak to you."

At this I opened the door and said: "Out! You've known me long enough. You should know I won't be blackmailed!" And with that I threw them both out.

That must have been on a Monday, because Dr. Klausen was here and had surgery hours, and I happened to catch up with her.

I say: "Aren't there any relatives left? Doesn't Gerd still live in B.?"

She says: "I'll drive you there. You have to talk to him."

So I ask the grandson: "Do you mean for your grandfather to have a socialist funeral?"

"No," he says, "not at all. But they were here and they said they'd take care of everything. I thought they'd order it, the church and everything."

And so I told him what they'd said.

"I can't believe it!"

I say: "Then you'll have to go to the mayor and tell him that."

"Yes. I'll do that! I'll be there in the morning."

By now it was evening. The next day was the pastors' conference, and still the bell hadn't been rung.

I said to him: "After you've been to the mayor, go to my wife and say that you've canceled the socialist funeral, and my wife will see to it that the bell is rung, so that people know what's going on."

* * *

Later, the grandson told me what happened. The mayor was holding the telephone receiver when he walked in. He said to him: "Siegfried, this is not right. Our grandfather is to get a church funeral." Right then the mayor dropped the telephone, probably from shock. Everything really was canceled. And the bell was rung at ten o'clock.

* * *

Then we held the funeral. All the party members stood on one side, the rest of the people on the other. None of the party members took off their hats or their caps, in order to make a point. Not even when the coffin was carried past them!

The next time I talked to the district council, I mentioned this and said: "You know, it didn't make a good impression on the inhabitants of the village that the comrades kept their hats on during the funeral. We're not used to that!" It has never happened again.

I have never hated anyone. One should avoid that. Of course, I did not like chicaneries like this being perpetrated on the church. But if you are convinced of something, then that's your right. And it's my right to have a different opinion. You have to have mutual respect.

And if someone today wants to be a stalwart PDS man, then that's what he should be, if he hasn't learned anything at all from the past. There are such people, you know. But others have experienced things differently.

* * *

I allow everyone their experiences. Somewhere in the villages around here we even have the so-called *Sixth Book of Moses,* which you can use to work magic. It got really bad in a neighboring village I was also responsible for. People said the cattle were bewitched. A lot of cows went into a decline, and then they fetched someone who was said to have certain powers, who knew white magic.

He had water with him; he had to beat himself on the nose until it bled, and then the blood had to flow into the water, and then there was something else, and then he went through the stalls and sprinkled everything.

I don't know if someone had secretly inherited this book from someone who practiced in earlier times. There are no more magic spells. There was a woman in A.; people from the entire neighborhood went to see her to be cured by incantation. Actually, I had a very good relationship with her otherwise. She also came to church services. One time when I was alone with her, we got onto the subject. She got really angry. She was doing good, she said. And then she said: "I'm old; I won't live long. I'll teach you."

Of course, I couldn't allow that. You shouldn't. There are often spiritual after-effects. People can't believe any more. Or they can't pray. They want to but can't. Or they have blasphemous thoughts and the like. Often the cause can be traced to occult stuff like this.

Of course, I don't believe everything I hear about such things. But that doesn't mean there aren't realities that can influence us. We can make these forces subservient to us, but these forces can also make human beings subservient to them. I've seen too much of that, even at home in Pomerania. None of this was new to me. I'm thinking especially of three people. None of them knew of the others' existence, and I never said who they were. But sometimes they could foresee who was going to be the next to die. Or they saw what was going to happen. One was a very pious man who suffered greatly from having seen all of that from the time he was five years old. Few people knew about it, because he would certainly have become a laughingstock.

So I've experienced a few things. You can laugh it off, you can believe it or not believe it — your salvation does not depend on it. But I believe that there are dark forces as well as good.

What is it that makes some people behave in the ways you read about sometimes or see on television? How abysmally dark can a person be?

Does it just come from the person himself? And why is someone else completely different? I really do believe we are exposed to certain forces and influences.

After 1970 there were some suicides here in the villages. A married couple, within a year of each other. A complete mystery. He was the mailman here in the parish. In C., some people walked out into the water. Even a young girl. Why? Because the mother was messing around with the girl's fiancé. By the way, the suicides in C. began to increase till there were so many that I was almost ready to say I wouldn't bury any more of them.

It was like an epidemic. So many of them. One almost every year. And they were all well-off people. You don't find any poor people doing that. They're very hardworking, very together. But it's a trait of a certain kind of person. Here they always say: They're from the Pfalz. That's where they come from. A settlement from the time of Frederick the Great.

When there's a celebration, the tables are groaning. Nothing is kept back. It just can't be big enough. And then there's this other side . . . I can't explain it.

In the old days, there were still huge weddings here in R. You can't imagine how many people gathered when the bridal couple came to the church with their guests. Or when there was a golden wedding anniversary. If the couple could still walk, then the whole church square was full and on up the street to the pub.

There haven't been any weddings for a long time. It has stagnated somehow. Since the changeover. Either people don't have the money, or they move away. And some, well, they just live together. Perhaps it'll all come back again . . . Who knows . . . Who knows? . . .

CHAPTER FOUR

THEY EVEN ACCUSE ME OF HAVING PLANNED MURDERS . . .

— Major Glewe, 45, retired State Security officer

R IGHT AFTER I BEGAN WORKING at the Ministry for State Security, I wanted to quit again, because I was given a position dealing with the church, and at that time, 1972, I felt it was unimportant. My thoughts ran like this: "Is this kind of work even necessary? Couldn't I do more for society in another profession?"

So I was seriously thinking about the possibility of getting out completely. But then I said to myself: "What if everyone did that? I mean, not liking your post and saying right away: I'm not going to do it." There are always tasks in society that are not particularly well liked but have to be done. That's the reason I stayed on in the beginning.

Anyway, in time, by the end of the seventies, a change had taken place. I really had the feeling that I was doing something significant, that I was making an important contribution to the defense of the GDR. Over and above doing my actual job, I had submitted certain suggestions for "operative work" to the other regional administrations of State Security.

It was only in the second half of the eighties that I began to reflect in general terms on the effectiveness of our work. At that time it seemed to us that our information on the evolution of "hostile negative forces," as we called them then, was not generating the appropriate political reactions. In early 1987, this culminated in my writing a proposal for dealing with all political groupings. I really thought that this would give me the chance to act for the good of society as a whole. This proved later to be a fallacy. But at that point in time I believed in it.

On your first day at the Ministry, you have to write out your statement of commitment, and you are told your place of work, your department, and the subject area you'll be dealing with.

Of course, you would have already been acting as an unofficial co-worker, or UC. In addition, I had been inducted into the reserve cadre of the Ministry three years earlier. That meant that I received eighty marks a month more stipend, among other things.

My inner motivation was always to be in intelligence. I believed in socialism and I saw the gathering of intelligence as an important job with which I could make a contribution to the strengthening of socialism.

I was born in 1948. For me, memories of the Second World War were connected to the struggle between capitalism and socialism. This contrast also determined my childhood experiences. Or to put it another way: as a child, I somehow reached an emotionally charged rapport with socialism. Because I was against fascism, against concentration camps, and against the oppression of other countries.

True, my father was also in the Party, but he in no way forced me to develop in a certain political direction. I had complete freedom of choice where that was concerned. I can't remember whether or not my father's past played a role in my childhood. I only knew that he had been very badly wounded in the war and was once almost buried alive. But that wasn't spoken of very often. Apart from the fact that he had "been there" and had gotten to know the "hardships of war." But he didn't speak of his motives, his thoughts and feelings, and it seems like I had no questions to ask him either.

Of course, I later saw contradictions in our society and addressed them, but I was always of the opinion that socialism was the better system.

There were also many discussions among the students in my year. At that time, I was even going out with a fellow student who was not a Party member, nor even a candidate for membership. But all that aside, she was, of course, positively disposed toward the GDR. Actually, critical questions were discussed within the Party. My attitude at the time was: "Even if the comrades criticize something from a political standpoint, that doesn't mean others are allowed to do the same." You see, some wanted to make things better, and others were the opposition. Yes, I do believe I was a little allergic to criticism from the outside, because these critics, so I thought, did not really want socialism.

* * *

But I didn't intend to be something special or become "famous." On the contrary: if you want to be in intelligence, you take the path diametrically opposed to that; you have to remain completely inconspicuous. At most, the only thing that can be important is the information you manage to gather without being detected yourself. I saw my study of physics as a good foundation. Because the natural sciences occupy a key position in the dispute between the systems, I was of the opinion that my training as a physicist could be a good qualification. Of course, I did not see the meaning of my work and my life to be in gathering information or becoming an intelligence officer, but, in the final analysis, in helping socialism to victory. I wanted to promote that with all my strength. To a great extent I was ready to subordinate my life to these goals. I didn't see it as "self-sacrifice." For me, the "correspondence of individual and societal interests in socialism" was actually a reality. The strengthening of socialism fit with my individual goals. And I was even willing to accept a whole host of personal disadvantages for it. I considered socialism to be a just society in which the exploitation of man by man had finally been eliminated . . . Well, should have been.

Of course, I was mired in "bloc" thought patterns. In the sixties, there was the war in Vietnam; the conflict between East and West was at its height. In 1968, of course, I was all for using the military to suppress . . . what was going on in Czechoslovakia because I believed that . . . what was happening there was an imperialist attack on socialism and not, of course, an inner development of the communist party itself.

Perhaps my attitude also has to do with how I grew up and was educated. Where we lived in the North, it wasn't possible to get good reception of West German TV channels, and anyway, as a child I once heard a program in which it was established that the West German channels were running down the GDR. I drew my own conclusion from this: "No, I'll not watch or listen to the West."

But I didn't see any sense in turning the TV antennas on the roofs away from the West, even back then. If I decide not to watch or listen to any West German channels, then I do it voluntarily. Conformity just for show went against my beliefs. I also thought the wholesale attack on long hair or jeans was not right. Of course, I didn't understand or defend "individual freedom." But, in my opinion, long hair was only an external matter that didn't necessarily have anything to do with the interior attitudes of the person. Actually, I was against long hair personally — but more for reasons of fashion, because I was brought up conservatively, you see. I didn't wear jeans either. But perhaps that was because I never had the chance to get any.

I do not see any contradiction between this view and my work in the Ministry. Even there, we did not want to intimidate anyone, or to force any external conformity. No. We did not want to quash the "outward trappings" of the opposition. In our understanding of "political underground activity," we assumed that the majority of the people were "misguided." This term was specifically used. Only a few "prominent operatives" were approached in a "hostile manner," as we called it, and they were the ones who wanted to bring down the socialist context as a whole. The majority were always "misguided" or "fellow travelers." That's why a great part of the analyses that we had to make consisted of working out the subjective aspect of the actions of these "fellow travelers."

* * *

My workweek was Monday through Friday, 8:00 A.M. to 5:00 P.M. When I started, I read the duty regulations and completed a basic course on the workings and structure of the Ministry for State Security. That's a course that employees from all areas have to take, from the cleaning staff up to operatives. This was followed by instructions specifically for "operative work." This was a theory course, in which you were familiarized with the various methods. At the same time, you had to continue studying all kinds of regulations. Marxism-Leninism also formed part of this basic training. Criminal law was also important, especially the "operative" part. Usually there was further training one day a week, and the other days were spent in your office.

I gave myself two years. I knew you couldn't judge this work after six months; that you needed a good length of time to get into the material. In this beginning phase, the work was very strained; it was no fun, I didn't feel stretched, I was envious of my co-workers who had "operative cases" and who were allowed to work on criminal trials. There were three of us in an office. The other two had already been there over twenty years.

I said to my wife that the work didn't satisfy me. But of course I didn't talk about the concrete subject matter at home. That was forbidden. And rightly so, in my opinion. My wife accepted this completely. In this respect, there was actually only one day a month when trust on her part was really necessary. Once a month, you see, we had night duty, but otherwise it was a life that ran very regularly. And she was fully prepared to accept this one little restriction.

We didn't do much in the evenings. At the beginning, when my wife was very pregnant, she herself had just begun to work, and that was certainly a very strong physical and psychological burden. We had little need for other activity. Sometimes a movie. After the child came, we had to stay home anyway or find someone to look after the child. So we were very limited.

* * *

I think that the first unofficial co-worker I was to train was given to me because I had to have something to do. It wasn't something important, but it was better than nothing. At least in this way I could stick my nose into operative work. I also went with another co-worker two or three times to meet this UC.

* * *

We always said "unofficial co-worker." The word "source" was only used within the Ministry for the purpose of further camouflaging the UC, because the Ministry also dealt with conspiracies on the inside. There were always cases where there was interest within the Ministry in directing an important UC, a bishop for instance, to another, higher, level of the Ministry. We, as staff members, tried to counter this. Because the more interesting the UCs were, or the higher the social milieu with which they interacted, the more insight we ourselves gained into certain societal processes. There was always a certain curiosity, an interest, or however you want to categorize it. And besides, having UCs who were designated as "top sources" increased the reputation of a staff member.

We didn't have any special psychological training at the Ministry. That was generally left up to the experience of the superior who gave you your start. And of course your own knowledge. You had to find your own ways and means and proceed in a more intuitive fashion. There were even cases where staff members couldn't handle the "operative work" and then they were moved into analysis or some other ancillary department.

* * *

The UCs worked with us for many different reasons and to differing degrees. I can't recall at all my psychological situation at the time I received my first UC; at least, I'm not sure if what I think I remember actually happened that way or if I'm now interpreting it with hindsight.

A UC delivered information to us. Not always, but most of the time. They were also sworn to silence. Fine.

So I never thought about alienation, about conflict. That depends on your standpoint at the time, you see. I see it quite neutrally as "UC activity." Others see it as "informant services" or something. It's always a case of how you see it, how you judge it.

In any case, I have to say that during my entire time at the Ministry I never had to deal with UCs who had been forced into working with us. There was rather a certain convergence of interests, to a certain degree and in certain areas. That's how I saw it then from my standpoint.

Now, with hindsight, I see it differently. Not very long ago, in a department store, quite by chance, I bumped into a UC that I worked with. He asked to speak with me. During our conversation, he told me that he had worked with us for completely different reasons and that he had been very afraid to come to our meetings. I hadn't noticed that at all during the meetings, in his case. That's why I say: From my subjective viewpoint I believed he worked with us voluntarily.

I don't know why I didn't notice he was afraid. Only with hindsight has it become clear to me that it is difficult to truly be able to judge another human being. It's true that I noticed that there were quite a few things that this particular person was not prepared to talk about. But in no way did I see fear as a motivator.

During this recent conversation, he told me that he had always been anti-communist. That was something I had never expected from his biography. He was one of those people who were very active in many areas, but I never had the feeling that there was a total aversion to our system.

For me and for us, the fact that he had a critical attitude to some issues was quite acceptable.

He said: "Really, I was always afraid."

The year 1953 must have been of great importance to him, because at that time he had had access to information of which I had absolutely no knowledge. About reprisals against Christians and so on. That had had a determining effect on his anti-communist attitude, he said.

I noticed nothing of this fear at the time. Nothing. Absolutely nothing. Why was he willing to work with us, then? He certainly didn't see it as "working together." He had told his bishop that we had had these conversations. I don't know exactly what he told the bishop. Perhaps that he had to be aware of how far he could go. Or something like that.

In all these years, the conversations had been very much to the point, and I had foreseen from the start that he was no "source" in the true sense of the word. Actually, we passed on to him a lot more information than went the other way. But that was a normal occurrence, especially where the church was concerned, in order to gain input into certain decisions. Of course, it wasn't as heavy-handed as that. We passed on things "to consider." We tried jointly "to analyze" developments in church politics in order to deduce the motivations behind his actions. But we mustn't misconstrue the procedure as being strictly mechanical. As I said, this UC gave almost no information. From this standpoint, the results were a complete catastrophe. But we didn't care. Of course it would have been better if he had passed on information. But I saw my job more and more in a political light. That's why I was not so concerned about gathering information. If the chance of having an impact presented itself, well that was enough. Of course we couldn't assume that he would always act under our influence. We were clear on that: but he was still an "unofficial co-worker."

You see, that term was first and foremost a technical category. We were not concerned with following the instructions on UCs one hundred percent. His still being called a "UC" despite the circumstances was a determination that emerged from formal procedures within the Ministry. That's something that the majority still don't know today.

Of course, the majority of the criteria for UCs did correspond with the work done. But I know that after many meetings I stopped taking notes, because nothing could be pinned down. I only noted that conversations had taken place. And that was accepted by my superiors.

With regard to the church, we had a lot of freedom, relatively speaking. One cannot ignore that. Standards that perhaps applied to other areas were not enforced with us.

Back then, even I knew that certain duties were considered "informant activities." But I saw it very differently, namely, that my activities were a chance to improve socialism. That's also the way I interpreted the motivations of the people who worked with us. At least, that's what was accepted by many people. Perhaps also out of fear.

Of course there were people who absolutely refused to work with us. But in my experience there were also people who didn't see it that way and now one has to live with many differing opinions.

If I declare myself willing to carry out an intelligence activity, then I must simply accept that things will play themselves out in a certain way and not differently! When all is said and done, even the Federal Intelligence Service won't be able to work any differently. From a political standpoint, I can say that some people were for socialism and others for capitalism. I accept that. But today they act like the Stasi was the spawn of the devil! That's something I cannot accept. As if there had been any application of ethics or morals on either side! I just don't get it. But I have to accept that that's the way it's represented in the media. But that's not the way it was.

I wouldn't have seen it at all as a, shall we say, breach of trust, if I had talked about my family. Why shouldn't I talk about people in my own circle who want the same thing as I do? I would have had no reservations about that. Of course, it depends on who I'm gathering the information for. Fine. Some were sent into those "peace and environmental groups." They, of course, had to pretend to be the friends of the people they were "handling." Others were already a part of these circles and were then "recruited." I don't know how many. So . . . no. I can more or less understand that those on the receiving end might see that as a betrayal or something like that. But I see it differently. Because I am not of the opinion that . . . how can I put it. I believed I was working *objectively* in the interests of those people.

I do understand that the concerned parties must find that ridiculous. But how socialism was applied: with that education mentality . . . If you aren't willing, we'll force you into socialism, turn you towards the Good, so to speak. I mean it in the figurative sense. I was convinced that GDR socialism was the social order made in the interest of the overwhelming majority of the GDR population, and I also believed that the majority of the population of the GDR was in agreement with it.

It wasn't until the mid-eighties, with Gorbachev, that my thinking began to undergo a change. When I look back, I see that I always developed in stages. An accumulation of contradictions, then a solution, then it started all over again. But I was very far from a decisive breakthrough. For me, that only came in the course of 1989.

* * *

But I came under investigation as early as 1988. For three weeks. A kind of custody within the Ministry. Even with hindsight, I have never been completely clear about the reason. I have drawn my conclusions more from the subsequent facts. The official word was that I had been sent on a business trip. Along with a colleague from the department. The interrogations were then carried out in a house on a piece of land somewhere. It was an attempt to accuse us of "criminal machinations." But I see the actual reason in the analysis I had written in early 1987. In the meantime there had been some big setbacks in the work of the regional administration and therefore in the work of the Ministry as a whole. Some negative hostiles were arrested, but then had to be set free again, and somehow they were looking for someone to blame for this whole development. In my opinion, a thing like my paper was very well suited to that. I made it very clear during the investigation that most of the employees in my office supported Gorbachev's ideas and were for glasnost and perestroika in the GDR. At the time, I couldn't have cared less what the consequences might be for me. I stood up for my views, even if that meant negative consequences. If they had thrown me out, then the matter would have been over for me. I didn't think about prison. I hadn't seen any of that kind of thing during my time in the Ministry, so I had no misgivings.

Nevertheless, it was a strange situation. Absolutely no accusations were made. The only question that was put to me again and again was: "Which official orders and directives have you disobeyed?"

In principle, we disobeyed such things every day, when we didn't fill out a form correctly or whatever. It never occurred to me that the consequence would be to incriminate oneself.

We approached it quite differently. We thought: There will be some problem or other and I want to try to solve it, or contribute as much as possible towards a resolution. After all, I was in the Ministry and I wanted to help the Ministry.

It turned out that they wanted to prove that we had had criminal dealings with UCs. I was outraged that they should insinuate that I had done such a thing. On the other hand, I wanted to help resolve the matter voluntarily. Till the end, they kept me in the dark about what was behind it all. Officially I was charged with neglecting my supervisory responsibility as the superior of the staff member who was interrogated after me. He was supposed to have made deals. I don't know. I was told that without proof. The result was that I was relieved of my position as department head for disciplinary reasons and was transferred to another office as an ordinary staff member.

Then I was told: "You're being transferred to Protection of Information."

So I said: "Then I'm leaving. That doesn't interest me at all." The time was long gone for things like: "Where society needs me, etc." I couldn't see any meaning in it any more.

Finally, I was transferred to the area of economics, also working on "operative material." I agreed to that, though with much uneasiness. I was not allowed to have any more contact with my comrades-in-arms in my former office. A ban on association was in force.

This experience was certainly one of the most important catalysts that made me totally rethink my attitude toward the Ministry. Apart from the political problems, which I understood in general. But it was only after Gorbachev himself expressed certain truths that they became acceptable for me. Before, when people came over from the West, there was a wall inside me: "Listen to them talk; the pot's calling the kettle black." In that vein.

I must say, however, that the process of being more critically aware started with me a little earlier with respect to the question of peace. Because of my area of work, I also had dealings with the peace movement "Swords to Ploughshares." I was forced to come to grips with the subject matter of these problems.

I wondered a lot at that time why the communists, who surely were equipped with the best worldview, were not able to foresee *before* the capitalists that a war was no longer feasible under the conditions of the atomic age. That amazed me, and made me think, and led to a change in my opinion between 1983 and 1985. In the seventies, I had still been a believer in military strength and had been living with the delusion: "All right, if they attack, we'll just counter-attack."

The questions posed by the peace movement were an important impetus for me. If we as communists feel we have morality on our side, and if I know that a second atomic strike means the destruction of humanity, then I have to come to the conclusion that I cannot launch a counter-strike, because that would result in the end of humanity. These were my thoughts at this stage.

I wasn't "infected" by the peace movement. No. I took in the things that were available to me, and dealing with the material led me to this way of thinking.

* * *

Of course it's a weight off my mind now that I didn't put anyone in prison. That's today. But I would have done it then. I wouldn't have had anything against it; on the contrary. In those days we were fighting against the enemy.

A lot of things appear different now that the GDR is no more. But feelings of guilt as such? Feelings of guilt? No. It's very difficult to put into words. But I wouldn't call it guilt.

First of all, I blame myself for having taken so long to recognize that socialism in the GDR was no socialism. Of course, I also did too little to bring about the necessary changes. But that was because, until as late as

1989, until after the changeover, I always believed that socialism could be reformed. And I have to say that I shared this mistaken belief with very many other people.

With hindsight, I have to say that I regret very much that I actually "handled" the wrong people. Back then. People belonging to the peace movement, people who wanted a democratic socialism. But I still believe that there were a whole lot of people who wanted nothing more than to get rid of socialism altogether.

* * *

When it is said that we wanted to convict people, to throw them in jail and condemn them, just because of their views, then I have to say that that was never my intention. It was always a matter of actions. True, even a lecture could be seen as an action. But they also accuse the Ministry of opposing forces on the left more that those on the right. Personally, I saw it differently. In terms of what they stood for, I preferred left-wingers. For this reason, I would have had no reason to move against them. But there were many unexplained things in the way an attempt was made to change that around. There were rumors of possible terrorist entanglements. Fine, these were never confirmed, but when you have grounds for suspicion, it lies in the nature of a secret service to clear up such matters. And of course we were haunted by that specter of terrorism that had had a certain influence on the politics of the Federal Republic. We wanted to nip that in the bud. Which is not to say that I am unaware that exactly the opposite was happening on many levels in the Ministry. There were cases in which left-wingers really were locked up.

But at the same time, my own personal experience tells me that in my area, the church, it never came to that. Of course, I regretted that from time to time. But looking back, I think it was a good thing. If I were to be recruited now, whether to combat terrorists or whatever, I would decline. For me, a position with the secret service would be out of the question now. I've had bad experiences, and that means I'll have nothing more to do with it. I haven't yet thought about what is behind this attitude. But even if the GDR had continued to exist and a true intelligence service had been set up . . . No. After all, I had already decided to leave before it all happened. That was in September 1989.

It all began with that three-week mess. But other things followed. In early 1989 an "operative dossier" landed on my desk. A team from a large factory had written to the Politburo of the SED. They had asked them to deal with various domestic policy matters. The subjects were West German money, Intershops, travel to the West, and pricing policy. I read the letter and said: "I support all of these points." Afterwards I read the answer that was forwarded from the Central Committee: "Anti-party tendencies."

I said to myself: "If that's 'anti-party tendencies' then my point of view is also anti-party."

That was the first time it became clear to me that I couldn't go on this way. You can't handle certain subjects as an "operative" when you yourself consider them to be correct. And I brought this out into the open in the new workgroup at the Ministry.

Then came the elections. I was so naive and believed that you couldn't do anything to rig that election. It just wasn't possible. There were just too many people there checking the counting. That would be politically untenable. I felt all the more stupid afterwards. I said: "Are they that crazy that they had to do it anyway? Eighty percent would have been a magnificent victory. Did they have to rig ninety-nine percent?" I didn't understand any more. How could one be so ignorant of the real problems? I even said: "Well, I can't vote for them in the next election." Of course, I just went nuts.

The next consequence was that if I couldn't vote for them anymore, then I couldn't be a staff member of the Ministry any more either. So one thing led to another, and I became more and more certain: "There's no point any more, I'm quitting."

I had already told my workgroup that I was thinking about it. There were two people in the new office I could discuss things with, because they were having similar thoughts.

Then, around October 7, 1989, I had a meeting with our department head, where I said that I didn't believe I could see any future for me in the Ministry. Because of the interrogation that had taken place, but also because of other things. After all, he had witnessed my political development through all our discussions.

So you were immediately suspended; you took your personal effects and were not allowed any more access to the operative documents. After that, you had to look for another job, and when you got one, you were formally let go. Of course, you had to sign a pledge of secrecy. That was on the Monday or Tuesday before the big demonstration in Berlin on November 4, 1989.

* * *

So when I'm asked about murders, kidnappings, executions, I have to say this. They even accuse me of having planned murders. There was this article in a magazine, middle of last year. It's nonsense of course. Things like that did not appear on the list of "operative harassment measures." Well, I mean . . . Let us say . . . With respect to that three-week period, it was the very harassment measures we were using that were the subject of the investigation. During that time, I more or less laid everything out on the table and also took a very firm stand on the issue of an "attack on the life

and health of persons." The point of departure at that time was Popieluszko. That "mess." There was a whole series of discussions in the Ministry on the topic. For me too it was a reason to consider: "Is something
like this in principle a way the Ministry should go?" I didn't make these
thoughts easy on myself. One can always say: "If you have the power, you
have to use it."

As a result of these reflections I came to the conclusion that it might
have been possible that people had been physically done away with, that
there had certainly been the possibility of doing it in such a way that scarcely
a trace would be left behind and proof would not have been possible.

But on the other hand I also realized that, in my opinion, those problems that had been hidden behind the inner opposition movement were
deeply political problems that had to be solved by political means. It
would even have been very beneficial for the development of socialism in
the GDR if the opposition had been brought to an end through political
means.

In addition, I was of the opinion that you always have to keep the
methods in proportion. I mean, if someone goes against the system using
political means, then you have to counter it by political means. In which I
would include a certain amount of "harassment measures." But that
would not have meant carrying out an attack on the life and health of
these persons.

Planned car accidents? That's exactly what we are supposed to have
done. Therefore . . . That was included in these reflections. We said that it
would surely be no problem to do such a thing . . . No . . .

That's why I say, you see . . . That newspaper . . . Well, anyone can
tell that something like that could not possibly have been the subject of
serious reflection. Those are, let's say, typical clichés that you get from
movies and such like and are, let's say, talked about afterward . . .

What does that mean, researched with respect to a car accident? Researched doesn't mean it happened!

There were meetings. About these kinds of things! And the minutes
were sold to the newspaper. And in my opinion by someone from the
Ministry who had access to them. That's what I think.

* * *

As for murder plans, my experience was different. In the setting where I
worked, such a thing was never demanded, not even by our superiors. On
the contrary; when such things were talked about, they were deliberately
opposed.

That's why I think that most of what is shown on the TV today is
hypocritical. I'm very skeptical about whether most of it's really factual or
not. You can see a lot of things from two sides.

It's a little different when it's a matter of the death sentences that were carried out. They were carried out according to the rule of law. There were rumors about that. But I only knew of one case, a Ministry officer called T., for whom a search was begun. Afterwards, there were rumors of a report saying that he had been executed. I'm sure that it was a kind of indirect disciplinary action.

But when it comes to these so-called moral problems, I say to myself: "What right does a bishop who, for instance, was a submarine commander in the Second World War and has perhaps hundreds of people on his conscience, what right does he have to reproach me?" That's what I ask myself. And primarily I have to wonder that the church made a man like that one of their bishops . . . When you see that in relation to what a certain staff member of the Ministry did, the one who is in the public eye today, I really have my doubts. For that reason, a lot of things leave me cold. I cannot understand the reproaches, and I assess it all exclusively from a political point of view. When I hear all that moral outrage, from the church, from the West German media or whatever, then I have to ask: "What right do they have?"

Of course, the question of morality is very important for me personally. But whether the question of morality gains social relevance and whether or not that is intentional, well, I'm a little skeptical. I don't think it matters whether one comes to grips with guilt in a really concrete manner or not. That's a secondary matter. That can only be meaningful for the individual. But in general? Is it really meaningful? I don't think so.

I myself had no personal ambitions where power was concerned. Of course, I was aware that I was a representative of a power-wielding establishment. But I saw the concrete power of the Ministry as very, very insignificant. Of course, the theoretical power was always great. But a general in our regional administration couldn't even levy a fine in the area I worked in, because that could only be decided by the Politburo. That's the thing about power. The potential threat, the intimidation, it was there, all right. But in the final analysis, we were all pretending. We always thought that was enough. But . . . Well, you saw what happened.

* * *

So I think it is necessary to contribute to an objective picture of the Ministry. I consider it a political mistake for the powers that have had quite a lot of importance since the changeover to see their main task as fighting against the Ministry. From what I know, there was a broad potential in the Ministry that would have been willing to go along with sweeping social changes under the name of socialism. If this oppositional attitude had not immediately taken hold. I believe that even at the level of general there would have been some who would have been open to things like that.

I do find fault with the Ministry in one respect. Looking back, I think General Mielke was very short-sighted, and I hold it against some generals that they did nothing. They must have seen what kind of a man he was. But that's the point: that Mielke managed to keep all that stuff under wraps.

Of course it's also a question of structure. What does "perhaps the individual members of the Gestapo didn't want certain things to happen either" mean? Yes, with respect to organizational structure there were similarities to the Gestapo. But with respect to subject matter, there were massive differences. In aims and methods. In our organization, there was never the wish to attack other countries. For me, Hitler stands for capitalism, behind him stands capital, and for this reason any comparison between the Ministry for State Security and the Gestapo is invalid.

I feel absolutely no sense of responsibility as such. I'm proceeding from my political aims. I wanted to make policy for socialism. I was aware that there were enemies. That's the way it is in politics. Each side fights against the other. In my life, I have simply seen it no other way, and the term "compassion" really has no meaning for me.

CHAPTER FIVE

I NEVER CARED MUCH FOR WORK JUST FOR THE SAKE OF WORK . . .

— **Hartmut L., 43, conscientious objector, social worker, insurance agent**

BRINGING DOWN THE GDR was absolutely not my plan. The Wall had to go, sure. But I was no anti-communist. In the seventies, I read a lot of works by Karl Marx, *Das Kapital,* the early manuscripts, and I liked many of his analyses and also his hopes and visions, because they matched my Christian way of looking at life. Of course, the GDR had installed a system that didn't work, there were party idiots and blockheads at the rudder, and the whole thing had very little to do with the theory.

For me at fourteen, the so-called "youth initiation," that wannabe rite of passage, was a radical experience. I was quite a good student, and after eighth grade I was supposed to go to the upper high school and take my final exams. Of course, submitting to this "youth initiation" was a prerequisite. My mother wanted me to take part, the teachers wanted it; everyone advised me to do it. I didn't have the strength back then to say no. I cowered, I bent over backwards, I conformed, although I knew it was wrong. It was and still is one of the biggest defeats of my life.

So when I went to the upper high school, I wanted to make up for this fiasco. In the ninth grade, I left the FDJ, as a provocation. I refused to take part in military exercises and marksmanship classes, and I finally even declared: "I will refuse to do military service." All of which were totally unacceptable in high school at that time. The teachers and the principal were very quick to make it clear to me: "*You* will not take the final exams here."

I had to leave school after tenth grade.

After that, with the help of a pastor who had quite an influence on me in this youthful phase, I went to one of the three church high schools in the GDR, where I got a good, basic humanistic education. I was there two years, took history of philosophy, Greek, and Latin, and moreover received very good training in German.

In 1970, after I had been at work for some months, I began to study Lutheran theology in Berlin. After that, I had absolutely nothing more to do with all those things everyone had to submit to: FDJ parades, all that union fuss, competitions between business collectives, or party meetings. I studied at this church college for five years, but I didn't graduate. I just couldn't finish my senior thesis. I read a lot, took notes, wrote individual chapters, but there was always more and more material and no finished thesis. Something in me fought against the idea of "being finished."

Then I officially quit and began to work part-time in a cemetery: digging graves, carrying coffins. It didn't take long for me to be made cemetery administrator. Actually, this was a cemetery that lay right along the Berlin Wall. The parish council had accepted me, but they needed the political "pass," a "certification of good standing" for the border area.

I had to apply officially at the local authority offices. When I got there, two men sat opposite me and informed me that my application had been denied.

I said again and again: "Give me an explanation." And one of them kept saying: "I can't give you an explanation; you'll have to be satisfied with that."

The other said nothing for a long time.

It was only after the conversation had worn itself out that the second guy started in: "We have a few questions to put to you in this regard."

"Yes, and what would they be?"

"You only work four hours at the cemetery."

"Yes, so what?"

"What do you earn?"

"380 marks."

"And what do you live on?"

"The money's enough for me. I don't need much to live. The apartment has an outside toilet and it's cheap, so are basic foodstuffs, and I can do without luxuries . . ."

"And where do you live?"

"Krausnick-Strasse."

"Ah."

"Besides, my mother helps support me, and I'm continuing my theology studies by correspondence, as well. I'm going to graduate and then I'll become a pastor and so . . ."

Then I was allowed to go.

One of them took me to the paternoster elevator and said: "Sorry, I would have liked to have given you the certification. But another agency has said I'm not allowed to." He said this in a whisper, outside in the corridor. He wanted to be friendly, but he didn't dare, things being as they were.

A few days later, I was thrown out of my apartment. Early in the morning, around seven thirty, two people from the housing administration came and said: "Show us your rental contract." Of course I didn't have one, because it was a condemned apartment, and I had two weeks to get out.

I think the second man, the Stasi guy who sat in on the meeting, had a hand in it.

After that, for a year I lived with a friend who was a verger for a congregation. He and his girlfriend and child lived in a six-room apartment belonging to the church; however, he cleared out to the West after six months. Illegally. Without his girlfriend, without his child. Two weeks later the telephone rang. I picked up: "Mayer residence."

"Ah, Herr L.! Nice to talk to you. I've been wanting to meet you for so long."

"Well, and who are you?"

"Criminal investigation. When can we get together, then?"

"If we have to, as soon as possible."

That was a typical Stasi contact.

So I went to Keibelstrasse, where the Stasi and police headquarters and detention unit were all together. Some young guy who was working off his military service there was to take me to the appropriate room, but he had gotten himself lost in the gigantic building. So I was half an hour late when I sat down opposite a man who was perhaps thirty years old and way too friendly at first: "Nice to meet you. I'm handling the Mayer case. He's cleared off. And since you live there, I've a few questions for you."

I say: "Well, you know, we didn't have much contact, I was just subletting from him. I don't know anything and anyway . . ."

He listened for a while, but then he became a little harsher: "If you think you can sit there and make an ass out of me . . ."

"But I've no intention of doing that," I say.

Then he explodes: "Stop slouching! Do you see me sitting like that?" Stuff like that.

Sure, I had been sitting there a little too casually. Nevertheless I hold my own and say to him: "Excuse me, but what's all this about? Am I in prison here? What do you mean by speaking to me like that?"

Then he's suddenly very friendly: "You have to understand my situation; my superior just walked through the room and I can't just . . ."

I say: "But that's your problem, not mine. I'm still not going to allow you to treat me that way."

When he realized I wasn't going to sign on for the usual tour, he became formal again: "And if Herr Mayer's girlfriend thinks she can follow him, then she's mistaken. Her emigration application will not be processed. And you can tell her that."

But I wasn't going to let them make me their message boy, and I said: "If you want to inform her of something, you'll have to do it yourself."

Then he tried to force me into a corner again: "What's going on with you anyway? What do you live on?"

I say: "First of all that's none of your business, and you probably know the answer already."

And when he said at the end: "We may have to summon you here again!" I shot back: "Was this a *summons* or an invitation?"

I was very finicky about language; I tried not to let myself be intimidated, and not to brownnose, either.

Actually, I was not at all afraid of the Stasi.

When I was active in a peace group during my "Berlin period" after college, we always took for granted that the Stasi was listening in, of course; that there were "bugs" everywhere. But we tried to ignore it. A secret service like that always functions by means of a mechanism of intimidation: *We know more than you think! We can do more than we're doing!*

And the most effective countermeasure was not to let yourself be intimidated. To say to yourself: They'll do what they want to anyway. We won't give them any real leverage against us. But what we do can't be forbidden. Reading some books, communicating, discussing, meeting . . .

Of course, everyone knew that they could arrest us on the flimsiest of excuses. The laws were drawn up in such a way that they could stick practically anyone in jail if they wanted to. Because of "incitement," "agitation hostile to the state," "contact with hostile organizations," or whatever. In my case you could add "refusal to do military service." Twice I spent twelve hours at the district military command. I had to constantly sign that I "continued in my refusal." Then another three hours, "in order to think it over." Finally, another hour's meeting, and again a couple of hours in the corridor. It was more of that intimidation stuff. I stood my ground: "I will not submit to any order. I will only do community service." There was no such thing at that time, and refusal meant jail time. But they left me in peace. Nothing happened.

* * *

What's more, after my interlude at the cemetery, I had no proper job any more. I washed windows a few days a week; that must have lasted five years, always without a contract, without insurance, without paying taxes. Illegally, if you will. At any time they could have "legally" picked me up and thrown me in the slammer for "antisocial behavior," as it was called then.

Somehow I never really took their threats seriously. To me, the Stasi meant more or less the same as the Party. They existed, sure, but they had absolutely nothing to do with me. When I realize today what they could have done, looking back, I get the occasional cold shiver running down my spine.

Somehow I was lucky in my life. There were many situations where something bad could have happened. I fell down a mountain, had a car accident, a motorcycle accident. But I was never injured, never broke a bone, was never in the hospital. I never even got seriously ill. Somewhere I got the idea: Nothing will happen — to *me*.

By the way, my confirmation verse, which the pastor I was telling you about picked out for me, reads: "We know that in everything God works for good with those who love him." And this has really been authoritative for my life.

In my "Berlin period" I went to concerts a lot, to exhibitions, to the opera, and I read a huge amount — literature, history, philosophy; I sat for days and weeks in the public library, or in the university library. Basically those five years after college were a kind of second education for me. Apart from the few hours in the week when I washed windows, I had the whole time to myself. But there came a time when this kind of life no longer satisfied me. I thought: "You have to do something more meaningful. Something to serve humankind." I wanted to selflessly serve other people.

At the same time, in about 1980, I took part in a two-week course in self-exploration, where I thought about myself intensively for the very first time. Here I became aware that I was living a very superficial life that no longer fulfilled me or satisfied me.

I could still have taken my exams and become a pastor, a few years late. But I didn't want to, and looking back I think it was a good decision. I would have been a neurotic pastor, not being completely honest with myself or others. That's how I see most of them. They can't stand up to the most serious questions, the ultimate questions. Perhaps no one can, and my expectations of pastors are far too high.

Anyway, in 1981 I moved away from Berlin and began to work for this Lutheran home in S. As a matter of fact, I had been exposed to Christian socialization from childhood on; my mother had already modeled this altruistic, selfless lifestyle for me. She was a nurse, a single mother, never allowing herself any luxury. Again and again I heard from her: "When I retire, then I'll begin to live." She died when she was sixty-two. Just when she wanted to begin to actually live. I never saw her happy.

After she had been dead for a few years, a therapist said to me during an exploratory meeting: "Now you are realizing that you not only grew up without a father, but also without a mother. Your mother treated you like a nurse would."

At the time that totally shocked me. I wept for the first time in years. That's just how it was. She took care of me, did what needed to be done, but nothing beyond that. No physical contact. No stroking. No hugs. And no conversations in which I might have been able to open up. I believe she couldn't love herself, and, in a subtle way, she always pulled away from me. That is one of the burdens that will weigh on me for years, and is quite probably the reason for my difficulties in really opening up to another person.

* * *

So I started work in this Lutheran home. I had studied long enough, surrounded myself mainly with aesthetic things for so many years, and now I wanted to work with my hands. At first I was employed as a kind of gardener for two years. Then I realized: I have to start using my head. For the next year and a half I worked as a teacher for the handicapped, and from 1984 onwards, after I had passed a vocational training course, I built up the geriatric department within the home and also directed it until 1990.

For the first few years, the work was very exciting and also very varied. There were many old people there who were extraordinarily interesting and with whom you could have deep conversations. But eventually the seniors' home was made into a proper nursing home. In my last two or three years there, there was hardly a soul with whom you could carry on a real conversation, and the work became limited to pure nursing care. More and more I missed the communication, some intellectual aspect.

There was also another reason why the work began to weigh on me over time. I noticed that I could not really live up to the expectations I had of myself — to do something for others.

During therapy in the mid-eighties, when my relationship with my mother became an important topic, I gradually became aware of my own attitudes. I discovered something completely unknown: the country within myself. Apart from that one-time self-exploration in Berlin, I had not yet found any true access to my inner being. In this therapy I was confronted with my attitudes, my fears, and my true desires. I no longer wanted to live with the external, learned desires and attitudes that are forced on you during your upbringing. I had internalized very deeply this church socialization, this "being selfless for others," this "neglect of the self," this "think not of yourself." Until then I hadn't learned to develop my own desires, and above all not to be ashamed of those desires but rather to stand up for them.

Actually, I'm still learning how to get to know and accept myself. I'm certainly not the selfless, friendly, lovable person I like to think I am. I also have my dark sides, my egotisms, my very strong need for power and many other things. In therapy, I also worked on the "helper neurosis" I had avoided seeing earlier. Helping also means: I stand by the bed and you lie on the bed. I am powerful and you are powerless. I do something for you — seemingly selfless, but really with the idea: For this, and for everything, you must be grateful to me.

How many people become caregivers, doctors, pastors, or teachers in order to receive respect and affection — not because of their humanitarian attitude, but because of their position, because of their work? They work so that they can be accepted as "people of worth." It was the same with me. In actual fact, I didn't think I had worth, that I wasn't important or worthy of love. So I had to do something that would give me respect and acceptance. I realized that "being selfless" is pretty hypocritical. Since then I have drawn my own conclusions and now I work in a field where two people actually sit opposite each other as business partners rather than, on one side, as a "helper" and, on the other, as someone who has to be helped.

But my situation in 1989 was like this: On the one hand I wanted to stay here in my town. Didn't want to emigrate. I had my house, and I had also "settled down" somehow. On the other hand I was becoming more and more dissatisfied. With my work as well as with the political climate. Something had to change. That much was clear. But everything was so deadlocked and set in concrete. Then in April 1989, Rolf Henrich's book *The Custodial State* came out in the West. A friend brought me a copy, I read it in two nights, and said to myself: "He has put into words the essence of my impressions of the last few years."

I went to see Henrich, and we talked for six hours. After that, eight people in S. got together over several evenings, reread the book and discussed it far into the night. It was a small group, like in years past, and it had — at first — no discernible consequences. But then September came, and New Forum was founded, and when I got the call, I went to see Henrich again. He said: "What am *I* supposed to do? Why don't *you* do it. Each in his own place."

In our town, the Lutheran home became the center of New Forum. The first twenty meetings took place there. The first mass rallies too. The church was filled to overflowing, thousands of people suddenly gathering at once, as if led by an invisible force. But what was really overwhelming was that the plane of thought and words had given way — overnight and completely unexpectedly — to a plane of action and change. Before, everything had been theoretical. You came to an understanding in a small group, clapped each other on the shoulder, were of one mind, and that was that. For years I had the feeling that I was constantly treading water. And suddenly I could do something!

We formed twelve task forces. I organized the task force on "media." You had to inform the people of what had to change, what you wanted to happen — or so I thought. But I quickly realized that you can't really change opinions and attitudes. Either you write what the people want to read, exploit the trend, put yourself out in front, or you're very quickly yesterday's news.

So at the beginning we fought to get space for New Forum in the SED regional newspaper. In November, we got a whole page, twice, and we were able to lay it out with complete freedom and independence.

From December on, we got the chance to put out our own newspaper. I already knew what an unbelievable workload it had been just to deal with one page every two weeks. And now we had to produce a whole newspaper every week! I did fifty percent of the work by myself. Others took on the other fifty percent, especially all the technical processing.

All this time I was still the director of the geriatric unit. In the first weeks, then months, the nurses simply took over my work. But not just that. In this early period, our telephone became the hub for all calls to do with New Forum. That meant that a staff member had to deal exclusively with the calls at all times.

At first they were very proud that I was constantly in the newspaper, both New Forum and the home. But there came a time when they blew their tops, understandably so, because for months I was to all intents and purposes an absentee.

* * *

Actually, the real shock didn't come until 1990, when the so-called "Block-Flute CDU," this SED splinter group, suddenly got the majority of the votes, but only because they waved bananas and the West German mark around and had Kohl behind them. At that time I was pitched into a terrible crisis. It wasn't about the GDR or socialism or some other mega-concept. No. What really got to me was that the people in this country had allowed themselves to be corrupted so quickly and so terribly. They were simply "turned around" overnight.

The true squaring of the shoulders, the really unbelievable freedom and opportunity only lasted for a few weeks. "We are the people!" — "We are somebody!" — "We will not let ourselves be used any longer!" — "Go to hell!" — "Now we're here!" — "The streets are ours!" — It was a fact that, for a few days, a breath of freedom blew through this entire musty country.

But then came the troublemakers, who shouted "Hello Helmut" and later: "We are one people." In December I still thought: it's only a few windbags and nutcases. To me, German unity seemed extremely far off and not so especially desirable, either. I wanted the GDR to become a proper nation, with a parliamentary democracy, with Round Tables and an effective economy. I could have imagined a confederation with West Germany sometime in the distant future, after a gradual rapprochement. Why have one big Germany? For what purpose? I wanted to be able to travel. But apart from that, the GDR could continue to exist. And in point of fact, I still see it that way.

* * *

When I went to West Berlin for the first time, I just felt good, not at all as if I were in a foreign country. Of course, everything was colorful and gaudy and smelled like in an Intershop. But people I didn't know and who I spoke with for a while said to me over and over again: "So, you're from the East? You don't act like it." I liked that, somehow.

As for unification, there came a time when I accepted it or, more accurately, I became resigned to it. The New Forum newspaper was abandoned by February, because the costs were too great and interest had waned quite a bit.

In early 1990, when the squabbling in the nursing home had gone from bad to worse, we agreed that I should sit out for two months and take unpaid leave. During that time I worked only for New Forum and lost all my illusions about the chance of changing things in society by means of a grass-roots movement. Although we were still receiving piles of mail from the West. New Forum was being taken extremely seriously over there, but over here it seemed to me that it was increasingly just a bunch of babbling idiots. In the end, it seemed to be all about organizational stuff, hardly any real content; it was almost impossible to build structures, because there were rumors everywhere of the "betrayal of grass-roots democracy." I had no interest in working on uncovering the Stasi past, and I also didn't want to go back to the nursing home. I had no idea what to do.

It so happened that a new newspaper had just been started. I wrote a few articles for them at first, and a short while later I was hired as editor. That was hard labor. Basically, there were two of us and we put out a weekly paper with sixteen pages. Hardly any ads. Then there were my high expectations for myself. I couldn't just type the text into the machine and sit back. I reworked it too often and changed it around and that cost me more time than was actually necessary. Still, it was fun. But this newspaper also went under after a short while.

An acquaintance I had made through my work on the newspaper offered me a job. I didn't make the decision easy on myself. I weighed the pros and cons for over a week.

I knew I wanted to stay on in the town where I'd been living. I couldn't just leave my house behind. I also didn't want to work on another newspaper, because writing didn't come easily to me. Social work was out of the question. Still, it needed to be a job where I'd be dealing with people. All this comes together in my new line of work.

So I've been working in a service industry more or less since 1991, well, that's how I'd categorize it anyway, and I feel good about the work, because it's not run on hypocritical lines like the so-called "helping professions" are. It's a business, and the people on both sides of the table are business partners. Besides, I have to say: All kinds of insurance are not equal.

I don't have to talk people into things they don't actually need. Even if I think they do need a certain kind of insurance, I won't force the issue.

Insurance work, as I do it, is a true service. I see it this way: "Some kinds of insurance are necessities, some make sense, some you can afford if you want to afford them."

Of course, I do have to earn something, that's clear. But I work in one spot, in my agency; I don't go around with a suitcase ringing doorbells and telling villagers: "You have to have life insurance!" talking them into it and disappearing again.

They went through that for a year. And that has had a big influence on the image of the insurance agent, more in the East than in the West. That's what's made most people think insurance is a rip-off. I've had to deal with this prejudice for a long time.

Of course, I also have to ring doorbells. But then I always say: "I know what you've experienced. I've been through it too — but I'm doing something serious here. You can talk to me about it. I'm not just passing through. I live here in town. My office is here. I can't afford to talk you into something that's a joke, only to raise my commission." And people find that convincing.

Of course, this profession does go against one of my inner tendencies. Deep down inside, I'm against any insurance. Doesn't matter what kind. Normally I would send any insurance agent packing, with or without an agency. I'd say: "I don't need any accident insurance." Intuitively.

But I know that insurance makes sense in theory. I need insurance for this house. And I carry a very high accident insurance. If anything were to happen to me . . . how would I pay back the loans I took out to remodel the house, etc., etc.? It's one thing after another.

It's as if there's a struggle between my more intuitive take on life and my more rational and intellectual deliberations.

If, ten years ago, I had known what I know now, about the Stasi, I would have been more fearful, in some cases more careful, and also more mistrustful of other people. I would have behaved more appropriately, in a rational manner. Would this have been better for me? Difficult to say . . . No, I don't believe so. But in any case, it would have been more rational. When it comes to insurance, I now behave in a more appropriate and rational manner. I do have accident insurance. And even if I don't have life insurance, I can still advocate it from a rational standpoint; I can recommend it to particular people.

I just have to deal with this tension between the intellectual and the intuitive. It can't be dismissed and it also has to do with other areas of life. Money is tight at the moment. But in the next five or six years, I'll definitely have enough money. Perhaps I won't be rich, but I'll probably be able to live with fewer money worries.

On the other hand, the time in Berlin when I had almost no money, relatively speaking, was the most carefree time of my life. I didn't have to make sure I had a good lock on the door; there was nothing for anyone to steal. Now I have this house, with all the loans, I drive a car, and I have ten times as many worries. Not just financial. When I go to Poland, I now have to wonder where I can park my car. When you have an old Japanese wreck, no one'll want to steal it. But a newer car?

But then again, I don't want to let myself be corrupted by this "having" mentality. "Things" and "money" will not possess me. I don't want to be asking myself someday: "Is it worth getting into this relationship? How much time will I be investing? Could I not be using that time to work? Couldn't I just talk a little about insurance while I'm sitting with friends?" I won't do that. I really want to try to keep that separate. I want to keep this anarchic philosophy of life that I've had all my days.

For instance, I don't get caught up in these little "hierarchy games" in insurance. I'm in the city, in our central office, once a week. There are a couple of permanent clerks there. Sometimes they want to play the "superior" or something. So I'm supposed to come and say: "May I please? And thank you! And would you be so kind?" And so on.

I mean, I'm a polite person. I say Please and Thank You. But *they* are there to support *me*! That's why they get their money! From me, no less! And I'm very clear about that: "You are here for me, because I write the contracts. I bring in the money you live on."

Of course, some of them can't stomach that. But I've stood my ground. Even if they've wanted to throw me out. I couldn't have cared less about *that*! Should I tie myself in knots because of them? Not me! For a while it was touch and go. I had two or three meetings with the boss, because the clerks had complained about my manner. I was friendly, polite, but in this respect I stood firm, didn't give an inch.

During the third meeting I thought: Now he's going to throw you out. But suddenly the boss said: "What would you say if I made you area manager? Then you'd be responsible for all the people with agency contracts in this district." I said: "Thanks for your offer. I'll think it over." From that day on I was left in peace. They accepted it. And I am polite and bring in my deals.

Of course, I have to play by certain rules. I don't really know whether I would have bought all of this insurance and in such high amounts if I hadn't been working in the field. On the other hand, I would really like to keep my lifestyle, even if I were to have an accident, if the house were to burn down, or if some other great misfortune were to strike me.

Today — and this has become very clear to me — we are all responsible for ourselves. One hundred percent. Even in the case of the unforeseen. We have been released from the shelter of the parental home, with the despotic father. We're now in the middle of real life. If you fall on your face, well, you fell on your face. There you have it! Then you get up again and continue on your way. Who are you going to shift the blame onto? Whose shoulder are you going to cry on? If something doesn't suit you, you have to do something to change it. That's part of my basic philosophy. Of course, there are people who get trampled on by others. You have to give them a little support. But the basic attitude has to be: "If *I* fail, then *I* have to accept it, without complaining about it." But the "typical" GDR citizen is still looking for others to blame: his wife . . . his neighbor . . . communism . . . the state . . . money . . . or politics.

Of course, there's this perpetual dynamic that says that the successful get richer and richer, while the poor get poorer and poorer, and I don't know how to counteract that.

From a personal standpoint, I can only say the following, and I hope that I'll see it the same way in ten years time: If I ever have five thousand marks to spare, I'll not invest it at eight percent or ten percent. I'll say: This is spare cash and I'll give it to charity. Then the money's there for others. It's not my life's goal to be a millionaire. Of course, I want to make sure that I can enjoy my old age, and in the future I would like to live with a few less material worries, to fulfill a few wishes. To travel, to go sailing, to fly, not in a passenger plane but in a balloon or a glider. Dreams that I had as a small boy. Those are really the essential things.

Of course, there are also "horizon shifts" in expectations, in the standard of living. But I still hope that the time will come where I do really have five thousand marks to spare. I hope.

I'll also need people, of course, friends who will point things out to me at the right moment. Much can change in five years. But I hope I manage to retain a certain identity.

Also, I don't discount the possibility that I can someday reduce my expectations after I have caught up on certain experiences. For instance, a long trip where I don't need to watch every penny. It doesn't have to be a five-star hotel. Perhaps one day I can do without a car again. I would like to think so. But at the moment I'm still in the catch-up phase.

Of course, this economic system makes certain countries get richer and richer while others get poorer and poorer. I don't have an answer to that either. When I can afford it, money-wise and time-wise, I'd like to go to Africa or India. Then I'll have to deal with what I experience there, and that will also have life-changing consequences. What kind I can't yet say.

When I hear people say: "Ah, the GDR — that was the lowest of the low, so poor and so awful," then I used to say — and I still say today: "In spite of everything, we were still one of the rich countries in the world. I too was born to riches." I don't think I'll lose *that* point of view.

There's a reason I take the *TAZ* rather than *Die Welt* or the *FAZ*. It's not just an affectation on my part. I read it, and I take in its anarchy and its criticism of the system every day.

As for my political commitment, my strength is very limited these days. For almost two years, I've only done insurance. Now they're building up the office, and after that it'll take at least three months to deal with what's been left undone. I hope to take a few weeks' vacation in November.

My wish is that I will have come so far in the next two years that I can work at a more leisurely pace. Perhaps two or three days a week. I've never cared much for work just for the sake of work. I'm just too lazy for that; or let's say, I'm not ambitious enough. . . .

CHAPTER SIX

AND THAT'S WHY YOU'D RATHER GIVE IN FIRST . . .

— Bärbel C., 28, daycare worker, wife of a former border guard

I THINK IT'S LOUSY that people are always hurting each other. We simply can't have a reasonable argument. One person is always hurting the other, and then gradually it becomes ingrained somehow.

My shift work means I have a lot to do, and I also want to get to grips with the housework. I'm pretty ambitious when it comes to that. Everything has to be clean and tidy. But it's no fun if the housework's all on my shoulders. What kind of a life is that? Always working and cleaning at home and that's it. Bernd goes to work too, but afterwards he takes photos. He says: "What's with all this endless cleaning?" But then he'll say: "It's really nice to have a clean, tidy home. When I see how other renters live." That's a huge contradiction somehow.

Earlier, back before we were married, he didn't take photos; everything just revolved around us. It took a while for me to get used to the fact that there is something else besides us that takes up a lot of time. For a while I was pretty jealous, but it's not so much of a problem any more.

We got married because we wouldn't have gotten an apartment together otherwise. My mother never wanted me to go over to Bernd's. Staying away all night was completely out of the question. There was absolutely no talking to her about it. She had been divorced for years; my brother and I were everything to her. She was probably jealous.

I mean, I don't want you to think I'm not happily married. But it's no longer the way I imagined it: all love and bliss. We have a lot of problems and we try to deal with them somehow. Our daughter always takes my side when we have a fight. Bernd thinks I influence her to do that. But it's just that children take the side of the weak, and they see their mother as the weaker one because men are always so quick to get loud.

* * *

We recently went to see a documentary. About four youths from our town. They couldn't deal with the old system. One ended up behind bars, one landed in reform school — now he's living in Kreuzberg — and the other two committed suicide. The movie was begun in 1981. But after that, filming was forbidden, and now the filmmaker wanted to show the film in our town.

One of the young men had already applied for permission to emigrate, but then he committed suicide. His girlfriend said he was probably afraid. Just wanted out of the GDR. But it didn't have to be West Berlin. He probably thought he wouldn't be able to deal with life there either and made short work of it. He never felt understood. It was really sad to see this in the movie.

In another scene, one of the young men said: "He could never turn his back when his father was around." He was constantly kicked and beaten by him while he was washing at the sink or in situations like that where he couldn't defend himself. His father had to make him hurt, even if there hadn't been any argument beforehand. This father was also there at the showing. Seems he had called up the organizers beforehand and said he thought it was appalling that they were showing the film in this town. He would be made to look really bad, he said, and his wife's nerves were shot and she wanted to turn on the gas tap.

There was a discussion after the movie. At first the director didn't want to comment. He said: "Why don't you start by telling me what you thought of the film." The people were flabbergasted. You see, they weren't used to having someone ask for their opinion. They just wanted something to be presented to them.

On TV, they normally watch one film after another, but they seldom discuss them. Nevertheless, a discussion got underway. Mainly because of the young people who were there. At twenty-eight, I suppose I'm no longer young in that sense. I also recognized a woman in the film. I used to ride the bus with her every morning at five thirty. She was said to work in the SED district administration. Now I ask myself why she went to work so early. Normally it would've been an office job. You noticed in the bus that something about her wasn't right. She was an alcoholic. Now she's selling tickets at the bus station.

Anyway, it came out in the film how no one really tried to understand the youth back then. "Standard behavior" was all that was expected. That carries over into the foreigner problem today: "Whatever isn't like us has to be re-educated." Basically, that's the way they think. Everything must fit in. "If they can't behave themselves here, they have to go." That's what you always hear.

It's difficult for people to tolerate strangers or people who are different. Sure, they'll say: "You have to be tolerant." But as soon as someone expresses a different opinion, everyone tries to re-educate them.

The amazing thing was that so many people came to an event. You see, the changeover was a shock for many people. Everyone had to come to terms with themselves first and no one had time to go anywhere. When this singer-songwriter came here a few months ago, there were maybe twenty people there.

We bought an LP, too, but the performance he gave here was much better. We're not so crazy about the background music. It's a little weird, with guitar and concertina. But the lyrics were very good. He takes on everything, even the changeover. How people are fitting in with the new era. The spending frenzy and: "Money is everything." You see a bit of yourself in it, as well. As bitter as that is.

But we grew up here. And somehow we've even been comfortable — well, at least since we moved into this modern apartment building. I used to live with Bernd in an old building. But I don't like old buildings very much. Perhaps because I've been used to modern buildings from the time I was a kid. It's funny that my brother, who grew up just like I did, thinks old buildings are great.

* * *

Actually, we always took the easy way out. That means we took what they gave us. Just like this apartment. I should add that the so-called "old apartment buildings" here were built in the fifties, at the same time as the big industrial plant. The pine trees were cut down, the plant was built, and people were brought in from all over the republic. Socialist town, large industry, and all that propaganda. Bernd's parents also moved here because the apartments were reasonably priced. They're sailors on the inland waterways. Bernd spent his childhood in a home, in the "sailors' children's home." He only saw his parents every two months. That's a sore subject. I think he's gradually come to terms with it a little. It surfaced again when we had a child ourselves and he saw how difficult it is to give away your own child. When you're a child yourself, you can't see it as clearly. Now, when his parents come to visit, after they've been traveling again for weeks, it's always disconcerting. It's different with my mother. Somehow she's right in the thick of things. But Bernd's parents are always on the sidelines and don't have the proper affection for their granddaughter. That makes Bernd a little bitter. When they come, they usually go straight to their allotment garden. At the very beginning, they would come by to pass out hugs and chocolate and so on. And then they'd be gone again. We wouldn't see them for days, until they took off again. And then they'd be angry that we didn't go over and say goodbye.

Bernd's father is the kind of person who could only ever deal with a two-person life. His parents really don't need any other people. Bernd's mother would maybe like to come by sometimes but she doesn't want to have a falling-out with his father. I turn a blind eye a bit and keep my thoughts to myself. After all, you can't keep falling out with people just because they're different. And they're not so bad that you can't get along with them.

Life in this town is difficult. There are no traditions, no fixed family structures; people have gathered here from all over. That's why there are so many identity problems now. I miss my extended family. My grandma, great-grandma, my uncle and aunt, they're all scattered over the entire republic. We've hardly any contact with them, because of the physical separation. In the early days, you see, there were hardly any telephones.

You can't really feel comfortable in this town. There's no infrastructure, no old houses, no stores, no small cafés, no shopping mall, no park, and no street pubs. There are none of the things here that I know about from other towns, especially in the old states, but cities like Leipzig have them too.

I mean, things are happening over there. There's stuff going on, both summer and winter. It's so very dreary here. The streets are wide and empty; you feel lost here, and that's why people sit tight in their apartments.

There are hardly any foreigners here. At least no "Indians," no "Chinese" where you could go to eat. There is a refugee home. It used to be a barracks for the riot police, with barbed wire and towers. The refugees don't find it quite so bad any more, now that they've found out what's going on outside.

Bernd was inside once and took photos. There are over thirty different nationalities under one roof. Iranians and Iraqis, Kurds and Turks, Muslims, Serbs and Croats, all together. You can imagine what the atmosphere's like. Sure, they're supposed to be physically separated a bit, but there's not enough space. It was built for six hundred, but it's always overcrowded. Bernd was very shocked. "The people in there live like dogs" That's what he said. Beds are set up in a giant gym, and the men lie around there all day. Everything's dirty, everything's a mess. They don't know what to do with themselves. Wait for something and lie around all day. Bernd says that he would rather hang himself than live like that. There are a lot of single men, a kind of vanguard, who want to bring their families over later.

But then there are also the Sinti and Roma, the gypsy families. Well, Bernd once photographed a whole family, in a meadow, from the baby up to the last old man. That was something out of the ordinary. I mean, they were very clean and even well dressed. The women looked attractive, as well. There were very good-looking people there. So there are differences. But their day often starts early, around five. Then they set off carrying their big blue sacks through the whole town, from dump site to dump site, opening the trashcans and picking out what they can still use. On the way, they probably find something better and they're constantly dropping the other ballast by the side of the road. That goes on every day.

People are frustrated enough, and then this. People are basically good. I think tolerance is in our makeup. But circumstances being as they are now? There's a young man living in our apartment building; he used to work in the big plant, as a skilled worker. Now he's got an ABM job and he has to rake lawns, clean up corners and such like. He's making seven hundred marks less than he used to. No more than nine hundred in his pocket. He says: "The refugees get everything handed to them on a platter."

There's a gigantic sense of frustration all over this town. Some people are still working, but many have no work at all. Add to that being shut up in these tiny, narrow apartments. As long as they were working and weren't at home all day, it was somehow all right. But now?

I would like to see foreigners moving to our town; it would be good for the town and good for the area. But they would have to really live here, really put down roots, open restaurants and so on. But the people oppose it with all their might. Everyone wants to go abroad for a vacation, but to get on with foreigners in their own country, well, no one wants to do that.

On October 7, 1989, when the demonstrations started in Berlin, I was about to travel to France. I got the trip through the FDJ. Bernd took me to Berlin that evening. Then I sat in the train and was extremely anxious, because I knew that Bernd would be walking through the city. Later he told me that he'd been really depressed that evening. Even on Unter den Linden, everything had been barricaded off by young men in civilian clothes. Later, he went to the Alexanderplatz, where some people wanted to start a demonstration. Basically, he was an onlooker. And then the police appeared on the square. We saw it again on TV later. They started in with unbelievable violence. It was crazy. At the time he was really furious, but luckily he got out of there and went home. Thank goodness, because I was really very scared.

You see, we already knew from experience, in our own family, that they would take action, and what means they would use. My brother's father-in-law, that's his wife's father, well, he spent a long time in jail. He got out in June 1989; his freedom was bought by the West. We never really found out why he was put in jail. He had applied for permission to emigrate, and then it seems he secretly printed out the Declaration of Human Rights and also the parts of the GDR constitution that deal with freedom of speech. He was also a member of certain circles and groups that held meetings, all emigration applicants. That probably had something to do with it.

In any case, his father-in-law and mother-in-law were taken from their apartment in the early morning. My brother's wife was not at home because she was studying in P., and one sister was at the Palucca school in Dresden; she wanted to be a dancer. But the youngest daughter, she was sixteen and still lived at home. So she comes home from school one afternoon and thinks: "This apartment's a real mess." The dishes hadn't been washed, the beds weren't made, and everything had been gone through. She waited until evening, but her parents didn't come home. Then she went to my brother and said: "I can't understand what's going on. There's something wrong."

Then my mother and my brother telephoned the Stasi. And they said: "The parents were arrested, and if they're not back by tomorrow morning, they will be staying here."

The next day, his mother-in-law came back. They kept his father-in-law. But legal proceedings against his mother-in-law went on the whole time. She had to accept that she too might go to jail. She became thinner and thinner, went downhill, as people do.

In the end, she didn't go to jail because of her bad health. One of her daughters, my brother's wife, was immediately thrown out of college. She was studying education. The other sister had to leave the Palucca School. That was how things went.

The worst thing was that my mother didn't tell me anything about it at first. I heard it from other people. "Hey, is it true that Gabi's father's in jail?"

I didn't know anything about it, so the other people told me. Then I talked to my mother. "Mom," I say, "you'll never guess what people are saying . . ."

And my mother said: "Yes, Bärbel, they're right."

"It can't be true!" I said. "Why didn't you tell me?"

Then my mother said: "I was just afraid, Bärbel. Please don't say a word. Not a word. I'm begging you." Suddenly there was this unbelievable fear within the whole family, because we had felt for the first time how quickly the system can strike. They had their ways of humiliating people. For days I felt as if I had a stone in my stomach. It was really bad. I didn't want to eat anything any more. For a long time I had lived in the belief that socialism was the right way. Sure, I realized that there were certain contradictions in the system, but you always thought something could be saved, and you never really had any contact with people who were persecuted for political reasons. There just weren't very many.

Anyway, we always thought that socialism would work somehow.

All these years we were mainly occupied with ourselves. With our family circumstances. We never thought the Wall would fall. When that started, we didn't know what to think; about the demonstrations in Leipzig with "Germany United Fatherland" and all that. I was a bit queasy about that. I thought it was too quick, and also that it was maybe not the right course. But there was no stopping it. We accepted that somehow. With the money and everything. The masses just wanted it that way.

But there was a lot that could have been done differently. You see, you couldn't throw the old powerbrokers out of all those organizations.

Before people had learned how to speak their minds, and trusted themselves to do so, everything was over. Most people were still anxious, and it's especially hard for women to say what they think openly. It's always done behind the scenes, with whispering and gossip. We had no idea how to exploit the situation. And now, most of the leaders who had a Stasi past or were in the SED are still there. The biggest socialists have now become the biggest supporters of free enterprise. That annoys me most, and I also blame the Wessis: they came to an agreement with those people pretty quickly. They wanted to do their business and they didn't worry overlong about who with. And of course the old powerbrokers support each other. They know each other from before: "If you don't help me, I'll leak something about you . . ." That's how it goes.

★ ★ ★

I was allowed to travel to the West for the first time in 1986. It was with a group. Whenever the train stopped, the two "tour guides" stood at the doors to the railcar and made sure no one could get out. They were afraid there could well be someone among us who would just get off the train. But everything had been prepared beforehand down to the smallest detail: everyone who had been chosen had to go to an official "party" a few weeks before departure. There was a delegation of young people from the West there and we had to converse with them. The people from the Stasi sat around inconspicuously and pricked up their ears. Whoever didn't discuss correctly, that is, socialistically, was simply separated out before the trip.

Nevertheless, they had to reckon with the fact that someone might be pretending and would cut and run. Many had their very own personal opinion that they didn't necessarily show openly. Even in West Germany, when we got to our partner town, "they" were constantly afraid that we would express an independent opinion. We were given detailed lectures every morning, about what we could say and how we were to behave. Any kind of personal contact was to be completely cut off before it ever began. If we were actually invited to a private home, we were under no circumstances to go alone. Always only in twos, and one had to watch over the other, so to speak.

Bernd had just gone into the army at that time. But he was given kitchen detail during my trip, so that he wouldn't be stationed directly at the border. He was a border guard but at the time you didn't think about it much, relatively speaking. When you see on television nowadays just what happened there, it's really disturbing, even in retrospect.

But I can also remember exactly what Bernd told us when he came home on leave. Every day it got rammed down their throats: "The people who want to go over, they have no scruples, they'll shoot you too." To all intents and purposes, the situation was: "Who shoots first?" Of course, he could have said at the outset that he didn't want to go to the border; they did have that chance. But you never knew what the consequences would be. If you got off easy you'd be left in peace, or else you'd be given a rough time and harassed all day. That's what you were always afraid of, and that's why you'd rather give in first. You tried to take the dull middle path, not totally red and not totally the other way. You just wanted to get through somehow. Besides, it was our country and in every army you're eventually going to be expected to shoot in an emergency. Of course, the difference was that over here people were locked up and such, but we grew up in this state and so we just came to terms with it and in part even identified with it.

Still, we did do a lot of discussing. Bernd had taken photos — head-shots — of the people he was at the border with. They included some very nice people. But all border guards were vilified in public, and that's the reason why they often came home in civilian clothes when they had leave, which the other soldiers were not allowed to do. You see, border guards were being beaten up on the train when they traveled in uniform. That's why Bernd asked himself the question: "Is what I do the right thing?"

The real question: "What would he do if someone actually turned up at the border?" He tried not to think about that. As much as he could. Still, we talked about it every time he had leave. We hoped no one would come. And they were completely cut off, of course. No television, no radio, for weeks at a time. And then they were shown pictures of long knives and sharpened shovels and so on. Bernd was afraid too. They were only human beings, after all, the border guards, and not murder machines or such like, as they are portrayed today.

Of course, he was running around with real bullets. But he didn't want to shoot anyone, just wanted to put in his eight hours every day, finish his year and a half. And luckily he was in a quiet spot, where not much happened. I was really very happy about that.

Normally he only had one weekend's leave every two months. But they wanted to keep the people there free of conflict so that no one would go crazy. So he could come home on extra leave sometimes.

We told the officials that I wanted a divorce. Of course, we couldn't use that excuse too often.

But he did tell me how many of them had bad stomachs, and he had to deal with this as well, at the time. It's often the case with men that stress goes to their stomachs.

I think others should bear the responsibility for the border, not the little people. I can't imagine that Bernd could have shot at a human being. Really I can't. But I'm sure there were also agitators, like everywhere else, I imagine, and Bernd told me about that too. They would have picked anyone off without blinking an eye. There was a cadet or something. He had already gone quite crazy in the head from all the training, from the army and stuff like that. And they earned a lot of money and everything. People like that were even allowed to go to the West side of the border. They also kept an eye on Bernd and the others. They were only allowed out in twos, each had to keep an eye on the other, and they were always put with different partners so that they couldn't come to an agreement.

That was so strange. You just went along with everything. It was so stupid somehow. And once we even talked about whether I should just take off when I was on my trip or something . . . Actually, this conflict was strongest before I went to France. In October 1989. After everything here had gotten so heated. Many people had already been in Hungary since the summer, remember. And we sat here on many an evening and thought: "Should we pack our bags today or not? Is staying here a mistake?" It was really strange. All these people just seemed to carry you along with them. I don't know. But we found it difficult to make a decision.

And it's the same today. There are no more prospects for me as an infant daycare worker, now that women can stay home for three years after the birth. I could perhaps keep working for another two or three years in this profession. I can't be fired, because I'm on the staff council. But I don't see the point any more. It's just managing something that's temporary anyway. I would rather start something new.

Right now we've got a good offer to go to West Germany, to Heidelberg, with an apartment and a job for Bernd. He would be very well paid and it's a very pretty area. I would also get a job as a caregiver there, because they're opening a daycare center. But Bernd thinks he would be losing his roots if we were to move somewhere else. We would always be second-class and couldn't have a say in anything because it wouldn't be our own society. I think it can only be a help to us to go somewhere else; I really want to try to come to terms with life there. Something like that can't help but develop our own personalities. And we can always come back to visit; we do have a car, after all.

But Bernd always says: "It's not only a different city, but the people are different, they speak a different language, they have different customs." I say we can come back if we don't like it, but we should at least give it a try. Anyway, we haven't decided yet.

★ ★ ★

On the evening of November 9, we didn't take the press conference with Schabowski at all seriously. We went to bed as usual, and early on the tenth Bernd went off to work. I got up later and then heard the news. On my way to work, Bernd met me with the moped: "What are we going to do? What are we going to do?"

I say: "We'll try to get a visa right away, so that we can drive over this weekend."

Like everyone else, we joined the line in front of the police station and got the stamp, although it would have been all right without one. But we didn't know that. Early on Saturday morning, at four o'clock — this was now November 11 — we took the train to Berlin. My grandmother had a sister living in West Berlin. She was absolutely delighted to see us standing at the door.

We crossed at Friedrichstrasse; some people were climbing over the Wall, there was a huge mass of people, and the lines stretched all the way back to the Hotel Metropol. We got in line anyway. But I was still afraid. You just couldn't imagine that everything would go off so peacefully. On the other hand, I didn't think that they — the military — would shoot at their own people. But there were always the agitators. And you just couldn't know what they had in mind.

Even Bernd's brother held it against him that Bernd had gone to a demonstration once, in L. At the time — this would have been October — he just couldn't understand it. And he wasn't even a really committed comrade.

I spoke to his wife after that documentary. About how much responsibility each of us had for the old system. I always say: "I'm also responsible. I too made it possible." But she rejects that. She never joined the party, she says. And now she really thinks she bears no guilt. I think everyone here made it possible, because not one of us said adamantly: "I'm going to take steps, I'm going to do something against it."

But, personally, I can still sleep well, in spite of this. But there are many people who absolutely cannot manage any more. Of course, I don't know whether it has to do with feelings of guilt or their economic circumstances and this uncertainty. "Guilt" is a huge concept, of course. I tell myself that people can be manipulated. By the media and all sorts of things. We let ourselves be influenced, we go along with it, and that's really bad. Doesn't matter which system. Every state tries to manipulate its people, and it usually succeeds. To be honest, I didn't draw great consequences for myself from my own experience. You try perhaps to be a little more aware. That sounds a bit silly perhaps. You try to watch everything with your eyes open wider. But it's doubtful whether that would work.

At the time, I wasn't aware that we were being manipulated in such a way. It's only now that I've become conscious of it. Okay, sometimes you noticed a bit of manipulation, but you thought at least it was in the right direction.

Everyone was always talking about the Nazi period, how people were manipulated then, and you were really aware of that. But as for being manipulated in my own state, I really didn't grasp that. Perhaps I was too young. Or it takes a changeover like this to really make you aware in the first place.

But I don't know either whether this social system, the way it's working now, is the correct way. Parties are voted in at the elections, and then nothing else happens. We all know where the power actually lies. Real power has to do with money. And people are continually kept busy with everyday things, and they're also distracted by the media.

Looking back, the thing I find strange is how long Erich Honecker managed to stay in power. After all, he couldn't say a word under his own steam. How a man like that kept his position at the top — that I find amazing.

My own guilt? Well, I also tried to opt out once. I didn't want to have anything to do with the German-Soviet friendship. Of course, the teachers had their quotas: one hundred percent membership. They really discriminated against you. For instance: "If your parents don't have the money for the membership fee, just come to my house and pick up some scrap, and you'll be able to pay your fee with that."

But my grandpa influenced me. He always said: "Why do we have to pay for friendship?" Somehow that made sense to me. So I said: "I'm not joining the GSF." But I joined eventually. I've just never been able to follow through. I did try to protest, but later I gave in and went along with it. You needed to have more courage.

Personally, I wasn't hurt too badly by the system. The worst thing that happened to me was that I found a lump in my breast. That was one of those things that you just can't come to terms with immediately, that really frightens you. It could have meant the end, and you suddenly realize that, although the doctors always let you believe that it's "benign." Fortunately, the lump really was benign, because if they find out that one single spot has degenerated, then they take off the entire breast.

Perhaps it happened because of the pill. My whole breast looked like it did during pregnancy, although I wasn't pregnant. And I've always been healthy. It was like a blow to the head. And the fear that something like this might happen again is always there. I don't mean that all my identity as a woman is wrapped up in my breasts, I don't mean that, but it is important.

My pregnancy with Julia went off well, but I suddenly got gallstones afterwards. Two years later. Well, I thought, I don't believe it, there's always something. I couldn't reconcile it with my age. I don't know if I would be able to bear it, if new things kept coming up over and over again. When you're young, somehow you think you should always be healthy.

I don't see these illnesses as a sign that I haven't lived my life correctly. At least not the breast lump. It's easier to see the connection with the gallstones. I'm always getting overexcited about everything really quickly, and you know it's people who are always impulsive who tend to form gallstones.

My personal wish is for fulfillment in my career. I'd like to start something new again, not to be an employee any more but somehow to have a bit of independence. I don't want to get these constant orders from on high and then have to carry them out. It just doesn't suit me somehow. I would like to be able to make decisions for myself and follow them through.

The city also needs to have more atmosphere, so that you can identify more with it. But I have real doubts that there would be any possibility of that here, with these big areas of new apartment buildings. I also wish that people would be more tolerant in their dealings with foreigners and even each other. I think that the narrow-minded mentality is stronger in the GDR than in the West, because egalitarianism was so huge here. In the West, everything was set up on so many different levels, and the people there are also more tolerant. I mean, if someone walks around here dressed a little differently, then everyone stares and says: "Eww, look at him!" People talk, you can't avoid it. In this respect, I saw my trip to France in 1989 as a great enrichment, and it will keep me going for a long time. People made contact with us, began conversations, and wanted to find out something about us. They took the time to do that. Even at meals — and you wouldn't believe how long those last — they took the time. Here, you eat quickly, clear the table, and you have to wash up immediately because everything has to be clean.

Here's how it is here: when company comes, everything is cleaned, everything has to be immaculate. You prepare everything by yourself, and then set it before your guests.

And there they said: "Today, we're going to make a pizza together. You make the fruit salad, and the two of us will go into the kitchen and make the pizza." That made an impression on me.

But we don't have company very often. We don't have a large circle of acquaintances, no real friends. Until two years ago, we were good friends with a couple and we really got on amazingly well with them. But Bernd and Rainer worked together and didn't get on at work. Working together with friends is not a good combination. Everything went sour because of that. Since then, we've been on the lookout for another couple we can be good friends with. But I've had people tell me a few times that you shouldn't just concentrate on couples. That doesn't work. It's better if you find a lot of people.

But right now I've been waiting for two hours again for Bernd to finally come home. . . .

CHAPTER SEVEN

SO WHAT'S CHANGED? PATRIARCHY HASN'T DISAPPEARED...

— Beate G., 45, institute employee and sculptor in metal

I SUFFERED FROM THIS "Wall syndrome" a long time, always felt hemmed in. I lived for years with the feeling that something amazingly important was being kept from me. I dreamed, I fantasized, I felt an indescribable longing. Intellectually I knew: that's unreal, excessive, utter nonsense. The West is no "savior," nor is it "paradise." But I couldn't make headway against this longing for the "other." I tried to fight it, I suffered, I was torn apart, I made my life difficult. I envied everyone who came over from the West, no matter what kind of a person they were. Why did she or he have something I couldn't have, just because she or he had a different passport? I was ashamed of myself for having these feelings, this longing and this envy. But I couldn't rise above it.

I often dreamed I was in West Berlin. I would walk through a supermarket and would see all the things I had wished for from time to time. But also a lot of kitsch, junk, useless stuff. Really realistic, you know. Or I would be sitting in a bus, traveling endlessly through West Berlin, but I wasn't allowed to get off. I didn't see any of the streets that were familiar to me from TV, and the scenery was also very strange. West Berlin was like a village; there were a lot of one-story houses, and it was always evening. I would see the neon ads, a lot of lights, and the houses were all tiny.

In another dream I went through huge, ancient gates. I ran and ran and I knew in my dream: "Now I'm in West Berlin!" That was as clear to me as if I were awake in my dream, and I knew while still dreaming that a train station would be coming up that I had to go through and then I would be in East Berlin again. But the station looked nothing like the one at Friedrichstrasse, the "palace of tears," as we called it, where I had so often taken friends to the border. The way back to the East Zone always led through narrow, winding alleys, past watch towers and barbed wire, just like it did in real life, although I had never been allowed to travel to the West, had never seen any of this with my own eyes.

I found these dreams infantile. I thought: Do you really need to do this? On the other hand, I was happy to see any images of the "other." I had completely fallen under the spell of that comfortable feeling you get between dreaming and waking. "I was really in West Berlin!" And when I was completely awake, I had to start crying, in bed in the mornings, and me a woman of forty.

These unbelievably intense feelings were not inspired by television. They came from way down deep within myself. Something was being kept from me and I wanted to experience it. I sometimes talked about my dreams. They were coming more and more frequently, but even then I didn't want to acknowledge that I was suffering so much because of the Wall.

* * *

In spite of all this, I witnessed the wave of refugees in the summer of 1989 with great inner distance. I would never have gone "over" in this way. That's not how I am, leaving everything behind and "solving" problems by running away. I would have found it dishonorable or hysterical or paranoid. Luckily, the problem solved itself in a way that made the most sense to me: by the opening of the Wall.

I already knew that the West could also be repulsive; I didn't want to live there, didn't want to take part in this "dance around the golden calf." And when I could travel at last, everything I had always felt was confirmed: my home is here in the East. In this little town on the river Oder, in this simple house. I live here very well, live life to the full, and material things are important to me only up to a point. In the West, on the other hand, I find a lot of things repulsive, inhumane, threatening to one's existence. But that someone set up a wall in front of my face — that was the truly awful thing.

* * *

Now the Wall is gone, and I can't imagine that we've become different people overnight. We have lived very different lives in the West and in the East, parallel, without really knowing anything about the other. For example, you can't imagine people in the West having dreams like I had. Or take the education system. So much was kept from me that I could have learned in the West. That's why I'm so sad sometimes. My niece, who has just turned fourteen, goes to a school in Bavaria. The last time I looked at her textbooks, I actually broke down in tears. You've no idea what she learns about in history! The way the material is taught there, you can really learn something for your life. And I learned so little, and what I did learn was garbage. For example, I have no feel for the English language. I couldn't imagine that I would ever in my life get to England, and now I have to acquire the language with difficulty, bit by bit. But I have to come to terms with this sorrow as well; I have to accept it, because it just so happened that I lived here.

* * *

The breakdown of the GDR was not as much of a shock for me as it was for many other people. The way I was brought up, I had nothing to do with the state. From my childhood onwards, I remember the whistle of the jamming transmitter that was always in the background when my father listened to RIAS on medium wave. Father told us: "They're all criminals, this government." He told us about bunkers. I remember these expressions and phrases exactly: "Ulbricht bunkers. The leaders are murderers; they make people disappear, beat them till they're crippled." Even back then he was telling us the stories about the Stasi that everyone knows now. He spoke quite openly in front of us kids. Mother would say: "Franz! Not in front of the children." And she would say to us: "Children, please don't say tell anyone any of this. Anyone! Otherwise we'll go to prison." I remember her words, her tone of voice, exactly. We heard a lot, very early on, and I thought it was marvelous. My father just couldn't keep it to himself; he let everything out, and I believed him.

I didn't become a Pioneer, and I was very proud of being different from the others. Later, I didn't join the FDJ, either. I never went along with any of that stuff. Nevertheless, I was looked up to and actually very well-liked. Of course, in the choir, during performances, I always had to stand at the back, hidden away, because I never wore the uniform. This principled upbringing was actually the most positive thing about my childhood, and I really admire my parents for that. "Thank God I don't have to be like the others!" Even as a little girl, this feeling was very strong.

At that time, there was a large weaving mill across from our apartment. On holidays, huge portraits of Ulbricht and Pieck and all those guys were hung up there. You got up early, looked out the window and had to look at those pictures. My father made a joke of it. "Come here, my dear children, and look at this. So, now we'll make a huge bow and say together: 'You are my morning and my evening prayer, my protection and my redemption, my help in times of trouble . . .'" That was his way, ridiculing everything.

My father was a Catholic priest who had had the misfortune to have fathered children. A highly educated man. He had lived in a Cistercian monastery that was destroyed during the war, then arrived in the East Zone, and later worked as a chaplain in the *Hofkirche* in D., where he also got to know my mother. He was a very sensual, good-looking man, who gave an impression of complete innocence. He entered the monastery in order to get a good education. My father's father was only a school caretaker and wanted at least one of his children to study. It fell to Franz, my father.

Well, in D. he met my mother, and the rest is history. Of course, he didn't want to have me. Later, I found a diary belonging to my mother. The abortion had already been arranged. Even the church would have turned a blind eye. It read him the riot act and said: "Fine, we'll take care of this. But it will never happen again." But my mother didn't play along. And after I arrived, she put pressure on him, actually blackmailed him, and he had to marry her.

From the beginning, I was made to feel that he didn't want me. But I knew how to handle this straightforwardness. He was an angry man and often swore at me, on many occasions just because I was there. I grew up with this. Still, I never developed any feelings of hatred towards him. Once, during puberty, I had a fit and said to him: "I hate you!" He just broke down altogether and actually started to cry. In fact I'd always had the feeling that it had nothing to do with me. It had to do with his life, with his relationship with this woman, my mother. I was only a little girl who somehow got in the middle, this unwanted child that had destroyed his life. He loved women and what was the harm in that, if only all these little kids didn't keep coming into the world all the time.

My mother never used contraception, never did the math, nothing. So he made another four children with my mother, and there would have been more if she had not said at one point: "So, now we're not going to sleep together any more." It was a brutal mess between the two of them. But I can also understand my mother. She was only a lowly pharmacy worker when she had me, and she would have been pretty much down and out. So they reached an agreement: my father would look after her until I was sixteen and then he could go his own way. Of course, they didn't plan to have any more children. They came along, but the agreement stood. Father became a hygiene inspector, played the organ every Sunday in church for years, but was not allowed to take communion. I think he found that very difficult.

Later, my mother studied pharmacy in college. In spite of us children. But when I was sixteen, my father didn't leave. That was a problem for my mother. She'd been hoping for years that he would finally leave. But he was no longer in a position to do so; he was drinking more and more. Then she sued for divorce and simply sent him packing when I was about twenty-three or twenty-four. That must have been a dreadful scene.

The monks saw to it that he could at least get back onto monastery premises. He spent many years there as caretaker. Later, he often went to the bishop, humbled himself in every possible way, and it seems that he was forgiven everything. He celebrated mass again and was very highly regarded. In this respect he died in peace. He became round and fat, everyone liked him, and no one could imagine that he had once been such a Cerberus. Today I am reconciled with him, and besides, he's dead. Died in 1979.

* * *

In actual fact, I like my brother and sisters. As a child I even had a very close relationship with my brother. But dealing with me always reminds him of his own misery. I once tried to talk to him about it, but I failed utterly. Then we gave it a rest for two years. With my mother, too. Now I accept it. They don't want to. They have their reasons and I don't want to force myself on them. I feel most sorry for my brother. He wet the bed until he was fourteen; he was an extremely sensitive boy and was thrashed so much. Our mother almost went berserk. He doesn't want to be reminded of that. Now he's a totally uncommunicative scientist; he has his doctorate and is a gene technician in some institute.

* * *

I did vocational training and passed my final exams, and then studied to be an agro-technician. Horrible word. Later I wanted to study psychology. But with my grades, a B average, I didn't have the slightest chance. Eleven applicants for one college place, and I was a non-conformist, had never ever been "societally active," as they called it. So I was rejected. An indefinable urgency remained: "You have to do something." I landed in mathematics, and that was the worst thing that could have happened to me. I'm not stupid, but that was simply not my subject. So this undertaking failed miserably after a year and a half. I hung around for a while, took part-time jobs in the office-machines plant; later I was an orderly in a hospital, did the lowest jobs, and felt like a fool. It was only the men that gave me a bit of a boost with my feeling of self-worth, with my self-confidence.

I cannot remember ever liking to talk about my life. I even found it difficult in therapy. I'm sure it has to do with my life story. I never needed to talk, never needed to make myself look impressive. I was always something special because of my strange upbringing. And I enjoyed that even as a child. My individuality had already blossomed while my best friends were still shouting: "Be prepared, always prepared," were standing to attention, and going along with everything. I thought it was dumb. At that time of my life I was totally healthy. Even the teachers tended to see it as a positive thing. I got the distinct impression that I was something incredibly special, and in actual fact I didn't need to do anything for it, simply be what I was. Strangely enough, I hardly ever experienced anything bad, either, was never put down, even by the teachers. On the contrary, they actually liked to argue with me in a constructive way. I even became friends with some of them. So I was pretty proud of myself, of my parents, and of the way I thought of myself as not being a "conformist." And no one could have foreseen at that time that things would ever change, that the Wall would come down, that the system would fall apart, and so on.

I thought being a Pioneer was ridiculous, that wearing a uniform was terrible, and that looking like everyone else was simply dreadful. It just could not be. After all, *I* was a human being, an individual.

This attitude has continued throughout my life. The only thing I sometimes wish: that I had been a radical. I envied the terrorists. Not because they killed people, but I was always too "well-behaved" even for myself. Basically, I became less and less special as time went on. When I worked in the regional institute for veterinary medicine in F., after my vocational training, everything was already a big mess, politically speaking. I couldn't clarify where I stood any more, because there was no one left who believed in all that ideological nonsense. Even as a child, I probably had this narcissistic need to stand out, to be different from the others, and politics were just right for that. Later, however, I met more and more people who were like me. The charm was gone.

My relationships with men were pretty neurotic. For a long time I went looking for them and needed them. Men as a father substitute. Most of them were much older and pretty worn out. That appealed to my masochistic tendencies. So, for a long time, I looked for men who repeated exactly what I had experienced in my childhood. That's why I went into therapy later. I wanted to grow up and stop looking for something in men that I couldn't find there. For years I fell in love with Catholic priests. I didn't let up until I got what I wanted. Not like a prostitute. No. In a very innocent way. . . . Today I would say I was a real bitch. But at the time there were many layers to it: revenge on my father, testing myself, and also hatred of men. All of this lay behind my behavior. I had to learn the hard way to treat myself and others with great care. But I know that I will never be fully successful.

* * *

I have absolutely no trust in patriarchy. It frightens me, because so far men have only messed things up. Of course, I mean male society, not men as individuals. I would like to talk more about it without it always being taken as an attack from the get-go. It starts as soon as my son comes back from a hunting expedition. "It's really great." That makes my hair stand on end. How can hunting be something really great? Something beautiful? To corner animals and then blow them away. That's only one example. But I see that as "typically male." No female human being would find pleasure in that. These are things that make me angry or aggressive. Then I drink a little too much, and Sebastian, my husband, gets the worst of it. He comes to me, makes with the smiling and the kissing and such, and I'm full of these kinds of thoughts. Actually, I would like to talk, but he cuts it off. I'm sure he has his reasons, because I really get very aggressive, or he feels himself attacked as a man, as a substitute for society, and that's really a shame.

I also like to be alone a lot. When I sit and listen to music, I live very intensely in my own thoughts, as if I were in another world, and this world is very alive in me. Of course, I'm still in the world that surrounds me. But it doesn't matter whether I'm reading the *Spiegel* or watching television, I encounter the same thing everywhere, over and over again: patriarchy. I think Sebastian embodies something patriarchal as well. Although he's no macho man in the true sense of the word. But he's a dark horse. He's wrapped himself so tightly and plays the softy, so gentle, loving, and tender. But I suspect there's an incredibly macho man inside him. I would like to let him out. It's all pretty difficult. Sometimes I'm a bit aggressive and provoking. But he doesn't let himself be drawn in. He says: "You're drunk or being silly." And then he sits down in his office and works. Whereas a real fight would be very important to me. I suspect he's extremely afraid of women. True, he does have a lot of female friends, but there's no real closeness there. He's "the good listener," the "dear"; he puts on a "good face," and women like him a lot. But he never really lets it all hang out.

* * *

In September 1989, I wasn't very politically committed at first. I met Henrich, the lawyer, read his book *The Custodial State,* went to see him a few times, and did a few courier runs. Delivered a message, dropped a few things off, or picked something up. But I wasn't very intensely involved. Later, I went to the church in F. I only knew: "It can't go on like this." With the Stasi, for instance. People like André, a young man who came from a Stasi family; he went to officer training school, cleared out after six weeks and turned up here. He lived with us for a year. Later, the Stasi tried to nail him again. With blackmail and everything. I found all this muck absolutely nauseating. It couldn't go on like this, and the Wall was a problem too; it just had to go. So even I took to the streets, but without any euphoria.

I observed people very carefully back then. What's happened now, all this huge disappointment and resignation, doesn't surprise me in the least. I don't know of anything where I could say: "That just cannot be true." They're still exactly the same people. Before the so-called change-over and also afterwards. It's just that back then, for a short while, they had an awful attitude of anticipation: "Now, finally, the great redemption will come!" That's what drove the people out into the streets, that's what gave them strength, gave them courage. They could even get loud; suddenly they even had a voice. But of course this simplistic attitude of anticipation could never be fulfilled.

There are some people who are still shouting, only they're now long-ing for the "great leader" who will finally put everything right for them. Because they've never learned to do anything for themselves, *to be* them-selves, because they've always been dependent. They are so completely helpless, without any powerful "superego."

And I feel sorry for the young people who are searching everywhere for their fathers and find that there's no real, true authority figure who is trustworthy and can give them direction. Whoever was lucky enough to be able to experience a real authority figure as a model in childhood will no longer need a "leader" later on. But as it is, the young people are still searching, as adults, as alleged adults, and that's the ridiculous thing about it. They haven't gone through that process by which a boy at some point no longer needs his father. That's why they're now taking to the streets, going around bellowing and running after any idiot who waves party slogans in front of their faces. Could be some kind of brownshirt or a fly-by-night guru or whatever. It's all the same mess. It has nothing to do with East and West any more. It's just the same over there as it is here. Only here it takes a more primitive form, that's very obvious. In the West it's a bit more hidden; over there this longing manifests itself as drug use, resignation, or consumer frenzy. These are only ways of playing the game. Here they're still bleating in the streets, acting out their power or aggres-sions and beating up foreigners. That's bad, but somewhere there's still something inside them shouting out loud. There's not only resignation and cold cynicism.

* * *

But I don't hold out much hope. So what's changed? Patriarchy hasn't dis-appeared! First of all it's important to get all the men out of politics. They can be quite ordinary husbands or lovers. Of course, that doesn't mean that women should go and do what men have been doing up to now. I'm thinking of a completely different kind of politics. I doubt whether the word "politics" will still exist then. There will be a completely different term. Not comparable to what has gone on for all these centuries. I imag-ine a matriarchy where the men have their place too. Nothing against men — on the contrary. But never again the way it has been up to now.

Perhaps waging war is inborn in men. But then a man should be placed in a position where he can let it out with toys. He shouldn't reach a position where human lives are suddenly on the line and nature, the earth, and the animal world become his victims. Just the idea that weap-ons are produced at all I find insanely threatening to human existence.

The matriarchy existed for six thousand years. It was way ahead of our time. Wasn't threatening to our existence, and the men had their place too. Could be it's a utopia. But does the earth have any other choice? When you watch television or read a magazine, it's enough to make you throw up. It just hurts to see and hear how everything is being de-stroyed. And we women play along and are absolutely unconscious of it.

That's the problem. Men are only able to run riot because women play along. We prepare the ground, bear the children, the sons, let ourselves be oppressed. That has very deep roots. I don't know how a breakthrough could be managed. I don't hold it against women, though; after all, they don't know anything else, women or men. They just grew up in a society like this. It's just that sometimes I listen to what is inside me and that's why I have such thoughts.

* * *

"Wall syndrome" is no longer relevant; that was on a different level. If someone had forbidden me to leave the house, I would have gotten some peculiar syndrome then too: "How great it must be to be able to run around in the street." It's no more than that. I can do without external motivators. There's nothing there that would be completely new to me. Of course there are lovely things I can enjoy; strolling through West Ber-lin with my friend Christiane — she's just so kind and affectionate. Or when I'm in nature, when I go for a walk here along the Oder.

I'm not a very intellectual person; I live more by feeling, letting things affect me differently. There are certain matters I should approach more objectively and systematically, perhaps, but I always think I really don't need to read up on things a lot, I don't need to listen to any lectures; I usually find everything within myself, if I only listen to my inner being. I'm often made aware of things in dreams. There's so much material in me, so much power, but this power is a little witch-like. It scares me sometimes, because much of what I feel lies outside reality, I mean, what is normally considered reality. I have a lot of intense dreams, every night; they fre-quently get to me, but should I write them all down? And read them again later? I shy away from that. It's hard to really get into dreams, to empathize intensely with that world. And I also ask myself: Why should I?

It's pretty seldom that one human being really takes an interest in another. There's often a lot of delusion, a lot of self-deceit. Isn't the other only interested as long as it has something to do with him? Then he's all ears, because something's happening within him. But when you tell someone else your dreams, they mostly block you out. When you are close to another person, then you sometimes force something on him that he can't bear. He goes crazy or leaves. And what is he to do with things he really doesn't want to know anything about? A woman like me is threatening, makes a lot of people afraid. Even I'm afraid sometimes, when things come up, unpredictable things.

* * *

Perhaps that's why I work with metals. At first I was struck by old roof gutters made of zinc. I noticed they had a lovely patina. I saw the various shades of gray as a symbol of weathering and morbidity, of fragility and decay. The metal reacts to influences from the environment in so many different ways. So many layers, shadings, transitions. That fascinated me. I sensed how much it had to do with life. We all have our patina, don't you think?

Later I began to sew scars into the material. Very small, fine seams. Scars like we all have and all carry around with us. The skins that we want to slough off and yet they stick to us. The power of time. This spoke to me from the metal, was suddenly completely obvious. And there was no longer anything cold, anything evil about the metal; it was something very alive that changes.

I'm fascinated by the green copper that used to be on the roofs. It has experienced so much and has still not been destroyed, just as changes don't destroy us but alter us greatly and leave their traces behind. Perhaps this is an explanation of why I make sculptures out of roof gutters and copper. Chrome and stainless steel deny their history, put up a pretense. You can't perceive time in them. So I prefer to take these "simple" materials and add something. Sometimes more, sometimes less.

I polished an old aluminum plate until it gleamed again. Also a symbol. It can't be what it is; the signs of age must be eliminated, it must shine once more. And sure enough, the old luster reappears. But there are very small pores that indicate, if you look very closely, that it is indeed old. You can see all of that and make something of it, if you want to, as a photographer or a philosopher.

It's important to me to do this work. But I still have to keep my job at the same time. The status in society grounds me. I have my salary and so I can afford certain things — this hobby, for example. If I had to rely on making money with my objects or having my husband support me, I don't know if I would still have the calmness to see things in this philosophical manner. I would feel bad if I were dependent upon selling. Some people would like me to sell all the time. "Metal is going to be big. Make this! Do that!" But I don't comply. "I can't be bought. I wasn't a Pioneer and I won't become one, no matter who or what happens along." I'd much rather give something away.

But I don't want to be arrogant even on the subject of selling. I have sold things, with a tear in my eye, when I knew it would be in good hands. I got a few thousand marks for a bit of metal. But the man understood me so well it was unbelievable. He wrote me very tender letters, and he simply had an eye for my work.

As for the junk, or rather what we now call junk, well, that came later. Mostly they're pieces that I found myself in the street or on the squares.

I look for "symbolic" junk. This steel helmet, for example, was used to shovel sewage. An incredible symbol, don't you think? I want to make something with it. I don't really need to change much. There's a handle welded on already.

Or a completely different subject: a woman made of metal. This dichotomy. On the one hand the whore-like quality of women, on the other hand, the wish to be sacred. Then somehow the Virgin Mary occurred to me. But with this amazing breast, not on the side of the heart, but intentionally on the other side. But I suspect that people wouldn't notice that or understand it, if it were exhibited at a gallery. Another is called "Scars." That one's made of zinc. As I was working on it, I lost a friend. I was very attached to this man. Sometimes I have extra-marital friendships, even a bit sexual, but actually more fatherly. The man simply broke down, and that's what I tried to express. But when I exhibit the piece, no one knows what to make of it. Perhaps it's easier to express all this with words, when you write a book. But with metal? You have to look a little closer, then. That's why I've kept a lot of things back, because no one would understand them anyway.

Those three strange, crazy-looking bodies welded onto steel, for example. Looks like an exposed skeleton. Man, woman, and child. Poor, broken, homeless people. I've tried to indicate what it's about with the title: "Refugees." These are things that matter to me. Whether it's the Kurds or whoever. I always feel bad when I see pictures like that. Again, just two days ago, people were evacuated from a city that was being bombed. The faces, of the children, of the old people: they are totally at the mercy of a terrifying power. That's what I was trying to express, and I would like to think a few visitors might get it.

Actually, I want to do some different things. I probably need that as balance. Design work. Not just these serious, melancholy topics: something with pep, flashy lamps for example, or a few other crazy things, without all that baggage. Giving old metal new impact by adding something or other. So that you think: Why is that so effective? Why don't I see that elsewhere?

I would also like to try store-window dressing. That's a field where I think that the Ossis are far too well-behaved and stuffy. They'd rather put a Santa Claus in their window than a nice, crazy copper lamp or something.

A little catalogue would be important, especially with particular objects where a few words might be useful. Not just to explain something; they'd have to be texts in their own right. I know what to do . . . Now I just need the people to help me. . . .

CHAPTER EIGHT

I ALWAYS HOPE I WON'T WAKE UP IN THE MORNING . . .

**— Rudi K., 39, former "unofficial co-worker"
of the Secret Police, now right-wing radical**

I WAS BORN IN 1953. Ever since I was a kid I wanted to be a radio announcer. When I was in the *Wehrmacht* I applied to the radio station in Berlin. I always say "*Wehrmacht*." Known at the time as the NPA: "National People's Army." Of course, I first needed permission to travel to Berlin. If you were in the military, you couldn't just go to Berlin. Not allowed. We had to stay at our posts and do our duty.

The people at Radio Berlin wrote back that I should apply to the radio station in C. So that's what I did. Finally, I got a letter saying they would take me. I was invited to Berlin, congratulated, and sent to the studio in C. I wasn't exactly overjoyed, but I said to myself: "Just go, then you're in radio and you'll get to Berlin somehow."

Actually, I didn't really understand the lay of the land yet. A studio like that was the end of the line. So I was forced to stay in this town.

Even back then I couldn't feel good about the work. We lied through our teeth. When there was a party conference, you always had to convince someone or other — a youth team, for example, who had competed for some honorary title — that they actually wanted it. They didn't want it, of course. At the usual preliminary meeting, people would speak quite freely. But in front of the microphone, they wouldn't say a thing. You practically had to stuff the words into their mouths: "The socialist state of workers and farmers is good, right?" etc. And somehow you'd put together your program. But there was almost always a party secretary there. Besides, the people had been "force-fed" beforehand so that they'd say what they were supposed to say. But if someone did ever express an honest opinion, it was certain to be cut out before the program aired.

* * *

I began drinking because it got to the point that I couldn't bear it any more. I would come home in the evenings and ask myself: "So what did you actually do today?" No one listened back then to East German stations anyway. Basically, you went to work in the morning because you needed the cash. And you came home at night knowing for a fact that you'd done nothing but shit.

So then you'd go to a bar in search of buddies you could talk to or whatever. And sometimes you'd find yourself talking to someone who'd say: "I've had it; I'm getting out of here."

Then I'd get scared and say to myself: "If anyone finds out you're mixing with this sort, you'll be fired." Well, then I . . . then, they recruited me. So to speak. I mean . . . In school I got through the tenth grade. Always got an A in citizenship. I lied, of course. I knew what the teachers wanted to hear. Listening to RIAS was forbidden in those days, and I wanted to look good. We had our instructions: If our parents listened to RIAS, we were to report it in school. That was in Frau Hauser's class, my homeroom teacher.

So I thought: To make a good impression, I'll just tell her we listen to RIAS at home.

My parents were called to the school, and when I came home they said to me: "You told them in school that we listen to RIAS. From now on there will be no more RIAS!"

But later I managed to get hold of an old receiver from the Second World War, from a buddy of mine. I could use it to listen to my RIAS again. My parents, of course, never knew.

* * *

Even back then I wanted to do radio. I wrote to the stations asking for music, greetings, and also pictures. I wrote to RIAS using a code name. I told myself the Stasi would never figure this one out. I called myself "Caesar." Code name: "Caesar."

Then one day I was called out of class by our principal. I went into his secretary's office, and there sat two gentlemen who unfolded their IDs: they were from the Stasi.

As I said, I had had contact with West German radio stations. What's more, I was dissatisfied with the political system and had begun putting out a kind of newspaper. Whether they had tracked me down because of the letters to RIAS or because of the newspaper, I don't know.

In any case, they tried to recruit me for the Stasi. I've never had much sympathy for them. For instance, I would never blow the whistle on someone for screwing up, or anything like that. Never.

But I went along with them at the time, at least I pretended to. Well . . . because . . . they paid me for it. Eighty marks was a lot of money back then. And most important, they would take me out to dinner, in a fancy restaurant. It was always a super evening with all the trimmings. Really great! But later I stopped. Well, I wanted to stop. But then along came my stepfather; he must have known something was up. He eventually worked with them as well. And he said I had to continue. I said: "No, I won't do it!" Then he threatened me: if I wasn't going to do it, then I didn't need to come home any more.

Even then there was a kind of frustration building up in me. For you never really knew who you could trust. I was always afraid. You couldn't find any straight-shooters, any real comrades-in-arms, I mean.

* * *

At some point I got interested in National Socialism. I liked it a lot. There was always some kind of feeling of betrayal, so you went looking for something to anchor yourself to. That's how I got into National Socialism.

But I lived in fear. I always hid all the materials I kept at home. You'd try to find like-minded people, of course. But you could never know: Is he really . . . or is he from the Stasi? You've no idea how horribly scared I was. It was unbelievable.

* * *

What they told you in school was all garbage. I never believed any of it. We had to learn the life stories of Ulbricht and the others. All crap. So I turned to the West. A pal I hung around with at the time had contacts. That's how we got the *Bildzeitung,* the *Deutsche Soldatenzeitung,* the *Nationalzeitung,* and so on. Eventually I thought to myself, man, what about you doing something, too. That's when I got the idea for the newspaper. We stole the articles and added a bit more. It was mostly a way of working off frustration. We were longing for a way to get rid of some of what was disturbing us.

* * *

Later, I was actually persecuted. By the Stasi. Three times I had run-ins with them. I was still being recruited even here in C., right up to the end and even afterwards. This is what happened: While I was still working at the radio station, I had to write reports and send them to the district headquarters of the People's Police. There was this press officer there, a man I got on with very well, in fact. At least I thought I did. He often invited me to join him after work for a glass of schnapps. Once, a strange "gentleman" suddenly joined us. The press officer said: "What d'you say all three of us go to a café, just around the corner? My treat."

"Sure," I said, "let's go." We just had a few drinks. Nothing else.

About a year later — I had long since forgotten about the "gentleman" — I had to go to the hospital for an operation. I had a boil, but I'd rather not talk about that. Anyway, I didn't like this hospital. So I asked the doctor if he couldn't let me go home early. On my own recognizance, so to speak. He said, if I signed something, then, yes. So I signed. Basically, only the doctor and myself knew about it.

I get home and I'm thinking, "It's nice to be home again," when all of a sudden the doorbell rings. There stands the "gentleman" I talked about. He's just there! Out of the blue! And I'm still unpacking. So I open the door and he says:

"Well, Rudi, we know each other, do we not?"

"Yes," I say, "that time in the café."

"Exactly," he says, and unfolds his ID.

So I say: "I suppose now I have to let you in."

He gives the apartment the once over and says: "Well now, doesn't this place look just great!"

He had seen, of course, that I had books from *back then*. And flags and things. And then he set about recruiting me. I mean, trying to recruit me. And I said: "Is there any point in saying 'no'?"

"It wouldn't make any difference."

Some time later, he also invited me to dinner, in a restaurant. By that point, I had absolutely no idea what I should do. I was simply scared.

I knew someone in Berlin, from my army days, so I called him up and said: "I have to talk to you."

He says to me: "You can't possibly become an informer."

I ask him: "So what should I do now?"

He says: "There's only do one thing to do, drink, drink, drink, so they don't want you any more." So that's what I did.

There was always, of course, this secret meeting place. So at one of our meetings I said to this "gentleman": "I can't go on, I don't want to, it's impossible. Surely you can see I've been drinking. You must have realized at our last meeting that I'm always drunk." And then he beat me up.

That was after the changeover. That's when I wanted to stop once and for all. This West German newspaper had just offered me a job. I thought I could do better journalism at this paper, and besides, they offered me a few other things to sweeten the deal. But this "gentleman" tried to convince me to go on working for the Stasi. I didn't want to. So he became more and more angry. We sat together over a cup of coffee and I said again and again: "No, I'm not going to continue."

And so he beat me up.

At the time he recruited me, I still lived in North C. There was a youth club there. I was supposed to watch the people who went in and out. But I told myself: "No. You're not going to betray them. You will never do that."

So I would think up stories at home, so that I wouldn't get them into trouble. I would tell myself: "These'll do," although I knew different. I always added, of course, a little something that I thought would interest this "gentleman." That's the kind of imbecilic things I did. But I really couldn't ever deal with it.

* * *

At the moment, I have no idea what I should do. I don't believe anything any more. They've also deceived me here at this West German newspaper. Someone let slip that I'm to be fired by December 31, at the latest. I broke my leg and was out on sick leave. When I got back, Mr. M. from West Berlin was already gone. Also thrown out. So I called him up privately and he told me: "It was all planned. All you East Germans were only there to get things rolling. You were to make the contacts. And now you'll be the first to be fired."

Well, *you* try to come to grips with so many problems!

Two months ago, I tried to commit suicide. It's so terrible, having this fear all the time . . . You know, of course, that it's going to end. Sooner or later. I just don't want to end up like some people, who hang around the streets here. Real bums. All in rags. At rock bottom. I'm too proud for that. I absolutely refuse to do that. But unfortunately I've yet to find the right suicide method.

First of all I bought bottles of sleeping pills, one after the other. Then, a bottle of brandy. One evening, I wolfed down the lot. But I woke up again the next morning. I felt terrible. The doctor had to be called, because I realized I was simply not going to die. Then they pumped my stomach and all of a sudden I had to go on living. I was on sick leave for some time. I asked the doctor not to write the real story on the sick note. She was good to me.

Now I sit at home every evening and wait for death to finally come. I always hope I won't wake up in the morning, but every morning I wake up again.

* * *

I'd like to give it one more try, working for the DVU. But, to be honest, I don't really know if it's the right thing. It's just that I strongly suspect you can at least find some grounding among people like that. And I seem to need something like that.

But does the DVU work? You don't find many people in C. who are interested in it. I've certainly tried to recruit, but most of them say: "No, we'd never join that party, they're too far right for us." Whereas, in my opinion, the DVU is not at all far right. But when you've only got yourself to rely on, when no one else will go along, then what sense is there in it? There's no future in that. Truth is, I've found it really difficult to convince other people of our aims.

I think I could go on a shooting spree. If I had a gun. I think . . . I would . . . I'm so furious with Honecker . . . with Ulbricht . . . with Pieck, and now also with Kohl. All of them betrayed us. Betrayed me. Their shitty politics even caused me to lose my family. Because I consistently saw politics differently than my parents, who always just wanted to be good citizens.

I would so much like to have a career I could enjoy. I would like to meet people I could talk to honestly. Not people who close the door behind you and then turn to someone else and say: "God, he's stupid!" I would like to be able to love . . . I can't love . . . I can only hate. And the whole psychologist thing doesn't do anything for me either.

You see, I wanted the SED regime to disappear. I wanted the Stasi to disappear. That's why I took to the streets in protest. But now there's no more real human connection any more. It was different then. I'm sure it's because we had the same enemy. We tried to solve our problems together. Like talking to my pal about the stuff with the Stasi, and things like that.

I have a two-room apartment. Modern building, with kitchen and bath. But how am I supposed to pay for it if I lose my job? I could go to the West, to Düsseldorf, I've had an offer from there, but I'm scared. That's a completely different world, and I can't even come to grips with the new circumstances here in the East.

The best thing to do would be to get myself a weapon and start another war. And just wait to be shot. Who would've thought I would go so far?

One time I met that "gentleman" again, the one who beat me up. There he stood with a gigantic shopping basket in the supermarket, with his stupid, arrogant laugh. And how he looked! So elegantly dressed.

So I went home thinking: "How's it possible that he's able to just walk around freely?" I was totally shattered. Well, he'd also be one I'd . . . I've sometimes thought about massacring people like that. But what would you gain from that?

He's got himself a business now. Like all those Stasi pigs. He's doing well again. They always lived well back then too. If you went down to the offices at city hall, you could just mow the lot down. They kept us down back then and they're still keeping us down today. Only now there's the West Germans as well. We are a betrayed generation. I'm now thirty-nine.

Basically I have no one left. My parents are dead. First my mother died, then my stepfather. One cousin killed himself. My other cousin, she's also dead. So I'm just living from day to day.

I still try to find meaning in the DVU. They're well represented in the West. Got a big percentage. But how long will it take to get them established in the East? I envy the young people who are strong enough to beat people up in the streets here. Unfortunately I can't do that. No. And I don't want to. But I would like to work with young people. You can teach them: Socialism is shit. What Lenin and Marx said is idiotic. You always have to be strong in life, work hard, and be proud to be German!

I can't identify with anything that smacks of the left. The PDS, for example. Or the Burger-Strasse. They're the left-wing independents that took over that house. I can't stand the sight of people like that: Hang the lot of them!

Why can foreigners come here and lead the good life but our German workers are thrown out on the streets? I have a few books about Hitler. Germany should be rebuilt like *he* imagined it. I still haven't been able to find a group of people who think like me. Sure, we have a little get-together at my place. But it's not enough yet. At home, I fly the war flag of the Reich, of course . . .

Once, my boss at the West German newspaper asked me if he could come by. I didn't clear everything away, of course. The flag was still there, the *Nationalzeitung,* the *Deutsche Woche.*

His reaction was really very ugly. He said: "Basically, it doesn't interest me what you do in your private life, but I have a feeling that you're a right-wing extremist."

So I said to him: "I don't like to call myself a 'right-wing extremist.' I would call myself a 'democrat.' Skinheads are right-wing extremists. As human beings we need to talk to each other more. We shouldn't be so hostile to one another. We need to feel a little warmth from each other again. Or maybe just embrace each other, so that this coldness is no longer there. This lack of feeling." That's what I said to him.

But I'm always afraid. Sure, you know the Stasi no longer exists, that you don't need to be afraid of them any more. But the other fear, that someone will find out that I'm also . . . I mean, if I now commit myself to working for "democracy" through the DVU, then I have to be afraid again that someone will report me. Perhaps someone will call up the newspaper and say: "Do you know you're employing a former Stasi collaborator, . . . or, a right-wing radical?" What do I know about what people are saying. Or, is it just that I'm still haunted by that old Stasi fear?

When the doorbell rings early in the morning and I'm not expecting anyone, I don't open the door. The same in the evening. Except when the group meets. But then I know about it ahead of time.

On the other hand, whenever I see people on the street who I know for certain were with the Stasi, I get mad. I could shoot them. Most of them. But I leave them be. I don't want to have any contact with that kind of person. For instance, if I happen to see one of them at a press conference, working for a rival newspaper, I don't say hello. But I do wonder how they've managed to stay in whatever positions they're in, in spite of everything.

* * *

My place is very tidy. I like everything to be clean and in its place. And I like to be able to rely on people. When I say we'll meet at three o'clock, I don't mean two fifty-nine and I don't mean three oh one! I go crazy if the other person shows up fifteen minutes late! I believe a little bit of discipline is simply a part of life. Discipline, obedience, and unconditional honesty. That is how people should be. You have to be able to rely on someone absolutely.

I would also join an army if I knew it was fighting for the right goals. However, I am not of the opinion that one has to start a war right away. OK, there are some people I could take a pistol or a machine gun to . . . But, to tell you the truth, if worst came to worst I think I might have difficulty killing. That's the contradiction. But does standing up for a new "understanding of democracy" within the DVU necessarily include being able to kill? I don't believe that the DVU . . . that Dr. Frey has any intention of suddenly going on the march. Of course, it's obvious that some things must be changed. Even the Poles say so themselves. Take, for example, this Polish woman I know, Mrs. L. I would guess she's about sixty. I'm not sure, because you don't ask women their age, right? In any case, she always says to me: "The Russians should give us back our lands, then we'd be very glad to leave German territory.

* * *

The point is, basically, people who become DVU members just want to lead a completely normal life. For instance, I was complaining a moment ago about there being so much coldness between people. We in the DVU want more community! More togetherness! To be perfectly honest, I don't much like the skinheads. We — the people I interact with and have conversations with — we really try to immerse ourselves in National Socialism. We want to deal with his ideas. I've read a few books about Hitler. "He" was not at all like "he" is often portrayed today. In one book, he's quoted at length, sometimes for pages. When I read his speeches, I can completely identify with him! Sometimes I even read them aloud. They could be my words. My problem is: I just can't seem to get other people excited. That's why I could never be a new Adolf Hitler.

The only thing I can't identify with at all is all the stuff about hating foreigners. In principle, of course, I wish foreigners wouldn't come here. We have enough economic problems of our own. But I was recently up where the immigrant shelter is now. I saw the little children. I couldn't do anything to *them*. Definitely not! Couldn't do it!

I can't even bear to see children being spanked. Children need warmth and love. I always wanted to have children. For a while I even had a stepson. But then my wife and I split up. Now he's nineteen, and I don't want to have any more to do with him. It's a case of politics getting in the way again. He's a total left-wing extremist, you see, and involved with some crappy group or other.

Before he left for good, we were constantly having discussions, because he had such absolutely *terrible* views. He was a musician and wrote
song lyrics and they were so totally leftist. I can't tell you how often I
tried to talk him out of it, very calmly. But it got worse and worse. And
all I heard from him was that I was a right-wing extremist. I said to him:
"Fine, I'll agree with you that I'm a bit more to the right than you are.
But you're a left-wing extremist." Finally he cleared off to the Burger-
Strasse. At first I had no idea he was hanging around there, but I soon
found out.

They're all pigs in there! Those leftists! They're the ones that go
rampaging about. Here in C. you hear almost nothing about right-wing
extremists. At least when it's not blown out of proportion, which happens
often enough. The only extremists here are the leftists. Of course, there
are a few skinheads who pick up those things and . . . But you can't really
put them in any category. They're not right-wing. No! They're simply
anti-social. As I've been saying, there's no real right-wing scene here!
That's what we want to build up!

In fact, a DVU district group is on the verge of being formed. And
not just with those skinheads . . . We have to have people join who have a
lick of sense in their heads, people who live for our ideology! Not simply
those who say: "We're right-wing!" My vision for the future is to build up
a completely new Germany. For that to happen, of course, there have to
be enough people willing to cooperate, that's clear. It's not going to be a
Germany that's red; it is going to be peaceful. A Germany — but now
I'm repeating myself — in which people can be friendly to one another.
Also a Germany in which there is no more hatred of foreigners. Of
course, only as many foreigners as are really needed should come. The
Sinti and Roma, for example, who come here and commit murder, those
are the kind of foreigners we do not need.

The foreigners should build up their own countries. The Poles have
the chance to do that, the Russians and the Yugoslavs would also, if they
weren't constantly fighting among themselves. Everyone has the chance
to build up their own country. And that's where they should stay, thank
you very much. We have to build up Germany ourselves. Only we Germans can do that.

As I always tell my people, "My own son could be lying in my doorway covered with blood, and I would step over him and simply leave him
lying there."

Don't get me wrong, I would take him in again if he were really to
come back and accept the DVU. But he won't accept it. I'm certain of
that. What can I do about it? I can't move an inch towards him, I simply
cannot. I will never be able to go in a leftist or socialist direction. I have
to say that in all honesty.

I never believed in socialism, you see. Well, perhaps when I was three years old, but I didn't know then what socialism was. But ever since I've been able to think for myself, I've never believed in it. I always knew — I can't say why — that socialism is quite simply garbage.

I think it might be possible at some point to put my son through a process of re-education. You have to put something sensible in its place. I think he just became a leftist because, as he saw it, the world fell apart. For him it was a world that was "whole." He was in the FDJ, although I was always against it. And he is very musical. So he played in a band. That was also through the FDJ. He could travel around a lot and perform and all that artsy-fartsy stuff. After the changeover, all that was finished because there was no money left. He never liked just going to the discos. So he looked for pals. Why they now have to be leftist, I don't know.

So what do you do with people like that? You have to re-educate them. Show them there's something better. And I believe the DVU, or let's say Dr. Frey, has very good ideas. As he says, "We have to convince the young people by offering them something." Only if they can't be convinced by words should you convince them by force! But now I'm starting to philosophize; we're not nearly that far yet.

Perhaps my son is just going through his *Sturm-und-Drang* period. Because at Christmas, or whenever there was another reason to give gifts, he always got books about Hitler from me. Back then, when the so-called GDR still existed, that wasn't so easy. You've no idea what kind of money I spent! You had to buy everything on the black market, remember. And he really enjoyed reading those books. I also recorded parts of historic speeches onto cassettes. Anything that had to do with the Third Reich. And he was very enthusiastic. But then, all at once there came this reversal. I didn't want to believe it at first. But after the changeover, quite suddenly, it didn't interest him any more.

I would really like to save him. If we can organize a group, I mean a group with real substance, not just five or six losers off the street, then I would try to bring him in. And I assume that the DVU has much more and very much better propaganda material than these leftist graffiti-scrawlers and vandals. Then perhaps we could actually convince him.

It does hurt that he's gone. Even though we grew in different political directions and fought tooth and nail. He once brought home a stupid leftist newspaper. *TAZ*, or something like that. So I said to him: "Don't you get it? We're all happy to be rid of that red SED system. Look at all that documentation that came out after the changeover! It shows what kind of a state it was! What kind of people they were! They weren't human beings, they were animals! Do you want to have something like that back again?"

"No. We're the New Left," he says.

Who knows what that entails? For me, one thing is clear, and no one can convince me otherwise any more: anything that has to do with the SED, the PDS, the KPD, the SPD, the Greens, the Alliance 90 is completely null and void for me. They ought to be run over with a steamroller. After the changeover, I joined the CDU. That was my first membership in any party. I've left since then. There are very few people there you can really get along with. People who also have reasonable political views. But what's most important for me are the comrades-in-arms I surround myself with now, who have an interest in building up a strong DVU group.

Fortunately, the *Nationalzeitung* can be found everywhere since the changeover. I have always been incredibly interested in it, because you can learn so much from it. And now I have a subscription, of course. I'm convinced, and no one can persuade me otherwise: I respect the DVU, I respect Dr. Frey as a capable and very intelligent man. Nothing better, nothing comparable exists for me.

And once we've got this DVU group, and once we're big enough and strong enough, then I know what I'd start: The ones we know worked for the Stasi, people like B., who had control of things here, what we'd do with them is. . . . I mean, they wouldn't have to be beaten to death right away, but they'd need to be at least half-dead, and someone would be telling them the whole time why they're getting a beating.

There's this incredible frustration in me, huge and uncontrollable, and it's got to come out somehow. Of course, it could be that when we have this group and when I've really found a new haven again, a haven politically speaking, that this frustration will die down. But at the moment I can't act any other way. . . .

CHAPTER NINE

SOMEHOW OR OTHER I WANT TO MAKE UP FOR THE MISTAKES I MADE BACK THEN . . .

— Peter D., 41, journalist, member of the SED, escaped to the West, returned in 1990, founder of a newspaper

I LIVE IN A MODERN GHETTO on the outskirts. A bit of green, good view, sixth floor. Brandenburger Strasse, center of the cultural left, is around the corner. Two hundred meters away as the crow flies is the haunt of the brown comrades. They rally in front of our building. They've bashed in our mailbox twice already. And also scrawled their graffiti: "asshole" and a swastika. You get real scared. Sometimes I say a bit casual-like: "Okay, the windows in our editorial room had to be replaced sometime anyway." Still, I'd rather not have a brick land on my desk, or on my head. When I hear that a lot of Stasi guys have now become browns, I wouldn't be surprised if the brakes on my car fail one day. Everything's possible. After all, they got a good education. On the other hand, I can't wear a straitjacket any more. I did that for forty years. The famous Biermann muzzle.

My nickname at fifteen was "correspondent." I began writing as a youth volunteer, then went to East Berlin, took a degree by correspondence, after catching up and getting my high-school diploma, and was a sports journalist for fourteen years. Always just one track, one horizon, one angle of vision. Didn't look right or left. The career's the thing. In the worst sense of the word. Influenced by those perennial comrades who said: "There is nothing without the Party. You are a good man. Come on in." At some point I was convinced. Of course, this conviction gradually crumbled away. One turning point was my divorce after twelve years of marriage; another was my transfer from the sports paper to a political daily.

The wife of the media czar sat twenty meters away in a large room, spouting forth. At the same time I got to know a new woman: well, if you can put all GDR citizens into twenty boxes, you would have to invent a twenty-first for this woman. Christiane was intellectual, clever, nonconformist, unpredictable, and amazingly hot as well . . . Italian blood. Deep brown at the first hint of the sun, a thick mane of hair, pitch-black eyes that were incredibly expressive. Everyone turned to look at her. I was proud and happy.

She had been trained as an interpreter, English-French, had been a dramaturge in television for years, and lovingly drew me into her green/purple circle of friends. These contacts did me good, but they only increased my distance from the SED. At the newspaper where I was working at the time, the gentlemen of the regional secretariat of the SED felt free to drop by during the weekly editorial meeting. They handed down their great sayings and were even honest once in a while. The gist of it was: "We're trusting you, comrades, and you will do well to keep it to yourselves."

It was an unbelievable psychological burden to know but not to be able to say anything. I looked for a way to let off steam at home and wrote down "daily minutes" about what I experienced every day. This pamphlet still exists, since I got it out through "criminal" channels, which included the West German embassy in East Berlin.

Before that, however, the documents were kept in my living-room cupboard. Whenever the door downstairs banged, I thought: "Now they're coming!" You see, you never knew whether the "Chekists" had discovered something or not. That put terrible pressure on Christiane and me. But I always said: "It just has to be. I'm a journalist. I can't express myself out loud, so I do it quietly."

But the tension in the editorial office and in our relationship was so great that I said to myself one day: "Okay, you're going on one of those dream trips again. This time you'll jump ship."

I was quite privileged, was allowed to go on a lot of trips to the West, not because I was a Party member but because of my skills. My final business trip was to Sweden. Beforehand, I took my leave of Christiane. At a supper in the "Forellenquintett" restaurant, in the Grand Hotel. She said: "It's okay."

And I said: "If you find it gets bad, then come after me. We'll find a way."

That was August 11. My August 11, 1989. I won't forget that day. It's fixed in my mind, like my date of birth. So I went away and stayed away. Beforehand, I finished up my daily work as a delegation leader, and, on the day of the return trip, at five in the morning, I went into the next room where the track and field athletes were sleeping, left a farewell letter, then legged it to the bus, drove to the ferry, and crossed. Trelleborg-Travemünde.

It just so happened that the track and field championships were being held in Hamburg. Everyone thought I was there as an observer. When I confided to someone that I wasn't returning to the GDR, there was a great uproar, interviews, even a report on the TV news. Two months later and I wouldn't have been worth the slightest bit of notice, that's obvious. But as it was I did the rounds a lot and got a job right away with a newspaper in Cologne.

In spite of this, I regretted leaving, for one thing because suddenly there was an amazing number of things going on in the GDR, and for another, because something stirred in my heart with regard to Christiane.

Three months later, in November, I traveled to Prague. On neutral ground, I see Christiane, my wife, again for the first time. And not only that. Precisely on that night, as I'm in the hotel with her and we're celebrating our own private and intimate union, the Wall falls in Berlin. The same night. How I felt was indescribable. These developments had been going on for weeks: "Something's happening, and you're not there." Although I had hoped for change for ten years. But there comes a time when you make a decision, make a break in your life, go away, and then someone says: "April fool!" and the Wall comes down.

I don't know how many emotional shadings there are, from deepest pain to total euphoria, but I cried enough tears to last until the year 2020. I had goose bumps, felt myself as big as Mount Everest, then as small as a child. I was happy and I bawled. I sat in front of the TV every day until two in the morning. An amazing feeling. And suddenly Christiane back in my arms; it was better than the best days that came before, and the Wall was gone.

At the time I thought everything would begin again. I went to Berlin every two weeks. After all, the border was open. But in the meantime Christiane had a new boyfriend. My disappointment was indescribable. Primarily because she turned out to be a woman who wanted to have her cake and eat it too. That meant a man who is constantly waiting for her, who in the meantime has a good income, his own car, a great apartment in Cologne, and at the same time her home and her circle of friends in Berlin. "Her Berlin." With which she was in love. And then this boyfriend, who also offered her security. Oh well. And there came a time when I got it at last.

* * *

In any case, after nine months in Cologne, I felt like I was in a golden cage. Sure, Cologne is a beautiful spot, and I will never again have another apartment like that one, but that's not everything. I wanted to go back.

Before the changeover, unfortunately, I never had the courage, never had the intestinal fortitude to express myself freely as a journalist. Now I told myself: "Do it!" I wrote to all the newspapers I knew of in the area of Berlin, and the chief editor of a weekly replied. He said: "Come to Berlin, we're starting a weekly paper that will stick it to that SED state and regional paper from C."

So I went to West Berlin and had a talk with the sponsors and publishers. They were all in agreement: "He's going to be the chief editor." I had one day to decide. That very night I sent a telegram to Cologne and asked them to release me from my contract at once. I then moved to C. right away, along with my garage-sale furniture. I was chief editor by August 1. Worked sixteen hours every day, took no notice of Saturdays or Sundays. But there was no good publicity man, no one to take care of the finances; the people had thrown a lot of money into it but hadn't looked into the environment, the media scene. By October it was clear that it would fold. And it folded. Finished and gone. Afterwards, I went to Turkey for a week with a friend. During a deep and long whisky-night we decided: "When we get home, we'll put out a newspaper!" We'll begin with a primitive advertising paper, but, being full-blooded journalists, we'll work out a good concept, put it gradually into practice, and make a real newspaper out of it. First of all we looked for delivery agents, then, on the day, we rented a hall, granted one hundred and twenty people the joy of our presence, and introduced our concept. We visited all the businesses in the area and told them we would be producing the best paper in the world. The first edition came out on November 1, 1990.

* * *

We had hardly any money, worked some of the time with bad checks, began with a modest eight pages and a circulation of thirty thousand. The last bills were written at three in the morning and the first customers got a visit at six. I conducted personnel interviews at home, in the kitchen, sitting on a beer crate.

We seized the opportunity: we had the right concept and found very good people. Right now circulation is up to a hundred and fifty thousand, fifteen thousand copies in Poland alone. The first newspaper from Germany that comes out every four weeks with three or four pages in Polish. Both ads and articles. Now it's no longer just an advertiser but a weekly paper with higher standards.

* * *

By the way, I met my present wife through this work. Back then, when I had to be able to charm the birds down from the trees — I mean, I had to make a newspaper that didn't even exist seem like a good prospect — I badgered some very odd clients. Including the director of a furniture show-room, the "World of Living," three floors, a hundred employees. The woman trusted me and gave me a super amount of advertising. Now she's our queen of sales. A kind of chief financial officer. Her daughter Janine is fifteen and calls me Dad. I feel more connected to her than to my children from my first marriage, simply because I witness her development day by day. Fifteen is an age where they are gradually developing into little ladies. Besides, she is very lucky and was quite spoiled by Mother Nature. The boys are constantly knocking on the door in the afternoons.

* * *

The thing that really disturbs me is that for an entire year I wasn't a journalist but an advertiser. But I can do a bit of research, go into the office, and knock out some text in half an hour. Good quality, too. Or another thing that annoys me: Someone calls up and says: "I've got an incredible story here. Yesterday, someone bashed in the windows of the refugee home, but there was a ruling: All the panes are back in within the hour, and no one is allowed to tell the press anything."

So I said: "Mr. Müller, it's really low of you to give me an exclusive on something like this when it's already three hours after our deadline." I was almost foaming at the mouth. That would have been my main story. One week later I was first runner-up, since my competitors had gotten wind of it in the meantime. I'm a maximalist. I want to be the winner. Not to come in second. That annoys me.

I would really like to start another daily from the ground up. Kind of a mixture between SPD and Alliance 90/ Greens. This region could take something like that. It would have to be well researched, serious, but much more lively with regard to diction than that forty-year-old SED paper with its endless by-the-numbers imitation of the German Press Agency. That's my ambition. I'm now forty-one. That's an age where you have to know what you're going to do with your life. As for my private life, I'm sure I've found the woman I want to grow old with. I feel at home in the region, my job has possibilities I can exploit, and I still have my strength.

Of course, I spent a lot of my strength that one year in Cologne. Worked sixteen hours every day. Didn't know anything about computers, had no idea how to run a tabloid, had no acquaintances, a lot of jealous colleagues because they realized that, being an Ossi, I was treated as a privileged person, with a salary of six thousand marks a month. So I had to prove myself every day and I also had to visit an awful lot of administrative offices, because the bureaucracy in the New Germany is ten times bigger than it was at the time of the GDR. I got a nasty case of psoriasis, psychosomatic disorders. But I experienced live the free market economy with its strengths, its weaknesses, and all its vagaries.

Sometimes I would wake up at three in the morning, bathed in sweat, and would see myself lying there as a skeleton. I drew on my reserves down to my last nerve. "What did I do right, what did I do wrong, how should I go on?" I took it to the limit of what I could bear. I'm sure I've aged about seven or eight years in the last two.

I would have preferred the change to have come fifteen years earlier. Then I would have been a young man and would have had more strength. But it's not too late. You can still correct a lot at forty.

* * *

In the GDR period, I was a careerist. I said to myself: "At twenty-five you'll have a 'Wartburg' at the door, a furnished four-room apartment, in a modern building of course, and a piece of land with a summerhouse." And that's what I had. And life was good and happy. I was good at my job, and as a sports journalist I wrote freelance for specialist magazines in my spare time.

Of course I knew that things were happening in the West, suspected that you could also live a different way. But for me the world was going along fine. Sure, I knew that State Security existed, but for a long time I neither noticed them nor felt their influence.

Fine, one time a gentleman came to me and said: "Wouldn't you like to work for us? You're a journalist, you have contact with many people and frequent the press club. We're all in the same boat . . . Couldn't you do a little . . . Just get a little information to us?"

I was uncomfortable with the whole thing, and then I had a flash of inspiration, I don't know where from: "Don't be angry with me, but I take it you've already done your homework on this old fool, done a bit of research in the meantime. I may be a nice guy, but I've got one big fault: I always speak my mind and so I won't be very useful to your institution."

That took me out of the running. Lucky for me. The next day, I was crafty enough to "confide" in the union leader and the Party secretary. I told them I had had a "visitor" and I knew for sure that they would pass it on.

* * *

Looking back, I envy all the people who were aware of things even then, because in the time between my twentieth and thirtieth birthdays I lived a complacent life. On the outside, everything was fine. I was married, had two little kids, and everything was nice and harmonious. But there was this obsession with gathering as many material things as I could in the shortest possible time. Because of this I was always pressed for time, often sat at my desk until eleven o'clock at night and neglected everything else. Of course, I was a happy-go-lucky guy; I made full use of the trips I took for my correspondence degree to sleep with other women here and there. It was an easy life, and the nasty wake-up call came when my wife said: "Sure, you're a good friend, but that's not enough any more." Then my world fell apart. First everything was hunky-dory, then suddenly: the end. I don't doubt I was eighty percent responsible for the breakdown of my relationship. Through superficiality, selfishness, and immaturity.

So I can't imagine — although I like to look at beautiful women, because I'm an aesthete — that I would disappoint my present wife and also myself by having a two-hour affair with another woman. I find the idea kind of attractive, but I believe I can do without that attractiveness because I have too much to lose. At this moment. You would never have heard this sentiment from me fifteen years ago.

* * *

In 1968 I was eighteen. I didn't experience the invasion of Czechoslovakia as consciously as others. But Biermann's expulsion in 1976 was a completely different matter. I was very irritated at what *Neues Deutschland* — that was the main mouthpiece of the SED — printed back then by the tram driver Alma Hockauf of Potsdam, who probably couldn't even have spelled the name Biermann: about how evil Biermann had always been. On the other hand I realized that the entire GDR stayed up till four in the morning in order to watch Biermann "live" on West German TV. Then there were those mean articles by the ND journalists and the extremely primitive if not ridiculous stances of all those union groups.

That's when I began to gather things. It could have meant three years in the slammer. "Tendentious newspaper analysis." That was the beginning of everything. Later I wrote those "daily minutes," sayings by colleagues and high flyers who came to the newspaper office. I felt an urgency: You have to keep this, even if it's only for yourself. You'll need this stuff some day, because something was going to have to change, in myself, in society, something. I read *The Language of the Third Reich* by Viktor Klemperer at least ten times. An unbelievable book, which for me described the entire media policy of the GDR.

* * *

I met Christiane in 1983 after my first divorce, at a kind of "alternative" party in Berlin. A party with unconventional types, red wine, gossip, and lots of topics considered at that time "hostile to the state." I found the people interesting and I felt a lot of humanity in these encounters. There was an honesty, an openness, a lack of pretense. Of course, I came under attack, as well, but I could live with that. The arguments were on an intellectual level. It wasn't vulgar or cynical, but rather soothing in a reflective sort of way. And then there was this woman. I fell in love with the lady on the very first evening. I strutted like an old rooster, pulled out all the stops, and it worked. Her jaw dropped for the first time when she heard I was in the Party. "With a red book." But by then our relationship was so secure that she said to herself: "He's still a very nice guy." If I had come out with it after three days, I wouldn't have stood a chance. She was and is still very suspicious of the whole thing. Later we lived in a small apartment off an inner courtyard, very cramped, like in a Zille drawing, Boxhagener Strasse, with stinking dumpsters under our noses. Nevertheless, that was my best time, because Christiane was simply the love of my life.

I never had the courage to throw out the Party book. Because . . . I don't know . . . because I just . . . I was too much of a journalist for that. I knew that if I were to pack it all in, and the time was ripe for that more than once, I would have found myself third clerk in a coal business. I didn't want that, nor could I have done it. But I was more consistent in other ways. I was right to go. Perhaps it was even too late.

Today I regret that I waited so long to act in a consistent manner. Other people gave up a lot of privileges and they now have a clear conscience. I don't have that strength. That's why I say to myself: "You did nothing before the changeover, so at least do something now."

* * *

My family was extreme. Father was a bookseller and a communist. A staunch believer. Mother came from a Christian background. Love thy neighbor and all that. Lutheran. But somehow they always found their way back to one another. As a young boy I lived on two fronts. I wanted to watch West German TV — "Beat-Club" was the rage at the time — but Father shook his fist: "No, not my son!" And when he was away, my mother allowed it.

She hardly ever went to services. But inside she was very bound to the church. I assume she was a bit inhibited because of the arguments with my father. But at Christmas even my father went to church, not because of the ritual but more something emotional.

* * *

Of course I was a Pioneer, in time also FDJ secretary and in the FDJ training camp in Halle/Bertingen. I was enthusiastic, all fired up and all that. Looking back on it today, it was a good time. Yes, we were abused, I know that now, my logic tells me that. But in my memory it was an adventure and that was exactly what fired up young people to go to the FDJ celebrations in Berlin. It wasn't about all that SED-FDJ roaring. It was about prowling through a city for once, casually, without ties, until two in the morning, about kissing some chick or drinking a bit of alcohol. You see, the young people were never controlled on such trips, apart from their ideological views. That's why they could get the people excited. At the time I didn't realize that we were being used by the Party as an advertisement. Today I know that.

* * *

In 1967 I went to a boarding school for my vocational training. I was studying to be a typesetter and the whole time I was carrying on an intense correspondence with a friend from Holstein. Using a post-office box and all that. Back then mail from the West was forbidden at the boarding school. At one point this friend sent me a pamphlet about the Beatles. In the words of *Neues Deutschland,* they were a monstrous off-shoot of capitalism, terrible hooligans, and I was a Beatles fan.

I remember one "talk." The ostensible topic was "The Beatles and the foreign policy of the SED." Of course I had long hair then and always wore a jacket three times too big, too loose, or too casual, so I looked a bit decadent. It was at this time that I first asked myself: "Why don't you just go to the West?"

A dreadful thing happened at this same time. Our boarding school lay right on a highway, and one night a convoy of Russian cars rolled by and the lead vehicle got a flat tire. Two days earlier, a marvelous — yet really crude — comedy had been on TV, in which a high voice was always shouting: "Hang 'em, hang 'em." The next day, I imitated this voice a few times as a joke. But it so happened that a collective of five Stasi-comrades were in training one floor above us. They heard this "Hang 'em, hang 'em," and of course immediately jumped to the conclusion: There's one at last! A big class enemy with all of seventeen summers behind him.

My mother had to come to the school; there was a lot of weeping and talking, it was just awful. I thought: How can you imitate a voice like that, carried away by your youthful fantasies, and immediately be declared an enemy of the Russians? Surely no one can be so primitive as to think like that? Add to that, of course: "Just look at your son; his hair's so long and he's wearing a nylon shirt. That comes from the West and so on and so on and so on. . . ." I don't remember how I got out of it. I probably strewed ashes on my head and swore to be a better person.

* * *

As for my political views, I was a late bloomer anyway. It could have something to do with my childhood. We lived on the outskirts of a county town, with a garden in front, with bike trips and tree houses. Those were really carefree years. Of course there were things that bothered me. When they gathered up Mickey Mouse comics in school, saying they were trash. Or when the teacher asked: "Does the clock you watch on TV at home have strokes or dots?" And stupid things like that. I remember thinking, I can't believe they want to pump us for information, but in my natural carefree state I didn't notice very much. I wrote my name very proudly on my Mickey Mouse comic, on the front page. There was a bag search in school. And it was gone. Magazines from the West, for God's sake. Back then my father was a city councilman and my mother ran to the principal the next day and asked to be allowed to tear off the front page, at least, so that our name wouldn't come up. You registered that something wasn't right, but you just didn't think about why.

I wasn't an easy child and sometimes got a beating. My father had a temper, but he was a man who was so sorry afterwards that he cried. I myself detest violence in any form, but I don't hold it against my father, even today. You can forgive certain things. There are things that make you who you are and then you have to hold a perpetual grudge because they hurt you and you can't accept that. But there are also things in life where I say: "Okay, he just slipped up and that's fine."

* * *

I was hurt in a completely different way in Cologne. I was to write a series about my feelings as a skilled Ossi, fresh in the Federal Republic. So I presented my case, without naming names. How I landed, first off, in a primitive summerhouse, without a toilet, without water, with a rent of six hundred marks a month. Showed a bit of how we're exploited. I received two death threats after that. It made me . . . Well . . . I just couldn't understand that there could be such extreme opposition to my opinion that they would send me two death threats. One addressed to the newspaper and one to my home. A picture by Dürer of some doves or a pheasant hanging on a rope, and the back read, in those notorious letters cut from the newspaper: "Asshole, you're the next one who'll hang." I suspected my landlord at the time. He was the only one who knew where I had moved to.

* * *

I've already received a death threat here in C., too. For my article on the Neo-Nazis. "How dare a German newspaper publish Polish articles . . ." I take these Fascist types absolutely seriously. It's a combination of stupidity and power. And they have power when they've got a baseball bat in their hands and turn up en masse. Thirty men can hold a whole city at bay. These are people who have no knowledge of tolerance. Only intent on themselves, only "my interest," only "my ideology is correct." I'm afraid of guys like that. But my fear is not as great as my will to do something about it. My office is insured against vandalism, but of course that's ridiculous. If they were really to come in here, they'd do more than just smash up my file cabinet. But if we don't stop them, it will just escalate.

On the other hand, when you look at these young people closely and as individuals, there are a lot of things they can't cope with. They feel the suffering in their families: the father has no job, he's recently taken to drinking, beats up the mother. Beforehand everything was hunky-dory. Or the lack of money. The girls can't buy themselves the same clothes their classmates have, the boys can't get into the clubs. They want to draw attention to themselves and then they start to play roulette with the police. Want to brag about how they were detained for a day and maybe even two. It's a completely different level compared with my childhood. Today they draw blood; today it's a matter of cold hard criminality. I don't want to whitewash the GDR period, but everything was more limited back then, easier to keep track of, even for the keepers of law and order.

* * *

I want to keep healthy, want to have enough strength so I'm not sitting in a wheelchair one day but can still achieve something at sixty or seventy. The state of Brandenburg shouldn't be the poorhouse of Germany but a really nice place where you can feel comfortable. A place where there is a little traffic back and forth across the border, where East and West, Poles and Germans accept each other, so that the bridge to Europe can continue here. I hope that the narrow-mindedness that was forced on us and instilled into us during forty years of the GDR will be sloughed off at last, and that people will no longer be spat upon or condemned because of their skin color or their ideology.

In a way, I feel guilty as well. We in the media supported the old system, no matter how you look at it; we highlighted top athletes who, as it turned out later, were doped. Sure, as sports journalists we were small fry because we just dealt in millimeters, meters, or seconds, thank goodness. But the members of the media are always those who influence and manipulate the people. Even today, and most certainly in the old system.

Sometimes I have very bad dreams. Then I think about things that lie far back in the past and ask myself what I could have done better? But I didn't have the courage then to stand up and say: "People, comrades, listen up, I've written a daily journal with the words of Regional Secretary so-and-so; this is bad rhetoric, conceited, arrogant to the nth power, and apart from all that I disagree completely with his ideas . . ."

I didn't have this courage at the time . . . The great Regional Secretary, with halo, one of those from the big house . . . I should have done it. I should have broken down the man's reserve with sound arguments and facts. Then I would have had a good feeling at some point. And in the evenings I would have drunk myself into a stupor, out of fear that the Stasi would come and take me away. But perhaps they wouldn't have done that.

I knew a man, a good friend of Christiane's. He was very active in a church parish. Wrote pamphlets, scrawled on walls: "Honny, open the Wall." I should have done something to help. But I wasn't mature enough and I was too afraid.

And sometimes, at night, I remember a few episodes. Then I'm pretty much wide awake, and I get up and drink a glass of wine, because I can't go back to sleep, because my skin creeps, because the old people are back in and writing and they shouldn't really be allowed to, because they're failures, because they avoided any consequences. And they keep on manipulating.

This one Stasi man, for example, he spilled everything for money. His wife was a school principal. They had a fat, greasy son who is probably even fatter and greasier today. And they were "Communists." Nice home, modern building, and money, a small car, and everything clean and fresh and livable. I get goose bumps just thinking about it. When people have been in the forefront for thirty years, all fat and mean, Party book in their pocket, living like parasites and with a thousand unearned privileges, then they need to take a step backwards now. They should feel sorry for what they did; they have to learn that they made big mistakes back then and pushed an entire nation off the cliff.

I was in the SED as well. But you have to make a distinction between someone who abused his function, who made people suffer and practiced psychological terror, and someone who did his job and traveled to Holland and France, because he was a good trade journalist. This was the case with me. I'm sure I would never have had the chance to become the head of the trade magazine if I hadn't had the Party book. That's shitty. But on the other hand, I wouldn't have traveled if I had been a bad journalist.

There are various positions and points of view. But I say: I am guilty. To whatever extent. But with me there was a break. I have begun to pay off my debt. And the rest, which I still bear on my shoulders, I want to pay off by doing something for this region, for this Ossi state. Somehow or other I want to make up for the mistakes I made back then. It's not so important whether others see the amount of my guilt as more or less. I feel a responsibility to myself. To my own conscience.

*　*　*

It's really a great feeling to be able to write at last what you want to and to know that a quarter of a million people are going to read it. I'm sure that the feeling of having power is also part of it. At least over the people who thought you were a fool a year ago. But I also have a very clear idea of the responsibility I bear. The press is an instrument of power. You can change things, but on the other hand you can also destroy lives. And I live on thin ice. I name names and addresses. That's why the magazine has many enemies as well as many friends. Recently we had seven court cases on our hands. We've won all of them so far. I think we have a pretty good moral compass and a pretty good conscience.

My best critic is my wife. She would beat me over the head with the paper if I slipped up, defamed someone who didn't deserve it. I couldn't do it.

Being a journalist is a wonderful thing. To communicate with people, to chat, to delve deeper sometimes, to get to know extremes you would never have guessed existed.

When I'm sixty or eighty or whatever — I hope I get that old — I want to be able to stand up and say: There was once a very bad time but then you accepted the consequences and you dealt with it. The scale between the good and bad actions must be balanced, so that you can say: Fine, now you can die in peace. You brought many things to fruition. I don't know if I will manage it. But I want to try.

Perhaps I'll succeed because I have a great wife and a good circle of friends. I can go to see N. or T. at four in the morning and have a good cry on their shoulders. They'll make me a strong coffee, listen to my whining for two hours and say: "Come on, let's go to bed and tomorrow you'll get up and everything will look different."

When you have people like that, you're in good shape. Nothing else is really as important as that. . . .

CHAPTER TEN

———————

SO HOW ARE PEOPLE EVER GOING TO CONNECT WITH EACH OTHER?

— Günter C., 56, laborer, unemployed and in debt

M Y FATHER OPERATED AN EXCAVATOR, in the mines. He built the house I still live in. He had four children and was given support by the state, by Adolf Hitler, for having so many children. My father himself never returned from the war, from Poland, no one knows how or where. Of my three brothers, one was in the air force and was shot down. My fat brother later became a workers' writer, in Berlin. He wrote for the farmers' newspaper and television and was a true believer. Socialism and such. The third became a schoolteacher, and I'm the only one who stayed here and became a miner. And suddenly the word was: Off to the army! To do "honorable service."

In the mornings, we weren't allowed to go straight down to the coalface but had to go to the "recruiting commission." That went on until we had signed. So you weren't worthy of hacking coal if you hadn't gone to the army. That was how they put it. And somehow, don't ask me how, they managed to convince us.

The rip-off was this: I wanted to be a driver and I was sent to the artillery. Also, I was into competitive sports. They said: "You can go on with your training." So there I was with my paddle and sandy wilderness as far as the eye could see.

That's when I said: "I'm not swearing another oath." That was in '55, when the "Riot Police" became the "National People's Army." I was discharged as an ordinary soldier. I always was a little out of step. That's why I was never promoted.

I lost my job as well. They only wanted to take people back who had been "discharged with distinction," not failures like me.

I found another position in the power plant near here. As a driver, actually. They said: "We need people to repair the power lines." After I had signed on, it turned out that they didn't have enough vehicles. But they said: "Why don't you stay here and become a boilerman." The boilers we stoked were from 1914, but every kilowatt hour was needed.

Later, I met a girl and said to myself: "This is crap. Others go out dancing on Saturdays and Sundays, and here I sit and have to slog through these shifts."

That's why I didn't hesitate when they asked: "Who wants to go into agriculture and drive a tractor?" You were to get a two thousand mark bonus if you committed yourself to five years.

The tractor still had to be cranked by hand. And the salary wasn't that great either. Two hundred and eighty marks gross if you were lucky. The top earners got three hundred and twenty, and for that you sat on the tractor from morning till night.

Later on, they were looking for people at the cement works. "You have a boilerman's certificate," they said, "we need boilermen and you can earn more money here." So I started at the cement works, and after that I worked as a painter, painting houses and such. That was in '61.

I didn't give a damn about all that Wall stuff, since I didn't have any ties to the other side or anything. I wanted to build a life for myself through my own work, and I was finally earning good money as a painter.

At first we painted high voltage pylons, then a textile factory had to be finished as quickly as possible. They said: "The best team will be moved up the waiting list for a Trabant." You would only need to wait two years! That was an incentive, of course, and we threw ourselves into it.

But we were screwed. When the factory was three-quarters finished, they sent us somewhere else, and what about all those promises? Nothing.

Shortly after that there was going to be some sort of an election, and I said: "Friends, if I don't get my Trabant, I'm going to do something nuts. I'm not going to vote."

My colleagues said: "You can't do that. We're a 'socialist team.' If *you* don't go, our bonus goes right down the drain."

"Okay then," I say, "this ballot's going to be invalid." So I take the ballot — we were to "declare openly and without reservation," remember — and openly exed it out on the window ledge.

Of course, that was considered "election provocation," because I did it "without reservation" on the window ledge, etc. Now I was definitely not worthy of driving a Trabant.

But, as if that wasn't enough, my zealous comrades reported this "election provocation." But the result was not what they expected: They themselves were made accountable. They should have reasoned with me until such a provocation could not even have happened.

So they sat there with long faces and I, in a fit of temper because I was not worthy of driving a Trabant, went and bought a Wartburg. Used, from some old farmer. Cost me ten thousand marks back then, but the car was only five years old. The comrades? Mad as fire.

Actually, the whole political scene didn't bother me much. But there was a lot of anger in me because of that stupid Trabant. After all, you made an effort, were ready to put in overtime, Saturdays, Sundays, all those extra shifts. And then nothing.

* * *

Later, when I was a house painter, I went to all their apartments, to their homes, those old comrades who shoved us into the army back then. Noses in the air, they would say: "We are a socialist people. A great community." And then you saw: They already had a television, a washing machine, a refrigerator, and even a real bathroom with a bathtub. All got through contacts. And us with our old boiler down in the cellar, that you had to heat with a wood fire when you wanted to take a bath. You could see back then how it was unraveling.

Sure, I earned money, but it all went back into the building. Put every mark into the house. It was built in 1932, shot to pieces in '45. The whole gable was gone when we came back after having to flee. First we covered it all with tarpaulins and we had an incredibly tough time getting it back into shape. My mother was still living here then, along with one brother and me.

* * *

There were always repairs to be done on the house. One time the chimney was about to fall down, then the windows had to be replaced; year in, year out, I worked on that fortress. After all, you want to make it a little comfortable and keep it clean. That became the central theme of my life. Then my daughter arrived. Actually, she grew up more with my mother-in-law, in the country. My wife also worked, you see, and we helped out at my mother-in-law's on weekends. She still worked a farm but had bad luck with her horses. She was the first to join the collective. The atmosphere in the village was always: "Traitor! Not an honorable bone in her body!" But what was she to do? Without horses. We helped out so that she could carry on somehow. Fed the pigs, took care of the chickens, the rabbits, and all that goes along with that. We'd often put the cow in the traces, but the stupid animal never went where you wanted it to go. Then I had the idea of building a tractor. I cobbled it together from eighteen different kinds of vehicles. Just "found" things all over the place. And the thing actually worked. Ran for over three years.

* * *

In the beginning we still traveled to my mother-in-law's by bike and by train. Then she said: "Why don't you buy a car."

Then we saved up and went into debt to the sum of two thousand marks. It cost 3200, an old DKW. With a soft top for summer. Even the old cattle trailer was hitched on the back; we fetched hay with it, delivered grain, and everything else you can think of.

Then came that election thing, when I said to myself: "Now you're going to buy yourself a Wartburg." That was a really modern vehicle, at the time. I transferred from painting to agricultural irrigation. We dug over the fields to drain them, and later I switched to a mobile crane. I was often on the road with it, loading wagons, pipes, posts, whatever was needed. And because I was traveling so much, I said to myself: "That's it, we have to have a proper car."

Then I actually got a note from the plant telling me that "because of my willingness to work and my achievements" I would be able to get a car early, a Lada, kind of like a Fiat. Because I was good. I earned the name "activist" four times as a painter. And three times in agricultural irrigation due to qualifications and competitions. That counted on a waiting list like this. I also got a telephone through the plant. You see, they had to be able to reach me at all times, even on weekends. Still, I often spent weeks at a time in a trailer when I was on a job. There came a time when I got fed up with the gypsy life.

At that time my wife was working in a savings bank, along with the wife of the site manager for the water supply, so we got to talking. He was looking for a crane operator, and I said: "Okay, if I earn as much as I do in irrigation, then I'll come." I'm still there after all these years, operating the crane and changing out the underwater pumps. The things were old, were being constantly patched up, and of course they were always giving out. Then it started. Saturdays, Sundays, holidays, always out switching pumps. So I became an "activist" another four times and once even "best worker."

It's been a good job, can't say any different, and there was even support for culture. I joined a photography club; I always liked to take photos, and the plant often needed pictures, to sell itself. The combat group, the Party, award presentations, whatever. Now, we didn't just photograph positive things for the bulletin board. They also needed something negative once in a while. Bad water treatment plants. Or we drew attention to particular mistakes. We slowly worked our way up to criticism, within limits, but criticism nonetheless. The game went so far that I had to take down my pictures from the bulletin board one day.

You see, we had this engineer, pretty crazy; he absolutely had to leave a nasty old thistle that was growing wild next to a shed. But the department head wanted the thistle gone, so that the courtyard would look clean and tidy. They went back and forth about this stupid thistle.

When the engineer had a birthday, we dug up the thistle, put it in a bucket, and left it in front of his office door. So there he had his thistle and could finally do what he wanted with it. As a joke, we hung a sign on it that said: "Many happy returns of the day/ from Greenpeace."

Then the department head came and roared at us: "How could you write Greenpeace on it? You'll have to delete it, and I mean immediately."

So we ex it out — making sure it's still legible —, photograph it and after a while the photo appears on the bulletin board. That was some fuss! The Party Secretary came: Why and wherefore, and did we not know what Greenpeace was. Enemy organization. What did we think we were doing? Striking it out so you could still read it? And then putting it on the bulletin board, even? That's hostility towards the state, that is, and the pictures have to go. As if everyone in the plant didn't already know all the ins and outs of the story.

* * *

Shortly before the collapse of the GDR there was one more cozy get-together in the plant. I took photos there too. Just like they had always wanted them: with medals from the combat group, awards, giving out certificates and all that. I developed the pictures myself as always, but when they were finished, four weeks later, no one wanted them any more. The changeover had made them very embarrassing all of a sudden.

* * *

After the changeover, I wanted to make myself independent, at fifty-four. I said to myself: There's a lot of dirt to be gotten rid of, there's a lot of building to be done. Let's get to it! You could say I was full of ideals.

But we didn't think that the agricultural system would collapse like that. The farmers no longer knew how to sell a simple tomato. They sold their sheep for one mark each. Now everything's lying fallow and over-grown. The stalls are empty, the old people are saying: "So what, we're retiring, let's leave everything the way it is." The young people are moving to the cities.

* * *

Everything wasn't fine before either. There were points of contention, a thousand little things. But you accepted that. You knew that nothing was going to change by and large, even if you went on the rampage. No one was interested in that, and you'd only be cutting off your nose to spite your face. So you were quiet.

I earned good money. Salary level eight. I got all the awards possible, could perhaps have gotten a few more bonuses, but there wasn't much more to be earned in the GDR. As a laborer. I had my livelihood, did some things after work, and still continued to build onto my home.

Of course, they didn't let me go over to visit the other side. I put in four applications and was pretty furious at the time. The cleaning lady, dumber than dirt, she was allowed to go. But my aunt was just not enough of an aunt — and that was that. If I'd had the chance to look around a bit on the other side, I wouldn't have stumbled into this racket.

So I thought: "There's a lot of building to be done; I'll buy a little digger." I wanted to use it to make footpaths and to renovate the old castle rampart. I thought everyone would get a telephone eventually. Sewer pipes would definitely have to be laid. The whole system of pipes is already eighty years old. A lot of work. We'll have to dig up in front of every house, I thought to myself, and a small digger could get into the little front yards without doing much damage.

But nothing at all is going on here. And if something does happen, they bring their machines with them and I've got egg on my face.

＊ ＊ ＊

So in the meantime, I go over to the other side and work in Dortmund for two weeks. Actually, I'm officially unemployed. So it was illegal work. I scratch your back . . . It was good to take a look behind the scenes. We built a house for a bartender, opening up the wiring shafts and other dirty work. One hundred marks a day — why not? We prettied up his motor yacht at the same time, when we couldn't get any further with his house. The motor alone cost 130,000 DM, and you wouldn't know it to look at the guy. "It's a privilege," he says, "some people keep horses and I've got a motor boat." With everything built in, of course: stereo, color TV, radar, and even sonar. He'll never need it. Has to have it though. When someone comes and opens the door he can say: "Here's this, that, and the other, and here's my sonar." Although he already knows how deep the lake is where he's out sailing, in Dortmund and the surrounding area.

＊ ＊ ＊

When the changeover came, many people knew that I did photography. Then you heard: "Can you just develop this real quick? Can you make ten copies? These were the first flyers. The petition from the artists in Berlin. Please sign and pass it on. No one was supposed to know and that's why I made the copies in my little darkroom at home. But there came a time when I said: "This is stupid. We're struggling with this photo paper, and it's far too expensive, as well. We'd be better printing them."

There were no copiers at that time, you know. So we wrote on stencil paper, and the stencil was cranked through a machine.

Now my colleagues in the plant were afraid. If someone were to come up and catch them at it, they'd be fired. So we made an agreement: I would take the print machine on Fridays and print at home. The machine had to be back in its place on Monday mornings and mustn't stink. That spirit alcohol was simply awful; the whole house reeked of the stuff for days.

Of course, people were being watched closely during those weeks; there were I.D. checks on the streets, cars were stopped and searched for banners or flyers. But I simply transported the print machine with my crane. No one cottoned on to that, of course.

It wasn't just for the thrill; the time had come. Whatever has to be done will be done: that was always my opinion. After all, we wanted to change things. When I see what came of it, looking back, I sometimes wish they would put the Wall up again. Basically, nothing's left of the ideals we took to the streets for. My idea was to make something of this economy. Work was to be made more meaningful, without all the Party rigmarole. Now we're told that the plants were uneconomical. I'm not convinced. We could simply have found another method of accounting. We built cranes for the Russians. I would like to bet that in two or three years' time we'll be building cranes for the Russians again. But by then they'll have found a sensible method of accounting. Introducing West German money so quickly was stupid. Of course it hurt now and then not have Western money, so you could buy decent tools in an Intershop, or so you could do something after work.

But there's not much left of the basic idea of the whole changeover: to make something better. On the contrary. We feel steamrolled. Many people I know think: "We did a crappy job. If we could only turn back the clock." You can't do that, of course. But there's still one possibility of changing something. With the help of the DVU, the German People's Union. They've got good ideas. They want to rebuild Germany in a responsible fashion. The farmer will plough his land again! Unemployment must go!

What I don't like is that they want to rehabilitate the old Nazis. In general, they're too damn far to the right, but I say to myself: Who else are you going to vote for? The CDU ripped us off; they made promises and kept none of them. The SPD doesn't help either, and don't even mention the FDP. The Greens are divided. If we want to help ourselves, we have to find someone who will take the reins.

It's just the same as before the changeover. If you look closely, the old forces that were in power before are everywhere. They're giving the orders again. That's what's so crappy. They put it this way: If they had been able to do what they wanted to back then, then everything would have been great.

In any case, unemployment was definitely not included in the plans. I don't see the point. Now we know: everything's produced on the other side, and all we need to do here is sell it. We're nothing but buyers and consumers. Our opinions are trodden underfoot. That's why we're now trying to regroup. Of course, it won't be easy. During the changeover we said: "It can't go on like this. You understand that. We want something different. Join in." The battle lines were clear. You knew: The Stasi's on one side and you're on the other. Today, everything's so scattered. It's not at all clear where you fit in, and besides, it's every man for himself, even at the bottom.

* * *

Well, I have to see to paying down my debt and putting the digger to work again. Eighty thousand marks. If I sell it now, I'll take a loss of fifty thousand. Those over in the West can be happy that they've made a good deal, and I'm the idiot. If only I could find a job, a decent one, then I could get on with my life.

We should have left the Wall up, that was the mistake. First of all we should have put the comrades into cold storage, and the Stasi. They had us completely in the palm of their hand. Looking back to when things were easing up a bit, some of them in the plant came out into the open; who'd been working secretly with them, whether official or unofficial or whatever. And now they're helping each other out. In security services for example. They can officially carry weapons, even. You know them. Up here in F. there's a base; they guard the industrial plants. "We're here for your protection. Do you have something against that?" No one asks how many weapons they've got strapped to their bellies. They've gone and re-grouped.

* * *

So the DVU will have to sow unrest. Of course, I'm not for the Republicans, who have their gangs of thugs and pinpoint refugee homes to attack. That can't be what it's all about! Whatever the nationality. They're human beings too. They're trying to live their lives, day in day out, just like us. Basically, they're just poor suckers like we are. Once they've gone, we'll not be any better off. It's just a political game. They need a scapegoat. As long as they're there, the politicians can distract us from the real problems. They're just pulling the wool over our eyes.

Well, if we're talking about a new *Führer:* In terms of the war — we don't want another Adolf. But he did cause an upswing, and that was good. He managed to get rid of unemployment, to provide people with a salary and food. The highways were good and we needed them, too. It was only much later that they were used for deployment.

Good God. We've got enough to build up here. Let's assume that the politicians are able to come to grips with it, that the fields are tilled again and the yield allotted to those who are starving and really need it. Wouldn't that be good? There have to be reasonable solutions and I believe that the DVU is a distinct alternative to all the others. God only knows what will come of it. But if they're successful, at least the others will see: "Hey, there's something happening there!" Perhaps then they'll make their policies with more common sense and primarily for the people. The DVU are gaining votes in the West, the Reps are too far to the right with all their hooliganism. Most people don't like that. Of course, the DVU also wants to go towards "Germany, awake." There's a lot of hollering that goes with it that I definitely don't like, but isn't it a real alternative to what's being done now? We can't foresee what will really come of it, that's true. But then again, we began the changeover with other ideas and it didn't turn out the way we wanted it to.

As for being unemployed, I now think: "To call it lousy would be high praise." Okay, on the one hand you have time to think. I read a lot, about the economy, but also about art and photography, and I do a bit of renovation from time to time. There's enough time but not enough money.

Twenty years younger would be better. Then you'd get a better start. How does it go? "Young, dynamic, successful." Now I can say: "Old, dynamic, and a failure." It's ridiculous, but I tell myself: So what? It'll get better somehow. I'm now retraining to be an insurance salesman.

It's the biggest swindle. I'm now on my fourth company. The first group was so hot they wanted to insure everything in order to get rich quick. They even tried to talk me into life insurance. The next lot wanted to do investments. They were after rich investors. If you don't have them, you won't get anywhere, and most of the people I know are unemployed. Who can manage to put aside a hundred marks a month? The third bunch, well that was kind of a systematic thing, where one person's always taking money out of someone else's pocket. Structured like a pyramid. Those on the bottom have to pay.

And how does it go from here? I'm trying to understand how the "economic miracle" works. I want to get to know the ropes. Today the successful person is the one who can conjure ten marks out of someone else's pocket. So, if I can manage to talk someone into insurance, then I'm successful! Whether he needs it or not doesn't matter in the slightest.

I could show you a "sales pitch" as a joke. With the looks and getting it onto the "YES-track," putting the pressure on ever so slightly and finally convincing you so much that you really believe in the end that you definitely need insurance. But what good would that do? I know deep down inside that the whole thing isn't right. You simply don't need most kinds of insurance. So I'm not "successful."

If you are going to cheat, you might as well cheat big. So that it doesn't hurt the individual. When I screw over my neighbor, I know it and he knows it too. But when the bank screws you out of a few percent, then you think that's the way it has to be. But first you have to get to the level where you can cheat without hurting anyone and still earn your money. You need a bit more upstairs to understand that. Perhaps studying would help. What did we have to count up back then? You knew what was in your wage packet. If you were good, you got more, if you had done an extra hour, even more. But now it's not a matter of physical labor any more. Now it's about who can scam who the quickest.

In the old days, I would say, people were more content, not so bitter. You could talk to each other. Now everyone's got their elbows into everyone else and no one will give anyone any breathing space.

When you meet an old colleague, the first question is: "How much do you earn?" You don't dare say you're out of work. They'll look down on you straight off. Then you're a failure. So I don't let anyone know. Fine. I haven't brownnosed the mayor so he'll give me a handout, some ABM position in the district. I did once offer my little digger. He says: "No. I can't do that, for God's sake."

The digger would do the work of ten men, and they'd be finished too quickly! They bought sixteen wheelbarrows instead. That's what it's like. I was at the unemployment office, to see what they would give me in terms of extra qualifications and such. Training in insurance, perhaps travel money.

"No. No. That kind of qualification is not supported by the unemployment office."

My future looks bleak. I have to get rid of the digger and get out from under my debts. They're at fifteen percent. I started at eleven, and if I'm not careful they'll take the house out from under me in the end.

I just have to try to get on the insurance track in spite of all this. We'll see if I manage it. I don't want to make a killing. I wrote on the questionnaire: I want to earn two thousand marks a month. You can live on that, in the present circumstances. There was an ad. You can earn between three and six thousand marks a month. —

What a con game!

I ask the man: "So, if it's all about commission, then what's this crap. We'll never reach amounts like these."

He says: "Well, then we'll see if the people are motivated and ambitious. And they're the ones we'll hire."

One guy wrote down "ten thousand marks." That's what he wants to earn in a month. How idiotic. You can get that much when you sit in an office and have fifty men to do the running about for you. But then you have to be shrewd enough to keep everyone in line. Most people earn a thousand marks and no more. Because you can only insure so many people. There just aren't that many.

The only possibility I see is that many GDR citizens don't know that AOK insurance isn't enough in an emergency. If you have a long illness — snap! You're hung out to dry. After eighteen months you get a friendly letter, you are hereby dropped. And then watch out. You become a welfare case. You get social security, but only after you've sold your car, your house, and only if your relatives can't help you out.

Then you're lower than dirt. Isn't worth going on. You have to be honest enough with yourself to put an end to it. Quite simple. To sink so far that the kids have to feed you; I can't have that. I'd rather bail out of the whole thing. They can go on alone! Then you've got no more problems at all! Screw the bank, the finance office, the taxes, all of it.

Lots of people tell themselves this. How many car accidents are really accidents? You insure yourself well first, and then you say: "'Bye. If I don't make it, at least I don't come out an idiot; I've got everything covered."

My God! How nice it would be, to look down from above and see them still fighting down below. I imagine the entire former GDR looking like a big ant hill. Everyone's running backwards and forwards and each person's trying to take something away from someone else and drag it back to his burrow. And once he's got it, then the others come and take it away from him again.

* * *

What do you ground yourself with? I never read Marxism. Horoscopes perhaps. You can't move your birthdate around. You are subject to the march of time. Never mind how big a fortress you build. The course of time is set. You, as an individual human being, are a little timing element. The only question is: Are you a good element or a bad element? But what do you do when you have the bad luck to be born in April, of all months? The dumbest birth month. When people are more successful or have more talent for business, I sometimes ask myself what makes the difference. There must be many explanations for that. But one thing is definite: when you have a partner you have to make deals with, you can understand him better when you know when he was born.

That's one of the reasons I didn't get on with my wife. I could never have built up a business with her. It is in her nature to be able to sort and categorize, but not to go along with things wholeheartedly. When you know your own faults — and this is what's good about it — you can take that into account and choose your partner accordingly. That's simply knowledge that has developed over centuries. You can really get something out of it for you personally. Marxism on the other hand . . . The ideas were good. But I don't think they would have worked in the long run. "Each according to his needs." First off, everyone would stuff a Mercedes under his arm and say: "I have the need to drive a Mercedes."

* * *

I have now found myself again. I begin with gymnastics. Every morning. Building up the body, keeping up the image. To get that "glowing management look." At fifty-six.

Thing is, you have to take it slow at the beginning. If you start off under pressure, you'll not get there. Sure, I'd like to be better off financially. Travel a bit, learn a bit and see the world. But right now it's about not getting steamrolled. Making sure that you're not left behind. Dreaming doesn't cut it: I wish. I would. I could. You'll just slide back down over and over again. But I want to find a foothold. To get back in. To finally have work again.

★ ★ ★

There's also no point in getting a new wife. I must first get through this alone. I tell myself: "If I have to eat dry bread, then I'll eat dry bread. If I have someone with me, I'll have to find some spread."

I have met a woman, actually. But she's also in a crappy situation. Her old man was an airplane mechanic with Erichs Machines. They always got privileges back then. That's why it has hit her much harder, coming to terms with the whole changeover. And the kids were in the Stasi. As a mother, she feels that, of course. Her "maternal feelings." All that whining: "My children, my children." Now she has absolutely no more contact with them. She does housework on the side for some old granny. That gives her a little bit extra. With her pension, she's got too little to live on and too much to die — you know how it goes.

★ ★ ★

But if I get back in properly, as a salesman, then I'll have to look for a person who'll go along with me. Otherwise I'll keep running in circles and won't get anywhere. It sounds harsh. But that's the way things are.

Sure, back then, you said: "I help you, you help me." That worked. When you ask today, no one has the time. They're all busy with themselves. The next thing is: "What are you paying?"

These days, you have to pay through the nose for any service. The first question's always: "What's in it for me? What's in it for me?"

Recently, I went to visit a former colleague for a bit of a chat. At first he said: "Yeah, yeah, come on over."

When I got there, it was: "You can have a cup of coffee as well. But you have to give me fifty pfennigs. I can't help it."

"No, no," I said, "that's okay. I have to go in a minute anyway. You don't have to make coffee. That's okay." That's how far it's come.

So how are people ever going to connect with each other? . . .

When I got home, I put my head in my hands and asked myself: What happened?

Everything here is completely screwed-up.

Is *he* crazy? Or am *I* crazy?

Or could it be that I just don't understand? . . . .

CHAPTER ELEVEN

YOU HAVE TO KEEP YOUR MOUTH SHUT AND DO YOUR JOB AS IF IT'S THE MOST FULFILLING THING IN YOUR LIFE . . .

— Peter B., 18, school student in
the East, trainee in the West

I'M A '74 MODEL. I graduated from school in the East in 1990. Tenth grade. I didn't think I absolutely had to go on and take the big end-of-school exams; I wanted to earn money instead, quite honestly.

First off, my mother found me a kind of environmental job, in water resources management. I'm sure it would have been interesting, but you had to be the right person. Greenpeace or something. I'm more cut out for the market economy, in contrast to my mother who's more of an environment-friendly person — the kind that wants to make the world a better place, as far as her political stance goes. She had read Marx and Lenin and stuff back then, but no matter, she always made up her own mind, I would say.

I played a lot of sports as a child. First swimming and canoeing, then six years of soccer; I really wanted to work with children, to be a trainer or something like that. But for that I needed a high-school diploma and a college degree in sports. I was pretty fed up with school; I get distracted pretty easily and there's a lot I can't follow. I have to learn everything by myself at home. And since I don't work very hard in this respect, it would've been pretty difficult to get through it anyway.

Actually, I was originally supposed to take the end-of-school exams. When I got to the meeting where we were to learn who was going to be allowed to take the exams and who wasn't, it turned out that everyone who'd been selected had a place reserved for them as "apprentice with high-school diploma" — apart from me. For a moment I was pretty shocked. "Why me?" But then I quickly got over it. As soon as I left the meeting I was kind of happy, — at least no longer sad. And anyway, I had a girlfriend back then and that also helped. So that's how I glossed over the entire problem. It was like: "Huh, who cares anyway." So, anyway, first off I go to the employment office and ask if I can get a position as an apprentice in West Berlin, as a sports equipment salesman. They said:

That's really, really difficult. But I hung in there and came out on top, as they say. I was accepted on the fourth try.

Our apprentice class is a study in extremes. East Berliners make up thirty percent, twenty percent are West Berliners, and the other fifty percent are foreigners. Logically enough, the West Berliners side with the majority and try to make a good impression on the foreigners. That's why they band together against us.

It's not normal to have so many foreigners in one class. I'm sure it has to do with the profession I've chosen. Many guys want to go into sports fields; most come from soccer or whatever. A lot of foreigners live in Berlin, and so they naturally get jobs in that area as well. To be honest, there are decent people in my class as well, I mean decent from my point of view, of course. But on the other hand, Serbs, Croats, and Muslims are all together. First they tear each other to pieces and then we're next: "The Easterners are taking our jobs away. Remember, us foreigners were here first."

And we're pushing back like this: "Foreigners were only let in to do the dirty work in the West." Of course, the reaction isn't rational "Hah, you're all stupid. You're Ossis. Why don't you go back to your own side?" That's how it goes.

Of course, it's more difficult now for foreigners to get an apprenticeship, and I can understand that. Department stores like Karstadt or Hertie prefer to take people who were trained in East Germany rather than a Turk. That's just how it is.

Anyway, people were constantly labeling us as Stasi types. "Spy" was the standard curse word. Made me puke, especially since the Stasi did so much shit. And then to be denounced as one. Of course, they also took it out on us in other ways. With martial arts, for example. Whenever they tried anything, you became a punching bag. If you were kicked from behind, everyone would laugh or seem happy about it, and you'd stand there not knowing what to do. The result was that I also took up martial arts.

* * *

Well, when I first went to school at age six, first grade, I was totally proud to be a Pioneer, of course. Suddenly you belonged to the big kids, with a Pioneer shirt and everything. But vacation camps with morning roll calls pretty much sucked, with everyone falling in and standing to attention. I asked myself: "Why does it have to be like this?" Back then my mother was studying at one of the Party colleges, SED of course, and when I was in the third grade more or less, there was one of these vacation camps and I wrote a card to my great-grandma in West Berlin, no big deal. But my mother had reported, sometime or other, that she didn't have any contacts in the West. My great-grandma, eighty-six back then, just imagine! I mean, it was just ridiculous, all that fuss about political contacts and such. Anyway, my mother was thrown out of the Party college, because she had kept this contact in the West a secret. Of course, I only got the connection a few years later. My parents divorced when I was five. When I went to visit my father, there was no West German television allowed. He was in the ZK, the Central Committee of the SED. Responsible for the Greens in West Berlin or for the Communist Party or whatever. Then after the situation eased up with Gorbachev, around 1985, I could watch a film from the West now and then, but no sports, no West German league games. He never could get over it all.

Well, I would have been happy if the Wall had fallen ten years earlier. I thought everything on the other side would look just like on TV. With neon signs and night life and everything. That was my childhood dream: to actually be on the other side for once, to be able to go shopping, to eat sweets, to run around and do really great stuff. Traveling to different countries wouldn't have been bad either. But Lithuania or Bulgaria were also fun back then. Or Hungary, for me the absolute experience: I drank Coca-Cola for the first time.

I always got on well with my mother. I'm sure she tried to kind of steer me away a bit from my consumer mentality, but on the other hand she got into it herself. Whenever she went over to West Berlin before the Wall was opened, to some kind of archives for her job, she brought me back great stuff. Of course, that escalated the whole thing. Once I got a reversible sweater, and then a pair of real jeans, and another time a T-shirt. I was totally proud of them. I ask myself how we ever managed without things from the West. As a normal person. With an off-brand generic sweater and East German jeans. When you compare what we wear today and what we thought was nice back then. The difference is pretty crass.

* * *

School was absolute shit after the seventh grade. We moved to a new house then and I ended up in a class of nonstop fighters. You were greeted straight off with a beating. If you had a different opinion, all you heard was: "Keep your trap shut!" That sure made me angry inside. And of course the others noticed whether you reacted or not. And they ground you down, not only with physical strength but also with words.

The political stuff was like water off a duck's back. Sure, we did take "citizenship" class, but even the teacher just rattled off the stuff from the textbook. An elderly lady. Meanwhile, we did other things, but that didn't disturb her. We had our own opinions anyway: The Wall has to be opened . . . the West is super . . . never mind what they say. Planned economy, *Aktuelle Kamera* — always the same shit, with quota fulfillment and all that jazz — we just laughed at it all.

Sure, in the eighth grade we had FDJ initiation. With preparatory training and everything. So that we could say — at precisely the right time — what they wanted to hear. We just turned it into a party. Of course I was worried about the disadvantages if I didn't join the FDJ. I wouldn't have been able to go to some dances or stuff like that. So I said to myself, okay, you'll just join, no sweat. There were twenty of us in the class; only one didn't join. His father was a craftsman. It was obvious to him that he'd also be a craftsman, that the FDJ was crap — and that was that . . .

For us, there was a kind of membership exam. We were asked: "Why do you want to join the FDJ?"

And I said: "Well, I want to change the world and stuff like that."

So then they asked: "How do you plan to do that?"

Then I let rip: "Well, I definitely want to fulfill the 'socialist plan' and help people come to the right way of thinking . . . and stuff."

They thought that was totally great, the FDJ card was in the bag, and the thing was over and done with. I never read the bylaws or anything. But if the GDR had lasted, perhaps it would have been important for my profession, but then again perhaps not. All in all, though, it brought me advantages: I got to go dancing a few times for free or to an interesting concert you could only get tickets to if you were in the FDJ.

Looking back, I'm not angry that I was in it, but I'm also not proud of it. Really, it all went totally over my head. Fine: my responsibility to my father also played a role. If he's in the Central Committee and his son isn't in the FDJ, then something's got to go wrong.

My father was in it out of conviction; that was his problem. Other people were slicker, made their cadre or personal file disappear as soon as the changeover happened. His still said: For such-and-such a time member of the Central Committee of the SED. For a while, of course, he couldn't get a job anywhere. He was always whining that things were going badly, that he didn't have a proper job or any money. The joke is that he now has a job as a teacher, in some kind of private school. Know what he's teaching? Social studies. I haven't said a word. You can't discuss stuff like that with him: he's too stubborn. I got used to that long ago. He's now forty-six and isn't going to change. In the old days we used to talk about Gorbachev now and then. I thought: An outstanding human being, upswing, *glasnost, perestroika,* everything's great. Then my father brought me back to earth, from my happy trip, so to speak. "Yes, Gorbachev is certainly doing some good things, but there will be a lot of conflict because of his policies." His attitude was really pessimistic. At first I tried to convince him: "We have to try, even if there are complications; we just can't keep running a Central Committee state in the Soviet Union like we've been doing. Sometime we'll have to introduce a market economy, and stuff like that . . ."

But at the time he was totally convinced of it all, dangled socialism and Marx and Lenin in front of me, and there came a time when I gave up. I don't ask him either if he used to be in the Stasi. Actually, I'm sure he wasn't. Perhaps he was shadowed himself? But what if he was an unofficial co-worker? I'm afraid to ask him, I don't really want to know. I would be pretty sad if he was . . . Actually, it would shock me. Because I've found out what the Stasi was up to here.

I mean, there's still time to ask him. But . . . I don't think I will. I'm afraid of hurting him. Maybe he'll think I'm accusing him of something?

Actually, I shouldn't stop asking uncomfortable questions even if I could hurt someone with them. That's a really big problem for me.

I even feel like, if I go and quit my job now, I'd think that I'd be hurting someone, that they'd get the wrong idea about me afterwards and I absolutely don't want that. But I'm slowly getting over that.

I just got a warning from my boss because he didn't think much of my work ethic. But that means shit to me at the moment. One day I wore a suit to work because I was going out afterwards. I'm in garden furniture right now, pretty dirty work. Anyway, some salesman said I was to bring up some goods from down below. I asked him politely whether he couldn't do it for me. "Look at me, in my suit, I've got plans later." Or something like that. He thought I was a big jerk and was absolutely furious with me, because he is, after all, a salesman, and I'm only a trainee. Besides, he wants to be boss one day and is in the "development circle" already. That's kind of an intermediate stage between boss and employee, he thinks. Anyway, he says to me: "That's refusal to work and grounds for dismissal."

Then I said he shouldn't be such a smart-ass. I couldn't help it. It was too much for one day. And then he chewed me out, in order to suck up to the boss or whatever.

You wouldn't believe what goes on: the sports department had done a lot of business, so the efficiency expert for the management wanted to set us up as a separate unit. But people come to a department store precisely because they can buy everything in one place. They don't want to leg it another hundred meters to get their sports equipment. We all spoke out against it. But they did it anyway. Now we're only taking in forty percent of our previous sales, personnel have been cut, contracts haven't been reissued. Many of my friends were let go, people I got on well with, and that means I more or less have to do their work as well as my own.

Then I was promised a day off. Two days beforehand word comes down: "You have to come in."

I said: "I've got plans."

"No, that's impossible. You have to come in."

The result was: I went to my doctor, around the corner here, told him about it, and he wrote me a sick note. No problem. Nothing happened. But it's a crappy job anyway. The only question is when I'll quit. For two years it's been: Sort the hangers, sort the hangers, sort the hangers . . . Always the same shit.

I do understand the principles of the market economy. Nothing comes from nothing, that's clear. But I only fight for something I believe in.

When I have my own business, when I'm an entrepreneur, then I'll fight for it too, no question.

I really worked hard for a year. But I simply didn't get any recognition. Besides, we thought that the new trainees would come in after that year and then they'd have to go through the first year. But that didn't happen. There weren't very many new hires and so we were still the idiots who had to sweep up the dirt.

In this respect I suppose they're right about my work ethic. It's not what it was at the beginning. And you can't talk to the big boss either: it's all turnover, turnover, turnover with him. He really does try to do what he can, but he just doesn't have the right feeling you have to have. When he comes up behind a customer and asks, "May I help you?" the customer almost has a heart attack. The boss has a really weird voice. Far too loud, to begin with, and also really mechanical, which makes it unpleasant.

Recently he was standing in front of the safe and couldn't get the key in the keyhole, he was trembling so much, because his nerves are completely shot. He just isn't bringing in enough business and he's being chewed out by the higher-ups. Of course, he takes it out on the staff. You have to keep your mouth shut and do your job as if it's the most fulfilling thing in your life.

* * *

Well, on November 9, I was sitting at home. At the press conference, Schabowski made that slip of the tongue. It registered, but we didn't really understand it. It was only the next day that I checked: "The borders are open? Hurray!" You've no idea how happy that made us. Of course we just let the teachers drone on and all the time we were thinking about what we were going to do. We went over that evening. Took the commuter train to Friedrichstrasse. You could hardly get off the train. You couldn't see any of the station, it was so full of people. And as claustrophobic as I am, I got completely hysterical. I always have to have my neck free and my head. Took twenty minutes but we got to the street at last. We crossed the border at Invalidenstrasse. A lot of people were crying for joy. Not me. And I don't know why. Sure, it was strange going through, not normal, somehow, like in a dream perhaps, but I still couldn't cry.

Of course we speculated about whether the Wall would be closed again. Then I would have gone directly to my uncle's place and stayed there. He was living in the West, you see. So we picked up our "welcome money" at once. I wanted to spend it slowly, this hundred mark note. But a week later I was at a soccer match and someone stole ninety marks from me. I had only spent ten by then.

* * *

Something I found really strange was the change from citizenship class to social studies. Must have been early in 1990. Anyway, it was winter and cold, I remember that. Fine, we hadn't had normal citizenship class in the months before either, only talked about politics, about the changeover etc. But I don't understand how the same teacher could just carry on. Of course, I was in the FDJ as well, but only to get the advantages, not from conviction. But if I'd been a citizenship teacher, surely I'd have wanted to be convinced that the state was right.

Looking back, I've often wondered: If the Stasi had asked me, would I have worked for them or not? After all, most of the soccer players were Unofficial Co-workers of the Stasi. Of course they were blackmailed: "Either you work for the Stasi *and* play soccer — or you can get lost." How would I have reacted? I would probably have gone along with them too. And I would have tried, like the soccer players did, not to do other people any harm. But you can't say that with certainty these days. Anyhow, my mother would have been around, and she would have definitely kept me from doing it. I talk to her about everything. But left to myself, I'm sure I would have given in to the blackmail. I would never have joined out of conviction, of course.

I'm sure there were many who were with the Stasi because they really believed they were protecting the state. They had the power to torture others, to beat them up, at a demonstration or in jail or whatever. I couldn't have done that; no, a human being can only do that under extreme duress . . . But on your own? . . .

Anyway, I was happy that the Wall was open and I had the contract for my apprenticeship in the bag. Seven hundred gross, six hundred and twenty in my hand. My pal in East Berlin, at Bergmann-Borsig, got eighty marks the same year. Now, in the third year of their apprenticeship, they're getting three hundred, but in the meantime I'm already getting eleven hundred.

Well, I survived the first three months trial period with flying colors. Then I thought, now you can take it a little slower, you can open your mouth once in a while without being fired right away. But once you're in that slimy circus, you can't get out again.

"You are a trainee in your first apprenticeship year, whether your first three months are over or not. You are to sort the hangers!" And then you just go and sort the hangers, whether you want to or not.

Everyone advises me to finish up my training, as a salesman, but it simply does nothing for me any more. The real apprenticeship is over after these two years, the third year is just review, and anyway the work is always the same thing over and over.

I talked to a friend who's with the Dresdner Bank and he told me that if I have a business concept that is supported by contracts, I'll get a loan. Even without training. No problem. So why should I complete my certification? Do a job that's no fun for a whole year?

* * *

I mean, I don't have to hand over any money at home, and I still owe the bank one thousand four hundred at the moment. I just got my driver's license and I bought a car the very same day. A Wartburg. Nice and cheap, 1985 model, one thousand seven hundred. But then I had to pay for insurance, the inspection sticker, and so on and so on. I got a thousand marks from my mother. Otherwise I would be at minus twenty-five hundred. I just put another three hundred into it. Water pump and cylinder head gasket. So you make a few mistakes.

I never thought it impossible that I could make myself independent one day. My goal is to have enough money one day to really be able to support a family. That's impossible with the salary I make at Karstadt. And I really don't know what I'm working for. Trained and certified, two thousand one hundred gross, leaving me perhaps one thousand six hundred take-home. Something's not right here.

A pal and I are busy working on a concept. We want to run a mail-order business, because then you can work with cellars and warehouses that are very much cheaper than the rent for a business on some street. I think mail-order is the wave of the future. We've really found a gap in the market, and it'll work, I'm convinced of it.

My personal goal is to be happy, not exactly poor, to have a family, a wife, and also children. I don't want to be dependent on money, don't want to have to stare at the bottom line at the end of the month and have to work out where we can still save a little.

When I look at my pay slip from Karstadt at the end of the month and think how hard we worked, I tell myself: There's no relation between the two. There are jobs that pay quite a bit more and for which you work less.

I was offered a job recently as a newspaper delivery agent. I would have gotten two thousand five hundred a month, without training, and would have had to work no more than six hours a day.

Of course, just having money isn't a goal. But I've seen at home what kind of problems there are when the money isn't enough. Fine, if you're in love you don't think about twenty years in the future. But if you want to have children and don't want to fight about every penny, then you really have to think about it today.

I don't have a steady girlfriend at the moment. I've had bad luck. She went on vacation and came back with another man. That was really weird, pretty stupid. We were together over a year. I didn't reckon anything would happen. A normal goodbye, things you usually say: "Don't be unfaithful, have a nice trip and stuff." She went to visit her cousin in Munich. She's been together with him now for two years. I did something wrong. I was really angry at myself because I didn't hang in there.

Back then I was playing a lot of soccer and just when I had decided to — not to give up soccer completely but to cut back a bit, because my girlfriend was more important, that's when it happened. It was just too late.

Since then I haven't met the right one. The women I want are already taken or don't want me, and the ones I can have I don't want.

As for AIDS, I think like anyone else: "That's not going to happen to me." I really don't know anyone who's had an AIDS test done. Sure, when I was donating plasma recently, they took some blood and did all sorts of tests. But they asked straight off whether I did marijuana, and that was that. That meant: I couldn't donate plasma and couldn't earn an extra thirty marks a week. I could come back in three weeks. But forget that. I mean, it's just that if you go to the vocational school in Kreuzberg you smoke it regularly. Now, I never do coke. But I've got this pal and I've warned him not to do so much of it. He's constantly stoned. I don't know whether it's too late already. He's now found himself a girlfriend. I hope she can maybe get him off it someday. He couldn't say a word to his parents about it. I'm completely open about all that, I talk to my mother about everything. Taboo or not. I don't treat this topic as taboo. I don't see marijuana as "dangerous." I think alcohol's much more dangerous. Here's a comparison. When you drink a few too many beers, then your head is clear but your body stops reacting to what your head wants; everything is slowed down for all practical purposes. When you smoke marijuana, you still can't drive a car, that's obvious, but your head is clear and you can move quite normally, you just speak a little differently. I mean you laugh about things you wouldn't normally laugh about. You're uninhibited, really happy. That lasts for two hours, and then you're pessimistic again. A real grouch, so to speak. But you're still able to function, and besides, you pay a lot less money. Your lungs don't exactly get better, obviously, but with alcohol it's the liver that goes bad.

I don't have to pay very often. My pal brings the stuff with him and then we smoke it. I pay for a movie or something once in a while. We're not so picky in that respect. Normally I'd have to hand over a ten for a joint.

We roll them ourselves. You take one gram of marijuana, crumble it up, add the tobacco from a normal cigarette, then you roll it and take a drag. Only thing is, it's about thirteen times more damaging than a normal cigarette — the tar content, I mean.

Difficult to say why I smoke at all. When I'm at school and accounting's the first class, I feel totally miserable afterwards because I have no clue about the subject. Then you sink into this stupid mood, and you sit down and talk drivel. But when you have a smoke, you feel happy again afterwards, and you go into the next class feeling quite different.

Besides, it's just fun to hang. Not to be stressed out. My role models are still John Lennon, The Doors, Woodstock and stuff. That whole time, when everything was more laid back and they didn't let themselves be jerked around by this stupid, bullheaded state. But if you want to get on here, you have to conform totally or become a complete dropout. Sure, I'm afraid now and then. Like a funny feeling in your stomach. And I'm absolutely sure that I won't be able to reach my goals if I switch to the harder stuff.

* * *

I don't think about the environment a lot. If push comes to shove, I'll run away from the problems and emigrate with my entire family, to New Zealand, for example, but you need money for that, too.

I really don't see how I could help solve the problems that dominate the world at the moment. It's probably impossible anyway, in capitalism. They'll just keep cutting down the rain forests if it brings in more profits than cutting down the forests in Sweden. That's the market economy for you. You can't change that in this social system. Since everything revolves around money, you can't convince people to pay more just to protect the environment. No one's interested in that.

I'm sure I would have scruples in that case, and that's why I'm not the ideal business man perhaps. And don't talk to me about political parties. I belong to the party of non-voters. You would have to take a little bit from each party, and then you could maybe make something decent happen. But at the moment you might as well vote for the German Beer Drinkers' Party, as a gag, so to speak. That would be pointless, of course. As far as ideas go, perhaps the Greens, but they're too divided to be effective.

You know what's a comfort to me sometimes? That this whole life is just a transition. I believe in life after death. This here is just a kind of intermediate step. I'm not a Christian. And I don't have the time to think about the problem so deeply that I could defend my opinion to someone with good arguments. If I were a Christian and had read the Bible fifteen times already, then perhaps I could use the Bible to make my argument. But there are so many unexplained things in this world, in this universe, and I just can't imagine that everything is based on coincidences, the whole earth, our whole lives. There's a certain hope within me, and the whole thing is supported by the documentation on life after death that scientists have collected in books.

Nevertheless, I'm sure there are problems we have to solve on this earth, in order to guarantee a life for those who come after us. But each person is his or her own neighbor. If I saw that the ozone layer was going to be destroyed in the next twenty years, then I'd do everything I could to save it, if I had the money or the strength to do it.

Of course, the old system was set up in such a way that it was to your advantage to join the FDJ. And it's now to your advantage not to contradict your boss, and it is also to your advantage to buy tropical woods. But I think you have to make a distinction. The FDJ and the boss, that's one thing, and you're not harming anyone else. But if you trade in tropical woods, then you're harming others. That's a matter of degree, where you have to make a distinction.

What annoys me is this violence everywhere. I think we should lock all these tough guys in a great big hall where they could beat each other up as long as they want to. The left and the right, as well as the hooligans. I don't care what their ideology is.

When I go to a soccer match, I want to watch soccer and not fight. I was beaten up once, by a whole lot of Turks. Over in Wedding. Our team scored two goals in the last minute; those were the equalizers and gave us victory in the tournament as well. The Turks went crazy, kicked our players in the ass, screamed at them and mobbed them. And, idiot that I am, I went down some narrow winding stairs and wanted to slip out. Stupid thing to do.

They caught me on the stairs; in the meantime the others were long gone and I couldn't get out. They came from above and below. They all piled on. But I didn't play along. The best martial arts won't help you when you're cornered. I screamed like a stuck pig. That's all you can think about in moments like that. Finally the trainers came, after an eternity. After that I just sat there, scared to death for hours. I tried to calm myself down a bit. I managed it outwardly, but not inwardly.

That's why I don't want to go to the army, because I wouldn't be able to stand battle situations. I'm just too soft for stuff like that. In the past I even used to get on with people who stand on street corners, drinking beer and yelling. But even this violence is too much for me now. I can tolerate everyone, whether right or left, as long as they're only giving their opinion — but without hassling other people.

On the one hand there's the thinkers, who are in the background. But then the ones who stand outside the corner bars, they beat people up afterwards. The thinkers don't do anyone any harm, at least not directly. But the real problems are the social catastrophes and the violence in families. The father is unemployed and drinks, the mother goes around whoring, the children run around in the street. They're still doing that later in life, simply because they grew up on the streets and learned how to make it there. I'm terrified of them and that's why I never go around outside without my sword. A small one; the big one's at home, for practice. I used to have a pistol, but I sold it. The metal sword isn't sharp, but when I draw it, it makes a definite impression.

They've already killed some people in the neighborhood. When I used to come home at night by street car, around eleven or so, and the street lamps weren't on, as often happened on the one street, then I'd walk with a blank gun at the ready, loaded with gas and flare ammunition, and I'd wheel around at every noise . . . I now feel safer with my sword. I keep it in my jacket or somewhere I can get to it in a hurry. If someone attacks me, he wants something from me, and I'm going to defend myself.

But if it's five men and you have one of those little teargas cans, they'll hold their hands over their eyes, run through the cloud, and come at you from the other side. When they see a sword like mine, I expect they'll be more afraid.

I was at a birthday party recently; some high school seniors were there and I struck up a conversation with them and we got into a discussion. One of them said he goes directly up to those groups and tries to find out why so many young people hang around in groups like that, what their aims and motivations are. I said to him: "If someone's beating me up, then I really could care shit about why he's doing it." These days you have to be careful what you wear. Good trainers, expensive jacket, great pants — they'll all get stolen. They'll rip them off you in the street. In effect, you're only dressing for other people now: as inconspicuously as possible so you won't be hassled.

It's exactly the same when you walk around with a short haircut, with your hair brushed back like this. They took me for a right-wing Nazi pig. Screamed at me. No matter what you do, you do something wrong.

I don't have the peace of mind that my friend has, for example. He is relatively right-wing. It all goes right over his head. I have friends in the leftist scene as well. I get on with everyone. That's not the problem. I just can't come to terms with those who want something from me. . . .

CHAPTER TWELVE

YOU CAN BEST CHANGE THE WORLD BY CHANGING YOURSELF . . .

— Lars, N., 40, pastor, philosopher, party founder

AT THE LATEST, IT SHOULD HAVE BEEN clear after the military suppression of the Prague Spring, if not before, that socialism as a societal model had failed. And after the exile of Wolf Biermann from the GDR, we should have said out loud: This system is not based upon any claim to truth. It will not reform itself, but will solidify more and more. The centralistic structures do not allow for any checks and balances or separation of powers.

I had achieved this clarity of insight a long time ago. But it had been suppressed over and over again by my emotions: Socialism was a good thing. Many West German left-wingers strengthened us in this, and we built up — as we have to put it today in the spirit of critique — an ideology of justification: There were good aspects to life in the GDR, we would say; there was a different social climate, a slower rhythm of life, not the hard competitiveness found in the West; we still had time to read books, we would say, even if we had to pass them on in secret and couldn't really check them out of the library.

This justification was even given philosophical validation: Even a restriction on freedom can have its good side. For a long time we — I — completely romanticized the situation.

We should have organized much earlier. Not only to reform the system, but also with the aim of bringing a system like that to its knees.

Nevertheless, along with this romanticization, we were still very sensitive to the social reality around us. I always saw it as my task to keep alive the consciousness of certain ethical values and to call for their implementation: human rights, separation of powers . . . But I saw this action as being more on a philosophical rather than a concrete political level, and addressed it as such.

* * *

I find it difficult to describe what made my family tick. Our mother loved us; our father was more concerned with himself and his work. He had been an enthusiastic officer in the Second World War and had had a lot of power as a young man. In Africa, he had command over large areas, and

I'm sure that left its mark on him. Later, he was captured by the Americans and had the chance to study economics in America. After his return, he was a committed member of the LDPD. On the one hand, we children were brought up to be very independent, and I'm grateful to my parents for that to this day; on the other hand, however, there was a very early rift. My older brother and I both refused to do military service. Father couldn't understand that at all, and we were almost thrown out of the house because of it. Besides, our decision also meant that we distanced ourselves a bit from what we were supposed to become according to our father's wishes, that is, from technology and the sciences. Someone who refused to bear arms, or, more precisely, a "construction soldier," was forbidden to study at an institution of higher education in the GDR, except for theology.

Originally I wanted to study graphic arts. I even applied, although I knew going in that I had no chance. After my rejection, I began to study theology in Berlin, primarily because there was a good drawing group there. I thought I could combine the two: graphic arts and theology. But then I began to enjoy my studies more.

After my brother and I moved away from home at eighteen, because we wanted to have our "freedom" and live our own lives, our relationship with our parents improved again. In fact, I had already been living my own kind of life while attending the upper high school. School was no fun for me; the atmosphere there was Stalinistic and hollow, and, looking back, those were wasted years.

But outside school there was a good student group that influenced me, even back then, from a Christian perspective. My parents were not especially pious. At the same time, this group was pretty committed to social causes. We organized aid to the elderly and wanted to effect something in society, most definitely with an exaggerated "service ethic." I graduated from high school in 1970.

* * *

During my studies, one professor, who read philosophy with us, was more influential in my life than any other. He was a guru, a teacher, both in his behavior and in his demands. Trained in ancient philology, he had just as much mastery of the ancient languages as he had of ecclesiastical and intellectual history.

What impressed me about this professor from the first moment on was that he could treat absolutely anyone he met equally: clever people and foolish people, well-read and ill-read, well-educated and uneducated. In addition, he lives a very consistent life in many respects. He's a vegetarian, makes do with very little money, and is living in a religious community today. For that reason, he also follows monastic vows. He is a person for whom the most important thing is not his career but rather a truthful life and knowledge: a very religious person who can, however, combine religion and scholarship. That was something fascinating and important for us and still is for me.

There was always a clear, purely teacher-student relationship between this professor and us, simply because he was so superior to us. And I felt this relationship even more strongly than the others, because I valued not only his scientific side but also his religious side very highly. As a student back then, I felt the need to attach myself to someone who had superior knowledge and who would take me a little further intellectually, because I had hardly any background in intellectual history from my parents.

* * *

Both during my studies and afterwards, philosophy was a kind of "safe haven." You could live completely in the intellectual history of humankind, even if you couldn't do anything practical on the societal level. After all, Plato says: The philosopher does not need the state, but the state needs the philosopher. The sheltered circumstances at that time were ideal for thorough, peaceful, and intensive studies. You had time, which not many young people in the West had, I'm sure, in that restless and hectic society.

You needed little money here in the East. The external things were ideally ordered — at least for people who didn't have great material expectations — those who "shirked their responsibilities," as it was called. Cheap rents, cheap basic foodstuffs — you only had to work at the most one or two days a week to earn the money you needed to live.

Of course, the devastating barbarity that went along with it was a different matter: the selling off of old primary texts, the neglected state of the libraries, so that there was hardly any intellectual history to be found in them. On the other hand, you didn't have to keep up with every fashion fad, didn't have to have read every new book that came on the market in the West. We saw things from an uncluttered perspective and could afford to read important primary texts. Aristotle, Plotinus, Nicholas of Cusa, Hegel, and Kant. . . .

* * *

Later, of course, during my time as a pastor, I struggled with the political realities near to home. I worked with peace groups, grappled with ecological challenges, but it was not as if I was preparing myself to found a party in the near future and to take over power.

I proceeded from the idea that the socialistic world system would last. And not only that. I also supported it emotionally. We consistently identified with the *claim* to justice, which was verbalized for us, as you know, and we were too lax in subjecting the system to a fundamental critique. Today, I reproach myself and other left-wing forces for that.

Of course, we also had our utopias. After all, we delve into history so that we can uncover future possibilities and put the various ideologies into perspective. It is precisely the task of philosophy and intellectual history to correct the prioritization of values that a society has set in place — and, not least, to *set ethical priorities* themselves. But we have written certain values especially large: that people under socialism should be taken care of. And in so doing we did not look closely enough at the extent to which the most massive dependence was created at the same time. We know that those who do not take care of themselves remain dependent. We have seen in no uncertain terms that there was absolutely no understanding of law in this state. Here, the law was nothing but a compliant instrument in the hands of those who ruled. That's exactly why we delved into Hegel's political philosophy. Consequently, even those of us in the philosophical working groups were close to the problems of our society. Moreover, as a village pastor in the eighties, I was also interested in dealing with those who possessed the power in society. I organized district youth conferences on questions of ecology and peace. There were intense arguments at these. At that time, Olof Palme's ideas on collective security were to be put into practice. So I did actually take on political responsibility in a concrete fashion. But as a pastor, not as a politician. And I continued to do so until the changeover, and later also as a college pastor.

It was never my aim to found a party and to work in society as a fulltime politician. In part because I believe that the important things in society can only be changed by people acting as individuals. Politics can certainly influence many things in society, but you can best change the world by changing yourself and perhaps by showing other people the way to being somewhat more selfless, more generous and just. And that is precisely the work of a pastor.

As much as I enjoyed getting into intellectual and philosophical questions with the working groups, even long after my studies, I also enjoyed just as much being challenged by the things that were right outside my front door. In my parish there were three broken-down churches, ugly and in need of repair. How could you sing "Hallelujah" in something like that? One large parsonage and a second parsonage, for which I was responsible, were to be set to rights and kept in good repair. Even the building jobs took a terrible toll. Our two children were small, and my wife, who was a doctor, was working more than eight hours a day. But I don't want to "dramatize" myself. I believe that retrospection must always possess a self-critical element.

In 1968 I was seventeen. Many people were already handing out political flyers at that age. But 1976, when Biermann was exiled, was a very decisive point for me. We worked towards getting the decision over-turned, called up the first signatories of the protest and looked up various authors ourselves. I went to see Anna Seghers, to convince her to add her signature to those of the ten writers who had already signed the appeal.

* * *

Also, you know, the so-called "basic anti-fascist position" in the GDR was poisoned from the start by a Stalinism that had not been fully processed. Reading the book *The Gulag Archipelago* by Solzhenitsyn in 1974 was a very important turning point in my life. A work of art with a deeply humanistic point of view, in spite of the many facts, and a wonderful translation. Of course, it was smuggled into the GDR.

There was a multi-faceted critique even in the GDR. But the crucial factor was that there was no overarching critique of socialist ideology. Bahro tried it in *The Alternative*. We read the book and passed it around, but it had many weaknesses, too.

In contrast, in Poland, in the circle of Catholic intellectuals who were characterized by faith and a particular nationality, a much more powerful kind of thought and analysis went into the battle with the system.

In the GDR, there were only the church-based grass-roots groups, who worked on questions of peace and ecology, but as for an analysis of the whole system, that only took place very sporadically and very much on the margins. That is something we neglected and I still reproach myself for it very much.

Of course, the GDR was never a "leftist state" for me. The system followed primarily right-wing visions that set the systematic ordering of an entire state above the dignity of the individual. On the other hand, I can't praise the "assertive individualism" in the liberal market economy to the skies either. Neither presents a good alternative for me. Rather, my political aim was to mediate between the interests of the individual and those of society; that was a vision we had already attached to socialism. At the time, my friends and I called it "democratic socialism."

In no way did we see this as being in conflict with the concrete political everyday reality in which we fought against educational policy, complained about the state of the libraries, and deplored the immaturity of the people. But you can also read in the writings of the socialist theoreticians that the free development of the individual is the prerequisite for the free development of everyone. And this was the claim with which we identified.

* * *

I felt like I belonged to the GDR, I never said: I was born in Germany. I was born in the GDR. Very different from the generation that was over

forty in 1989 and had experienced the open Wall. There's a real generation gap there.

It was a great moment of discovery for me to travel to Bavaria and to
find out that there was a completely different German way of life from
that of Prussia, a different culture that reached right into everyday life.
For such a long time I had had no experience of Germany being so much
bigger and comprising so much more than the Prussian Protestantism
that I knew. During the GDR period, I had no phantom pains, in the
sense that I didn't feel that there was anything missing.

In December 1988, I found an article by Rolf Schneider, "On German Identity as an Emotion," very thought-provoking. I felt that there
was quite a bit of truth in it and I tried to incorporate it later into the
founding articles of the SDP. So one sibylline phrase read: "Recognition
of two nations as a result of the culpability of the past" and in the consequent clause: "Which does not exclude the possibility of change within
the framework of a European peace order."

If I often think or say "we," I'm sure there are many reasons for that.
There are people who would rather hide and others who would rather re-
veal themselves. I myself don't often reflect on my history or my life story.
I'm certainly one of those who would rather hide than hang out their
dirty laundry for everyone to see.

And I think that there's another reason for the "we." In the GDR —
which was not an open society — there were certain groups that had gone
through similar experiences with the state. There was often a very simplistic opposition between church and state. It was quite clear that you had
to criticize many things if you wanted to remain true to yourself. This
gave rise to the formation of many groups. Now, in this open society,
with such varied political convictions, it's all much more differentiated
and difficult. For example, in the old days it was quite simple for the
church to stand up for justice or honesty, but today you have to explain in
much more detail what you actually mean by that.

Of course, parts of the church administration had been infiltrated by the
Stasi. But you knew that. After all, the same phenomenon had happened
during the Nazi Reich. When you realized how the various consistories
did deals with the state back then, you couldn't keep any illusions . . .

But it was a very different story with the pastors or lay staff. You knew
them by their work, and you could trust them implicitly. I would have cut
off my right hand for some of them to prove they weren't in the Stasi.
And there were a lot of them. They did such difficult jobs for so many
years with very little social recognition — and when you looked closely at
how much effort these people put in, although there was absolutely nothing to be gained, then you could give them your trust, and there was also
a feeling of community or a esprit de corps among them.

* * *

I got to know the West even before the Wall was opened. I was on disability because of a serious operation and could therefore travel to the West from 1985 onwards. But I didn't take advantage of it very often and, in retrospect, I was somewhat reticent in my behavior back then, in the West. Fortunately we had friends in West Germany who lived very modest lives out of principle, so that I hardly noticed a difference between them and people who lived in the GDR. That made the transition easier. I never traveled to any other country back then, with one exception. There was not enough time, nor could I take my wife along, which would have only been half as much fun.

When I look at it more closely, I went very systematically to galleries, exhibitions, and the various libraries in every city I visited. It was really important to me. Today I'm not so sure that I didn't want keep myself away from that society. For whatever reason. For example, I didn't seek any contact with people I knew who had emigrated from the GDR. I did not want to be confronted with their experiences and their perceptions. That, too, is a little tragic, that we kept aloof from those people who had left the GDR.

True, I had always agreed with them from an intellectual standpoint and had stood up for them: "Every person has the right to be able to leave his or her country and to go back again."

Especially in response to people inside and outside the church who thought that leaving the country, I mean the GDR, was treason. I took this stance intellectually and I always said: Everyone must have this freedom. But it was only later, during conversations with Jürgen Fuchs and others, that I noticed I had shut myself down and cut myself off from those who had taken advantage of that right. Perhaps, among other reasons, so that I didn't have to question myself and my attitude. Even today there's a lot that I haven't come to terms with.

But on the whole, all of this travel to the West did not play a large role in my life at that time. I'm sure it was different for a worker who could visit his relatives and see what kind of salary they were getting for comparable work. He would probably have asked himself why he was earning so little money compared to them with all his hard work, year in, year out.

* * *

For me, Gorbachev was no great hope. True, there were signs of a certain liberalization, but the militarization of society continued at first. Indeed, training in the schools became more hard-line under the regime of Margot Honecker. I read Gorbachev's speeches, of course, cut out the articles in the newspaper, but I didn't see such a great caesura coming.

Did he really come to power to dissolve the socialist world system? No one could imagine that. But that was exactly his historical task, we can say today, and at some point or other Gorbachev himself must have grasped that and consciously given it form. But back then?

All I knew was that, if he really put this liberalization into practice in a consistent manner, if he actually opened up the Stalin period for reappraisal, then the whole system would begin to slide. But did he really want that? Who could say? On an intellectual level, I saw Gorbachev as someone who supported culture and did a lot for the press. But for the workers, nothing changed at first. And it was very uncertain how long he would remain in power and how deep it all went. I just thought it was a miracle how a man like that could make it to the top of such a system, and I knew what kind of a huge apparatus he was confronting in his own country. I was in sympathy with his approach, but I also saw how dangerous his situation was.

It was an especially difficult time for me at home, because I had to fight on two fronts: on the one hand against the state and the Department of Internal Affairs, which summoned me regularly, and on the other hand against the regional church organization, which in this instance was working especially closely with the state. In the interests of the church, of course — as the leaders of the regional organization understood it at the time. They received in return better terms for the conversion or expansion of churches and things like that, but I never agreed with church policy taking such a course.

* * *

At one point I really wanted to be a college pastor. Primarily because it was much simpler to reach a consensus in a student congregation, even when it came to political questions, because of the homogeneity of the group. And then you could also act as a group. The pastor in a "normal" congregation fought by himself much more often. In my student congregation we had both a literary and a philosophical reading circle. The aim was of course always to relate what we had read to our own time, to our present, and also, of course, to cast a glance back over our century in order to be better able to understand its peculiarities: the loneliness of human existence; the destruction of family structures; individualism; many things that developed through industrialization and others that were now being reappraised due to the crisis of technological culture. It has to go that deep, otherwise there's no point in dealing with literature or philosophy.

* * *

The trans-regional working groups always ran parallel to whatever work I was doing at the time: The Hegel discussion group, the theological-philosophical working group. In these we worked intensively together on a topic, but the contacts between us were not very personal. We discussed content and not so much ourselves and our situations. On this level there was a clear distancing, and we valued it. We knew that we were all on the same intellectual wavelength, that we could trust one another, but otherwise everyone had his or her own work at home.

Nevertheless, I never saw it as a "scholars' club." I'm sure that had something to do with the fact that I expect more of the intellect. There is nothing more practical than a decent idea. The idea of nuclear power, which was put together at some desk or other, changed the world. And a truth spoken aloud at the right time — it changes the world just as much. That's why I can't comprehend the distinction between theory and practice. In the sense of Platonic philosophy, one thinks towards the ethical, towards the good — not solely for the sake of thinking itself.

The intellectual work, the intellectual growth, was always one aspect, but, on the other hand, that did not keep us from tackling real political problems at home or fighting for real outcomes.

But of course we didn't believe that our ideas would change the entire situation in the GDR, that, to exaggerate a bit, we were the very ones for whom the world was waiting.

Even today, I don't think that the social order is the ultimate determining factor, but rather the spirit that governs a society. The deciding question is always what you think the political sphere capable of. The peace movement, for example, really brought about a depoliticization, because it pushed back the universal politicization of all social areas. Politics is only *one* modest part of life.

In this regard, the hope that kept us going was more that of making something happen through ideas and individual people. And I still think that's important.

Of course, we were also able to exchange ideas with intellectual leftists from the West, about the West German state.

I've always said: the margin for tolerance is bigger over there, but in spite of this we have to criticize the system as an economy of injustice — one that can no longer provide a decent life in the southern hemisphere.

And even back then the question arose of how far the scope of democracy really extended, whether it can influence economic processes or whether it is merely influenced by them. As far as West German society was concerned, we were never euphoric.

* * *

In 1989, at a conference on the occasion of the two-hundredth anniversary of the declaration of human rights during the French Revolution, it became clear that the time had come to get involved directly in the political sphere as well. The situation was incredibly tense, the pressure to emigrate enormous, and Kurt Hager's comment about the change of scene in Moscow that we surely didn't need to put into practice over here put it over the top. Even the Lutheran Church had been talking very cautiously about "irregularities" during the local elections in May 1989.

Two friends from the philosophical-theological working group had already finished a report but had not yet published it. The first evening of our two-day meeting we ate in a restaurant, and they gave me their report to read. I said: "This is just what we need at this point in time. There'll never be a more advantageous moment, and even historically speaking, the time is right."

Every detail had been considered and it was clear to us that what we were trying to found at that moment had to be a party. Definitive structures had to be put in place, so that we could react effectively to state interference. And it had to be a social-democratic party in order to challenge the legacy of the SED. It would be the sharpest thorn in their side if we could say: "The SED is wrong when it says it is based on socialist ideals."

* * *

Anyway, the human-rights conference was very explosive with regard to its topic. So the pastor who organized it had quite a lot to answer for in his community, even in advance. Shortly after the publication of our report, he said: "Now I can start looking around for another job, and here I am a sixty-year-old pastor."

It was a pretty tense situation, and we made our first big mistake right away. Instead of jumping full throttle into working with the media, we asked the only journalist from the West in attendance not to report anything yet. We set up a term of copyright for the report so that the connection between it and our conference would not be so obvious.

Another reason was to make sure the report was not published in the West before it had become known through informal channels in the GDR. We knew that word of the report would get around in the GDR very quickly — we had experience in such matters.

But we were still anxious enough. The report was run off in the office of the parish youth ministry that very evening. The journalist from the West even drove us there, but we didn't hand over the report. And he was very unhappy when he left.

We soon realized that this vacillation on our part was not the right thing. You see, some news reports did actually come out after that. Bärbel Bohley spoke about us, as did Eppelmann, and of course not exactly as we would have wished. That's why we decided two weeks later to work with the press after all.

As an excuse, we can say today: Back then we were thinking in terms of much longer periods of time. We wanted — over years — to build up a party. It never entered our heads — nor anyone else's — that the system would crumble so quickly.

* * *

On that very evening, I had to leave Berlin to take my children home, and I didn't think I would even get out of the city. I was pretty sure I would be arrested right there in the car, since I had the copies of the report in the car with me so that I could distribute them outside Berlin. At the time I said to my children: "Listen, if the car is stopped and I'm taken away, it's not the end of the world. You'll be taken home and things will go on somehow."

But I arrived home safely.

The official launch of the party took place on October 7, 1989. The big question at the time was when and where. Just a week before our launch, "Democratic Awakening" had tried its own launch. Three different stratagems had been secretly agreed upon. But even the final one, which no one but the innermost circle was privy to, became known and the launch was stopped when state security placed the people under house arrest.

* * *

We worked in a relatively secret manner as well. We did publicly announce the launch date; I mean, we sent word in writing to a group of people, but we kept the place a secret. In addition, we designated four other people who were to carry on in case the four of us from the innermost circle were arrested.

We later found out that even among the four of us was someone who had been an unofficial informant for the Stasi for years. He was present at even the most private discussions. Even today I'm still not entirely certain what happened back then. Either nothing penetrated to the outside because he was no longer working for the Stasi at that point, or they didn't want to interfere with the launch, which is hard for me to imagine.

Just as a precaution, I left home two days before the launch date so as not to be placed under house arrest at the last moment.

The evening before, I introduced the Social Democratic Party — SDP — in an overcrowded church in Schwerin, and parallel to that Sebastian Pflugbeil introduced New Forum. The atmosphere in the church was tense. State security heckled non-stop; anyone who stepped up to speak was sworn at, sometimes whistled down, and to top it all we hadn't yet learned how to deal with such huge crowds of people. The situation was touch and go, and it was obvious that the meeting was going to be blown apart by a huge mass of Stasi people. Then we had the idea that saved us; to bring a few of those Stasi people to the microphone. They were really weak at debating and that's how we managed to contain the whole thing to some degree.

I had driven my car to this meeting. After the meeting, I left by a back door, abandoned my car, and drove away in another one to shake off the Stasi.

In Schwandte, where the launch took place, an automobile rally was going on at the same time and there was a lot of commotion as a result. That's one of the reasons why I was able to get there without being harassed, at first. Of course, we reckoned that the meeting would be broken up any minute; however, I was able to keep my fear within bounds at that point. It was clear that, what with all conceivable problems escalating at that time, it would be difficult to arrest a pastor and thus risk an open conflict with the church, especially since the West German church would have certainly gotten involved.

After this inaugural meeting, of course, I received a summons at home from the Department of Internal Affairs. I was told: "There will never be social democracy in the GDR." They wanted to intimidate me; from that day forwards, the Stasi watched the house entrance without a break, and even settled into the house opposite.

But we reckoned with a short-term internment or arrest at the most, and had no great fear at the thought. As a pastor, too, I didn't have to fear for my job like other people had to. So my risk was much smaller and consequently my responsibility to do something that much greater.

From then on I was in Berlin at least once and sometimes twice a week for the entire time I was part of the party leadership. I would leave at four in the morning from the Berlin-Lichtenberg railway station, so that I would be back here, at home, at eight, because I had lectures to give at the School of Church Music. It was a difficult, but also very wonderful, time.

* * *

I didn't see October 9 in Leipzig as a true turning point in the process. It was only when the demonstration of November 4 became possible and this demonstration was broadcast on television that I thought that we had pretty well made it.

Right from the start, there was a discussion within the leadership of the SDP about how grass-roots forms of democratic action could be developed and strengthened, how important a tightening of the party structure was, and what the advantages and disadvantages of this would be. We clearly understood that the model of democratic politics in the Federal Republic had to be expanded by means of grass-roots elements.

But it's quite another question whether this particular radical phase of the changeover was the right point at which to invent completely new political forms. The nightly meetings almost always lasted more than ten hours and were tough and rigorous, but when it came to the content, I felt that it presented me with very little challenge. Very often it was more a question of organization than content. Creativity was less in demand than I had hoped. And also, I have to say with hindsight, we didn't give enough consideration to the needs of the time.

Revolution doesn't ask whether the agenda has been carried out, and so, around Christmas, we broke it off. There were various reasons for this. The biggest was the opening of the Wall in November. That meant that the political pressure from the inside was gone.

But at the time I was also grappling with the fact that the "revolution" was so peaceful — something that the West praised so highly. This made it impossible for those who were politically responsible to be brought to justice with any severity. I believe that was a big mistake. The old "cadre" was still in place in all the important positions, in businesses, for example, or in the universities. Instead of urging that these people actually be deposed, the many "moderate" pastors were praised. But they all had their Christmas sermons to give, and so the "revolution" foundered. That was also *one* of the reasons why the party that thoughtlessly steered towards a quick annexation was elected in March of 1990.

It was just as tragic that it never came to a coalition between the SDP and the citizens' movements against the SED and the old block parties. This despite the fact that an electoral coalition among all the opposition parties and grass-roots movements had been arranged. But, before the party base could be consulted — that is, even before January 14, 1990, before the delegates' conference of the SDP in the East Berlin congress hall — someone from the SDP leadership had begun negotiations. That most definitely should have been made the subject of discussion at the conference. Along with asking who from the leadership had made the agreement, and when, and under which circumstances. As it was, all we heard was a curt: "No, the electoral coalition will not be done that way." The agreement was called into question simply because it had not been previously agreed upon by the members. I'm sure a certain amount of arrogance also played a role, because the SDP was very popular at that time. They thought they could go it alone, without the grass-roots movements. It was all pretty tragically interwoven. Instead of dealing with the truly important questions, we got caught up in an endless debate on statutes and stuff.

In this context, the discussion over the name of the party — SDP or SPD — was also pretty dramatic. Of course, most of the leadership wanted to continue as the SDP. But at that point in time, there was a danger that the SED would suddenly start calling itself SPD, that is, "the Socialist Party of Germany." That's why the leadership simply wanted to change the party abbreviation from SDP to SPD — "the Social-Democratic Party in the GDR."

But that's when we suddenly became aware of and began to experience just how distant the leadership, which consisted mostly of intellectuals, was from the party base. The leadership sat up on the stage, and just as much as we wanted to hold on to the words "in the GDR" as a matter of course, so the whole hall expected, also as a matter of course, to change the name of the party to "the Social-Democratic Party of *Germany.*" We were totally shocked, but we couldn't do anything to stop it. All we could do was recognize the distance between the leadership and the expectations of the party base. The "Declaration of German Unity" was worked out at the same conference of delegates, the same night. A very far-reaching text, a fundamental profession of unity, but coupled with a warning about the great social tensions to which a rapid unification process would lead. The declaration was shuffled back and forth across the table. No one really wanted to read it aloud because it went too far for the sensibilities of most of us back then. So it fell to me, since I could stand behind it.

Despite this, the hope of making something really independent happen was still very strong. But we could only have managed it if we had held together, all the grass-roots movements and the SDP . . . At least, we would have been able to do a little more . . . Even so, we might not have gotten a majority. Thanks to the open borders, history was going too far in a different direction for that and was pushing many things towards the quickest annexation possible.

Perhaps the ordinary people also anticipated the right thing, perhaps there was really only a short historical opportunity, a narrow doorway, through which we entered into unity.

As early as February 1990, I stepped down from the party leadership at the SPD Party Conference in Leipzig. For one, I was noticing a great dissatisfaction in my congregation, and I would have had to give up my work as pastor to students if I had wanted to continue to take part in the leadership. For another, the lack of intellectual challenge I felt in this kind of party work played a great role in my decision. The party conferences, all that applause, the negotiating . . . Or introducing the manifesto to the country. That may be necessary, but it wasn't my thing. You drive somewhere quickly by car, you're forced to say the same thing over and over again wherever you are, and then you drive back again.

It's impersonal and not down to earth enough. Besides, you have to present a lot of things in a very, very simplified form if you want to reach a lot of people.

Sure, politics can make quite a few things happen, but in the end it always remains tied to the ideas of the majority of the population and what they want for their lives, and that limits quite radically the forms it can take.

That became clear during the changeover. Last but not least, it is, of course, always a question of how much self-alienation you are capable of. I mean alienation from direct human contacts and involvement in institutionalization — in a party apparatus.

I didn't want to do that, and I found that now that I had experienced the really exciting time, I just wanted to turn back to the more down-to-earth things in life. . . .

ANNOTATIONS

CHAPTER ONE

I think it comes from keeping everything bottled up inside and never opening your mouth . . .

Page 4: *Real "fellow travelers."* The word emphasized here is *Mitläufer*. Immediately after the Second World War, it came to describe those who never exercised power in Nazi Germany but who passively supported the regime and turned a blind eye to its atrocities. In the German Democratic Republic (GDR), it was similarly used to characterize passive supporters of the regime.

Page 5: *My father . . . taught physical education at the vocational school.* The GDR organized its system of education around "general polytechnical schools," encompassing ten grades and equipping graduates with the equivalent of an American high-school education. Most students in the GDR completed the polytechnical school before moving into an apprenticeship in the line of work in which they would make their career. Klara indicates that her father worked at a *Berufsschule*, a "vocational school" that students might enter upon graduation from a polytechnical school for additional years of training tied to an apprenticeship (*Lehrstelle*) in a particular trade. Students who followed this track could also hope to take the *Abitur* (the comprehensive examinations taken at the end of one's secondary education, akin to A-levels in England, that certify competence in several subject areas and that are required for entrance to university) at the conclusion of the *Berufsschule*. Students might thereby obtain certification in a particular trade as well as verification of their readiness to pursue higher technical or university study.

Page 5: *We were all in the Pioneers.* The Pioneer organization was a state-sponsored youth group for those between the ages of six and thirteen. It consisted of two tiers, the *Jungpioniere* (Young Pioneers) for children in grades one to three and the *Thälmann-pioniere* (Thälmann Pioneers) for grades four through seven. It sought to structure the leisure activities of these young people in order to prepare them for membership in the ruling party and to shape them into proper citizens of the socialist state.

Page 5: *We were all in the FDJ. But my older brothers and sisters didn't take part in the initiation.* The *Freie Deutsche Jugend* (Free German Youth or FDJ) recruited young people from the ages of fourteen to twenty-five. Like the Pioneers, it was primarily concerned with the political socialization and moral formation of a socialist citizenry. It also played a key role in recruiting and educating the rising generation of leadership for the ruling party. The *Jugendweihe* (literally, "youth initiation") to which Klara refers served as a rite-of-passage ceremony that marked a youth's entrance into the FDJ. It was conceived as a replacement for the Christian practice of confirmation and as a ceremony that would attach young people to the ideals of the socialist state. Participation in the FDJ was the gateway to every kind of political career in the GDR, and usually a prerequisite of the best educational opportunities as well. It was from the ranks of the FDJ that fresh leadership for the SED was recruited. The FDJ also controlled the resort areas for young people, as well as recreational and entertainment facilities in the GDR.

Page 6: *"Klara does not take a clear stand on issues of class."* The official ideology of the German Democratic Republic represented its socialist order as the means by which the class divisions endemic to capitalist society would be overcome and a classless or fully just society finally achieved. This reference to Klara's apparent lack of commitment to the East German regime and its defining purposes implies a deficit of moral character, an evaluation that would likely preclude access to higher education.

Page 6: *I told my mother I was going to the town of D. to see a girlfriend.* The convention of only using initials for small towns has been used in German literature at least since the eighteenth century. It emphasizes the fact that the particulars of the town have no relevance to the account in which it figures.

Page 6: *Like* Kabale und Liebe *and so on.* Friedrich von Schiller's 1784 drama *Kabale und Liebe* (English title: *Love and Intrigue*) is an example of the eighteenth-century, pre-romantic literary movement in Germany known as *Sturm und Drang* (Storm and Stress). The play concerns the tragic love and socially problematic relationship between a musician's daughter and a young aristocrat.

Page 7: *dressed completely in black, which was pure provocation in those days . . .* In 1982, a party official publicly denounced the dissemination of "pessimistic views about our life and future" by East German cultural and intellectual figures, railing at the same time against the taste displayed by some for black and gray as the colors best suited to the reality of life in the GDR.

Page 7: *Nevertheless, after that the cops or the Stasi . . .* The dreaded "Stasi" were the secret police of the GDR. The word derives from *Staats-*

sicherheitsdienst (State Security Service); it is the vernacular abbreviation by which agents of the Ministry for State Security came to be called. The Ministry employed some ninety thousand agents, who were primarily concerned with the political policing of East Germany's citizenry in the name of defending the state against subversion and ideological corruption. Agents of the Ministry, however, also engaged in political and industrial espionage abroad.

Page 7: *When the entire troupe went off to N. for the Whitsun holiday* . . . The Whitsun or Pentecost holiday is celebrated seven weeks after Easter. In many of the countries of Northern Europe it remains a national holiday that falls on the Monday (or Whitmonday) following the Sunday of Pentecost. Even in the GDR, a regime with an ideological commitment to atheism, traditional holidays and celebrations, most of them originally religious in nature, continued to be observed.

Page 8: *I did not get an apprenticeship as an interior decorator because I had my diploma.* Klara alludes to the fact that her formal education had culminated in receipt of the *Abitur*, a diploma awarded only after successful completion of additional education beyond the mandatory ten years and a set of examinations meant to establish a student's fitness for university study. She is thus overqualified for an apprenticeship as a *Dekorateurin*. See also the note on "the vocational school" at page 159, above.

Page 8: *'Our' Karl and 'our' Rosa were taken to their graves, . . . the usual obligatory demonstration.* Karl Liebknecht (1871–1919) and Rosa Luxemburg (1871–1919) were left-wing intellectuals and political activists who organized the Communist Party of Germany in 1918. Both were killed on the night of 15 January 1919, while leading a failed uprising of proletarian revolutionaries that sought to imitate in Germany the achievement of Lenin in Russia. They were memorialized in the GDR as martyrs to the cause of international communism. The demonstration Klara mentions took the form of a march to the gravesites of Luxemburg and Liebknecht, an annual event staged on the Sunday before the anniversary of their deaths.

Page 9: *when the Russians marched into Afghanistan* . . . In December of 1979, the Soviet Union sent troops into Afghanistan to shore up a pro-Soviet government beset by a fundamentalist Muslim insurgency. The invasion rekindled tensions between the Western allies and Eastern-bloc nations, which had improved significantly during the détente of the 1970s.

Page 9: *to warble songs from the Zupfgeigenhansl.* This word, based on an obsolete Germanic word for the guitar (*Zupfgeige*, literally "plucked violin"), is the playful title of a famous book of folksongs first compiled in 1909 for the *Wandervögel*, the nature-loving and guitar-strumming youth who wandered the German countryside in one of the early youth movements protesting modern, bourgeois life. The *Wandervögel* typically looked back to a romanticized, preindustrial Germany for inspiration.

Page 9: *The problem with the West ... when the packages came at Christmas.* To stem a mass migration to the West, East German officials began erecting the Berlin Wall on 13 August 1961. Thereafter, consumer goods that were not available or were in short supply in East Germany often arrived as Christmas gifts from friends and relatives in the West.

Page 9: *Like signing the Biermann petition.* In 1965, the GDR officially banned public performances by Wolf Biermann of his popular and politically charged ballads. In 1976, he was allowed to give his first performance in eleven years and to travel to West Germany to take part in a concert tour. But once Biermann was in West Germany, officials abruptly announced that he would no longer be allowed to reside in the GDR. A dozen of East Germany's best-known literary figures sent an open letter to the party leadership protesting the action. Copies of the letter circulated widely and were eventually signed by some of the nation's most distinguished artists and intellectuals, all of whom were subsequently disciplined for protesting Biermann's expatriation. See also the introduction (page xiii).

Page 9: *the founding of "Solidarity."* In September of 1980, a coalition of shipyard workers organized an independent labor union to press their demands with the Soviet-backed government of Poland. They named their organization *Solidariność* (Solidarity). By 1981, the political movement spawned by Solidarity claimed over ten million members, posing a formidable opposition to the communist regime. In response, Polish officials outlawed the labor union and imposed martial law. This crisis led the neighboring GDR to impose restrictions on travel to Poland, something it had traditionally encouraged in order to promote an eastward orientation through increased contacts between its citizens and those of Poland and Czechoslovakia.

Page 10: *non-incriminating coffee filters ... with stencils cut into raw potatoes.* Coffee filters and potatoes could be easily obtained almost anywhere and without drawing the notice of the authorities, while having paper flyers professionally printed would necessarily have meant running the risk of being turned in to the Stasi.

Page 10: *in the shopping arcade on the Alexanderplatz ...* The Alexanderplatz, or "Alex" as it is commonly known, is a broad plaza at the center of Berlin. It served as the central square and commercial heart of the socialist capital (boasting the largest and best-stocked department store in the entire GDR), as well as a showcase of the modernist movement in architecture with which officials sought to identify their metropolis in the 1960s.

Page 10: *a shirt and "Präsent 20" pants . . . dressing for Carnival.* Klara names a brand of pants that were made and sold only in the GDR. The originally Catholic festival that Germans call *Fasching* (Carnival) is an annual celebration like Mardi Gras, which culminates in masquerade parties and parades of elaborately costumed revelers during the week prior to the beginning of Lent.

Page 10: *We met up again at the Hackescher Markt.* The *Hackescher Markt,* named after the officer appointed by Friedrich the Great to oversee the expansion of Berlin in the 1750s, represents an important intersection that lies near the center of Berlin. The *Linienstrasse* is one of the major streets running through this part of the city.

Page 10: *but they had bought his freedom.* In 1963, the West German government initiated a practice of paying the GDR in order to secure the release of East Germans imprisoned for political reasons. From 1964 to 1990, the Federal Republic of Germany (FRG) paid over $2 billion in exchange for the release to the West of some thirty-three thousand prisoners, as well as about two hundred thousand others, mostly relatives of the prisoners.

Page 11: *to hang an accusation of "illegal emigration" on them and us . . .* In criminalizing emigration, the East German regime coined the word *Republikflucht,* the term Klara uses here, which literally rendered is "flight from the [German Democratic] Republic."

Page 11: *That was seen as "subversive agitation." Yet most people weren't "dissidents" at all, in the true sense of the word.* Klara again employs official, legal terminology. In the first case, she says *staatsfeindliche Hetze,* the name given by the East German regime to political offenses like circulating cultural products from the West. In the second instance, the term is *Oppositionelle,* denoting an assertive and confirmed opposition to the political order of the GDR.

Page 13: *That very evening he took us to the Kurfürstendamm . . .* The *Kurfürstendamm* is a major avenue that runs through the western quarter of Berlin. Lined with ritzy shops, boutiques, and galleries, and crowded with bars and cafes that spill out onto the sidewalk, the "Ku'damm" was the best-known commercial strip of West Berlin. As such, it served as a kind of ideological prop, symbolizing for many the dazzle, glitz, and energy of Western capitalism as opposed to the drabness of East Berlin.

Page 13: *Even when we'd go to a concert at the Quasimodo . . .* Famous for its live jazz and the cosmopolitan variety of the musicians it regularly features, the Quasimodo is one of the best-known nightclubs in West Berlin.

Page 13: *we traveled to Italy while living on aid from the state.* By "aid from the state"(*Stütze*), Klara means the social insurance for the unemployed paid out by the West German government. The social-welfare system erected by the FRG in the 1950s and 60s continues to be one of the most extensive and generous in the industrialized world.

Page 14: *about the "hardship case"* . . . The word translated here as "hardship case" (*Sozialfall*) designates a legal category that is typically applied to individuals who have some disability or have suffered misfortune, and who therefore seek special consideration in their application for a public benefit.

Page 15: *how long they'd had to save for their Trabi* . . . The Trabant (or "Trabi") was the cheaper of the two makes of East German automobiles that citizens of the GDR could purchase. It had a tiny, box-like body made of a type of plastic, and a smoky two-stroke engine.

Page 15: *They stood in long lines in front of the banks* . . . After the opening of the Berlin Wall on 9 November 1989, East Germans crossing into West Germany received "welcome money" (*Begrüßungsgeld*) from the West German government to enable them to purchase goods and services in the West. East Germans were eligible for at least one hundred marks each. However, the flood of people who crossed into West Berlin immediately after the Wall was opened faced standing in long lines in cold weather to obtain their money.

Page 17: *as the Turks are in the West.* Over seven million foreign residents, most of them foreign workers or their dependents, reside in Germany. The largest number (about two million) come from Turkey. In the major cities of West Germany, foreign workers typically make up a conspicuous majority of those employed in the jobs deemed least desirable. In the 1960s, West Germany actively recruited Turks as "guest workers" to cope with a labor shortage. Some residents are now third-generation, German-born Turks, who speak fluent German and have little thought of leaving Germany for Turkey. However, because German identity has traditionally been tightly linked to bloodline, rather than to behavior or even citizenship, Turks have often found themselves limited in employment and other opportunities by their ethnicity.

Page 17: *Never mind about the Two-Thirds World.* The expression "Two-Thirds World" is equivalent to the term "Third World," but it underscores the percentage of the world population that lives outside the borders of the developed West. It is widely used in Europe, especially among those concerned with environmental and social causes.

CHAPTER TWO

So much of the really good life was lost to us . . .

Page 18: *and of course I was a member of the Pioneer organization.* See the note on "the Pioneers" for chapter 1, page 159, above.

Page 18: *the "antifascist protective barrier."* East German authorities explained their building of a wall along the line dividing the Soviet-controlled sector of Berlin from those under the supervision of the western allies as a defensive measure against threats from the capitalist West. Official propaganda thus labeled the Berlin Wall, a structure erected in 1961 to keep East Germans from fleeing the GDR, as the "antifascist protective barrier."

Page 18: *because the town of M. took heavy bombing.* On the convention of referring to towns only by their first initial, see the note concerning "the town of D." for chapter 1, page 160, above.

Page 18: *Every year on the "Day of the National People's Army,"* . . . The military of the GDR, which included ground, naval, and air forces, was known officially as the "National People's Army" (*Nationale Volksarmee*). Commemorating its founding on 1 March 1956, an annual "Day of the National People's Army" was celebrated each year on that date. Once conscription was introduced in 1962, every male between the ages of eighteen and twenty-six became subject to an eighteen-month service requirement.

Page 19: *About all those marksmen at the Wall.* Specially trained armed guards patrolled the Berlin Wall with orders to "shoot on sight" anyone attempting to breach it (the notorious *Schießbefehl*). Petra alludes here to the fact that most East Germans learned only after the collapse of the GDR of the hundreds of individuals shot while trying to escape during the almost thirty years of the Wall's existence. In its final form, the Wall was actually a series of barriers over a width of about a hundred yards that included anti-vehicle trenches, mines, watch towers, and a lighted "death strip" providing guards with a clear field of fire at anyone trying to scale the final obstacle, a fifteen-foot concrete structure that most people identified as the Wall.

Page 19: *the "Felix Dzierzynski" watch regiment.* An elite guard unit of around seven thousand men named after the Polish-born founder of the Cheka, the original secret police organization in Soviet Russia. This regiment was controlled by the Ministry for State Security. It functioned as the military arm of the Stasi, suppressing unrest or protecting government buildings and party leaders. It was likewise considered the most politically reliable security force in the GDR.

Page 19: *Although where he was posted, in Wandlitz* . . . The party leadership of the GDR maintained a residential compound in Wandlitz, a for-

ested suburb of Berlin, where SED officials lived in comparative luxury, secluded from the scrutiny of their countrymen and guarded by
members of the Felix Dzierzynski watch regiment.

Page 19: *Of course I joined the FDJ.* See the note on "the FDJ" for chapter 1,
page 160, above.

Page 19: *the World Festival of Youth in Berlin* . . . A "World Festival of Youth
and Students" has been staged every few years since 1947. In 1973,
the tenth such festival was held in East Berlin with over twenty-five
thousand participants from 140 countries, including members of
communist youth organizations based in Western Europe and in developing countries like Angola. This international collection of participants afforded young people from the GDR the exhilarating
experience of contact and conversation with peers from around the
world. The organization responsible for these events was founded in
1945 as a broad-based movement aiming to unite progressive youth
groups from across the globe in "the struggle against imperialism
and war." It fell under the control of Soviet-aligned communist parties during the Cold War, however, which resulted in declining participation by citizens from Western nations.

Page 20: *where our Politburo and foreign guests were standing* . . . The Politburo was the highest policy-implementing and decision-making
body of East Germany's ruling party — the Socialist Unity Party
(SED). It consisted of the top officials in the party together with
leading officials from the principal ministries, mass organizations,
and other centers of power within the regime. The Politburo reported on its weekly meetings to the Central Committee, the execu-
tive organ of the SED composed of about 165 party officials charged
with responsibility for carrying out the directives of party congresses.
The General Secretary was the highest ranking official in the SED,
presiding over both the Central Committee and the Politburo. After
1960, the General Secretary also served as head of state.

Page 20: *To march with the youth of our country, past Erich Honecker* . . . Born
in 1912 to a working-class family, Erich Honecker joined the Communist Party of Germany at the age of seventeen. From 1946 to
1955, he headed up the FDJ. In 1961, it fell to Honecker as chief of
East Germany's security apparatus to direct construction of the Berlin Wall. Later, he became the leader (or General Secretary) of the
ruling Socialist Unity Party and the official head of state, positions he
held until shortly before the collapse of the GDR in 1989.

Page 20: *I went to the FDJ Youth College.* The FDJ located its lavish *Jugendhochschule* or youth college in a forested enclave next to the idyllic
lake *Bogensee*, where Nazi propaganda minister Goebbels once built a
grand *Landhaus* (country house). The campus included elegant cul-

tural and dining halls and a vast sports complex, as well as dormitories, lecture halls, and extensive facilities for the study of foreign languages. The FDJ's *Jugendhochschule* was primarily used for leadership recruitment and training. Those selected for a career within the leadership structure or cadre system of the SED would normally begin an extensive program of training and political formation upon graduating from a secondary institution. This education aimed at preparing students for entrance into the state and party apparatus.

Page 20: *Our professors came from the Party University* . . . The Party University, officially known as the "Party University 'Karl Marx' for the Central Committee of the SED" (*Parteihochschule "Karl Marx" beim ZK der SED*), was established in the Soviet occupation zone in 1946. With the founding of the German Democratic Republic in 1949, it became the party's premier institution of higher education, standing atop a complex of schools spread across the fifteen regions of the GDR to train and to mold, in particular, the leadership of the governing SED. It offered diplomas in Marxist-Leninist social science (*Gesellschaftswissenschaften*) that were considered the equivalent of the highest degrees bestowed by the regular universities and colleges of the GDR. It therefore played a key role in educating the instructors and researchers who filled up the various regionally based party schools as well as the faculty of the FDJ Youth College.

Page 20: *At that time, the "FDJ-Initiative Berlin" was taking place.* In pursuit of its goal to shape East Germany's youth into an "active helper and reserve force" of the SED, the FDJ sponsored numerous training, paramilitary, and leisure activities. The "Berlin Initiative" was a program instituted by the FDJ in 1976 that brought some twenty thousand adolescent "delegates" from across the GDR to Berlin each summer, where they labored together with young Berliners as construction workers to aid in rebuilding the national capital. Many came only for the summer months, but others for periods of up to two years. The program thus contributed to labor shortages in some regions of East Germany, making it a less than popular enterprise among many living outside Berlin.

Page 21: *in the same breath as the SED* . . . The acronym SED stands for *Sozialistiche Einheitspartei Deutschlands,* or Socialist Unity Party of Germany. Established in 1946 at the behest of the Soviets in the occupied territory that became East Germany, it merged members of the Communist Party (KP) and the Social Democratic Party (SPD). With the founding of the GDR in 1949, it functioned as its ruling political body.

Page 23: *the "Black Channel" with Karl Eduard von Schnitzler* . . . Petra recalls an East German television program that based its reports on stories and footage appropriated from Western media to score ideological points against the West. Its clumsy manipulation of Western sources, and the implicitly condescending stance it took towards its audience, made it increasingly unpopular.

Page 26: *a "reclamation plan" had to be worked out for each person.* The official East German term, used here, was *Rückgewinnungskonzeption* (literally, a "conception of [how the state might succeed at] winning back" the applicant seeking to emigrate).

Page 28: *That was in spring 1988, eighteen months before the changeover.* The word Germans typically use to refer to the demise of the GDR is *Wende.* For East Germans, it names an irreversible "changeover" on the historical path that led to political dissolution and, finally, unification with West Germany. However, the word can also convey the idea of a 180° turn or "turnaround," a connotation often at the fore when employed by West Germans. Upon taking charge of the GDR in late 1989, the last man to hold the combined offices of General Secretary and head of state, Egon Krenz, also used this word to signal that a new direction would guide a now reform-minded SED.

Page 28: *a travel law . . . passed shortly before the opening of the border.* Desperate to placate widespread demands for complete freedom of movement, beleaguered SED officials announced new regulations on 6 November 1989 to govern the travel of GDR citizens. The effort failed, largely because rising expectations had already outpaced the incomplete reforms. The new provisions were rejected the following day by a newly assertive *Volkskammer* (People's Congress). However, the proposal represented a significant liberalization of restrictions that had historically confined foreign travel by East Germans to fellow Soviet-bloc states. See also the introduction (page xx), and the note on the "People's Congress" for chapter 3, page 171, below.

Page 28: *When Egon Krenz was elected* . . . The crisis that eventuated in the collapse of the GDR precipitated the resignation of longtime General Secretary and head of state Erich Honecker on 18 October 1989. The governing body of the SED chose Egon Krenz as his successor, but Krenz proved unable to convince a skeptical public that he could be an agent of reform, or to quell the popular revolt underway. On 3 December, just six weeks after his appointment, Krenz resigned from all party and state offices.

Page 28: *After the currency union* . . . At midnight on 30 June 1990, a few months after parliamentary elections in East Germany established an overwhelming consensus for unification with the Federal Republic of Germany, the West German mark became the legal tender of East Germany as well. The move initiated the process of formal unification completed later that year.

Page 28: *in the ABM . . .* This acronym refers to *Arbeitsbeschaffungsmaßnahmen,* or "job-creation measures." These "measures" were primarily government-created jobs meant to ease the transition of former citizens of the GDR into the West German economy.

Page 28: *those revelations about the privileges held by the party leadership . . .* When the material perks enjoyed by party leaders, cloistered in their official residences at Wandlitz, first came to public attention, these revelations fueled growing resentment of the SED-regime, if not also public enthusiasm for unification. What came to light, however, was a set of relatively modest benefits — fully stocked food stores for the exclusive use of residents in a well-tended and well-guarded enclave of houses that were spacious by East German standards. See also the note on "Wandlitz" at pages 165–66, above.

Page 29: *My daughter had her coming-of-age ceremony this year.* On the secular "youth initiation" ceremony, or *Jugendweihe,* instituted by officials in 1954 as an alternative to religious confirmation (Protestant), or first communion (Catholic), see the note to chapter 1, page 160, above.

CHAPTER THREE

You should know I won't be blackmailed . . .

Page 31: *but on Sunday March 6, in K. . . .* On the convention of referring to towns only by their first initial, see the note on "the town of D." for chapter 1, page 160, above.

Page 31: *Because these "recruitment teams" would come . . .* The government of East Germany began its drive to collectivize agriculture in 1952. By the early 1960s, approximately ninety percent of its arable land had been organized into some type of collective farm. To promote collectivization, officials undertook a massive campaign to persuade private farmers to relinquish their property to the collectives. They also employed political pressure and threats of coercion to make reluctant farmers comply. So-called "recruitment teams" (*Werbetrupps*) visited farming villages across the GDR, issuing threats of imprisonment in some cases to win compliance.

Page 32: *and it's the job of the grandchild or the son-in-law to ask . . .* The pastor here alludes to the fact that the State Security Service or "Stasi" maintained an elaborate network of informants and collaborators called IM's or *inoffizielle Mitarbeiter* ("unofficial co-workers," hereafter abbreviated as UC), which enabled it to compile files documenting aspects of the private lives and activities of almost two-thirds of the adult population of the GDR. See also the note on "the Stasi" for chapter 1, pages 160–61, above.

Page 32: *And when the migrations started in the summer* . . . Thousands of East Germans took advantage of the GDR's open border with Hungary, a fellow Soviet-bloc nation, to make their way to West Germany, after a liberalizing government in Budapest opened Hungary's western border in May, 1989. From Hungary, visiting East Germans sought to enter neighboring Austria and, from there, the Federal Republic of Germany, where they were guaranteed citizenship. See also the introduction (pages xvi–xvii).

Page 33: *as well as several from the block parties* . . . Four minor or "alliance parties," referred to collectively as the *Blockparteien* (block parties), functioned as junior partners to East Germany's ruling Socialist Unity Party (SED). These four parties — an East German version of the Christian Democratic Union (CDU); the Liberal Democratic Party of Germany (LDPD); the Democratic Peasants' Party of Germany (DBD); and the National Democratic Party of Germany (NDPD) — provided the GDR with the appearance of a multi-party system of government and assisted the SED in bringing certain sectors of society under its influence. In practice, however, the "block parties" adhered unswervingly to the dictates of the SED. See the note on "the SED" for chapter 2, page 167, above.

Page 33: *On October 7, I watched a bit of the military parade on TV.* The German Democratic Republic came formally into existence on 7 October 1949. Its founding was commemorated annually on 7 October, usually with an ostentatious parade of military weaponry and goose-stepping soldiers. The demonstrations against the government that galvanized the popular uprising that eventually toppled East Germany's communist regime began in Leipzig on 25 September 1989. On 7 October, thousands of demonstrators massed in Berlin, where they confronted some sixteen thousand police deployed to safeguard the celebration of the GDR's fortieth anniversary. The confrontation turned violent when police tried to beat back the protestors with their billy clubs; hundreds were taken into custody.

Page 33: *we had a son in the "People's Army"* . . . For a note on the "People's Army," see chapter 2, page 165, above.

Page 33: *Will it happen like it did in China?* The allusion here is to pro-democracy demonstrations by university students at Tiananmen Square that began in April 1989. Those demonstrations were eventually put down by force, when the Chinese military was called in on 4 June to break up the event. Hundreds of protesters were killed.

Page 34: *we didn't vote for the "National Front" candidates!* Created at the urging of the Soviet Union as political parties were being re-established in postwar Germany, the National Front functioned originally as an umbrella structure to facilitate the common "anti-fascist" goals of the different parties and mass organizations being put together. In the GDR, it became a means by which the ruling SED coordinated the activities of the other "alliance parties" and controlled the election of representatives to the national congress. See the note on "the block parties" at page 170, above; see also the note on the "People's Congress" immediately below.

Page 34: *the elections for the so-called People's Congress.* The *Volkskammer* (People's Congress) was a unicameral national legislature of elected officials charged by the constitution with lawmaking in the GDR. In theory, it was the highest organ of the government, but in practice the SED controlled the *Volkskammer* and directed every aspect of the regime. Elections in the GDR were tightly orchestrated events in which voters were presented with a single slate of candidates for their approval, insuring always an absolute majority for the SED. See the note on the "National Front" immediately above.

Page 34: *"All right, we'll become candidates for the CDU . . . we'll try for the SPD."* The Christian Democratic Union (CDU) and the Social Democratic Party of Germany (SPD) are the two largest parties in the Federal Republic of Germany and have historically dominated its parliamentary system. Since its founding in 1949, governing coalitions in the Federal Republic have always coalesced around either the right-of-center CDU or the left-of-center SPD. In East German parliamentary elections that were convened on 18 March 1990 to decide the future course of the nation, the CDU (which favored unification as soon as possible) and the SPD (which did not) sponsored candidates who had no formal party affiliation in regions where they did not have sufficient membership to fill out their candidate lists.

Page 34: *Unification Day, which was October 3, 1990 . . .* 3 October, the date on which Germany officially commemorates unification, marks the day on which East Germans formally became citizens of the FRG.

Page 35: *The band struck up "Einigkeit und Recht und Freiheit."* These words — "unity and right and freedom" — make up the first line of the third stanza of the traditional German national anthem, or *Deutschlandlied*. The lyrics, composed in 1841 by Hoffmann von Fallersleben under the title "Das Lied der Deutschen" and set to the music of Haydn's "Kaiser-Quartet," became Germany's official anthem in 1922. The *Deutschlandlied* was banned in 1945 because the words of the first stanza ("Deutschland, Deutschland über alles . . .") had come to be identified with the Nazi philosophy of conquest. However, the third stanza was rehabilitated in 1952 as the text for a version of the *Deutschlandlied* adopted by West Germany as its national anthem. The GDR, on the other hand, made no official use of the "Deutschlandlied" but commissioned a completely original composition — "Auferstanden aus Ruinen" — for its anthem.

Page 36: *I was still employed in B. around June 17, 1953.* This date was identified in East German history with the "June Uprising," a strike by Berlin construction workers against an increase in "work quotas" that led to an outbreak of protests nationwide. It came to symbolize for many the initial popular revolt against a Soviet-backed political order in Eastern Europe. The strike by workers in Berlin that began on 16 June was violently quashed the following day with the help of Soviet tanks and troops. Demonstrations outside the capital, however, continued well into July. See also the introduction (pages x–xi).

Page 36: *Very set against the "Junge Gemeinde"* . . . Germany's Lutheran and Reformed churches use the term *Junge Gemeinde* (literally, "youth community") to designate their youth programs. Beginning in the early 1950s, SED officials and operatives began actively to discourage participation in church-based youth groups, threatening in particular to exclude participants from the best educational opportunities. See the note on "the upper high school" on this page, below.

Page 38: *"Only we* tread *our hens," as the proverb goes.* The German saying that the pastor here recites is *Unsere Hühner treten wir alleine* (literally, "we tread our hens by ourselves"). The German verb *treten* (like its English cognate "to tread") can mean "to copulate," when applied to roosters. The pastor's meaning here is, we won't give up our girls to the boys from the next village without a fight.

Page 38: *they didn't get to go to the upper high school* . . . At the end of the eighth grade, students judged capable of the highest level of education might be invited to attend an "upper high school" (*Erweiterte Oberschule*), which encompassed grades 9 through 12 and led to the *Abitur,* or comprehensive end-of-school examinations, by which fitness for university study was assessed. As the pastor here notes, however, political considerations also factored into the decision to place students on this educational track. See also the note on "the vocational school" for chapter 1, page 159, above.

Page 39: *Primarily about the "youth initiation."* For an explanation of *Jugendweihe* (youth initiation), see chapter 1, page 160, above.

Page 42: *But he always paid his church taxes* . . . As in many other northern European nations, "church taxes" have been levied upon churchgoers in Germany since the nineteenth century. These taxes have traditionally been collected by the state, which then turns them over to the relevant church authorities. The government of the GDR, however, refused to assist East German churches in collecting these taxes, making it necessary for each church to collect them directly.

Page 44: *a stalwart PDS man* . . . The PDS or Party of Democratic Socialism (*Partei des demokratischen Sozialismus*) is a regional political party in eastern Germany that was formed after unification out of remnants of the SED. It thus represents the extreme left of Germany's contemporary political spectrum and champions a socialist politics that is often at odds with the liberal-democratic order of the Federal Republic.

Page 44: *the so-called* Sixth Book of Moses, *which you can use to work magic.* The *Sixth Book of Moses* is a record of magical knowledge supposedly revealed to Moses on Mount Sinai. It was allegedly by means of this knowledge that Moses obtained the power to command spirits and thereby to perform his miracles. The text was actually compiled by Johann Scheibel from medieval occult sources and first published in 1849.

Page 45: *Since the changeover.* On the term "changeover" (*Wende*), see the note for chapter 2, page 168, above.

CHAPTER FOUR

They even accuse me of having planned murders . . .

Page 46: *the Ministry for State Security* . . . Officially designated the *Ministerium für Staatssicherheit,* this agency housed the army of secret police known as "the Stasi." It became one of the key institutions in the government of the GDR. See the note on "the Stasi" for chapter 1, pages 160–61, above.

Page 46: *an unofficial co-worker, or UC.* On so-called *Inoffizielle Mitarbeiter,* or "unofficial co-workers," see the note on "the job of the grandchild" for chapter 3, page 169, above.

Page 47: *True, my father was also in the Party* . . . The reference here is to the Socialist Unity Party of Germany (SED), the organization that governed the GDR. It was established shortly after the Second World War in Soviet-controlled East Germany, paving the way for the founding of the GDR in October, 1949. See the note on "the SED" for chapter 2, page 167, above.

Page 48: *I was mired in "bloc" thought patterns.* The Major alludes to the political and ideological competition of the Soviet-led "East bloc" nations with the American-led "West bloc."

Page 48: *what was going on in Czechoslovakia* . . . Early in 1968, officials in the Socialist Republic of Czechoslovakia announced a package of political and economic reforms, kindling an enthusiasm for liberalization and democratization that soon threatened the communist regime's autocratic control. The episode came to be called "Prague Spring" in the Western press. On 21 August, Soviet tanks rolled into Prague as several hundred thousand Warsaw Pact troops marched across the Czech border to reassert Soviet control over Czechoslovakia. Thousands of East German soldiers took part in this invasion. See also the introduction (page xii).

Page 48: *The majority were always "misguided" or "fellow travelers."* The Major seems to attach a positive valence here to "fellow travelers," who were by this reckoning at least implicitly committed to the cause of universal justice that the state supposedly embodied. For a discussion of the usual meaning of the term "fellow traveler," see the note at chapter 1, page 159, above.

Page 51: *1953 must have been of great importance to him* ... On the 1953 uprising, see the note on "June 17, 1953" for chapter 3, page 172, above.

Page 52: *the Federal Intelligence Service* ... The BND (*Bundesnachrichtendienst*) or Federal Intelligence Service was formally created in 1956. Today it represents the foreign intelligence agency of a newly united Germany. During the Cold War, it was the West German counterpart to the Stasi or East German State Security Service.

Page 53: *Protection of Information.* The German term here is *Geheimnisschutz,* a shorthand reference to what was called the *Arbeitsgruppe Geheimnisschutz* (literally, "Working Group for the Protection of Secrets"), which was a division of the Ministry for State Security.

Page 54: *the peace movement "Swords to Ploughshares."* In the early 1980s, an autonomous peace movement sprang up in the GDR, taking its name from the biblical image of "swords [being hammered] into ploughshares" (Isaiah 2:4). Earlier the Soviet Union had presented the United Nations with a piece of sculpture based on the theme that inspired the adoption of these words. See also the introduction (page xiv).

Page 55: *the Politburo of the SED.* See the note on the "Politburo" for chapter 2, page 166, above.

Page 55: *Intershops* ... These hard-currency stores sold Western goods, not otherwise available in the GDR, for West German marks. Access was initially limited to Western visitors and select loyalists of the regime, but as the need for Western currency grew, it became possible for anyone who had money from the West (usually obtained from West German relatives) to gain access to the Intershops. East German shoppers found particularly enticing the exotic collection of aromas emanating from the soaps, cosmetics, and other Western goods made to stimulate an olfactory response.

Page 56: *the big demonstration in Berlin on November 4, 1989.* The huge rally in Berlin on 4 November at the Alexanderplatz brought together half a million protesters, who listened to a host of East German intellectuals, writers, and artists level criticisms at the regime and call for more reforms, particularly in the area of freedom to travel. It was the largest in a succession of mass demonstrations that had begun in Leipzig about a month earlier. See also the introduction (page xx).

Page 57: *The point of departure at that time was Popieluszko.* In late 1984, the Catholic priest Jerzy Popieluszko, who had become a leading voice in the resistance movement to Poland's communist regime, was brutally murdered by members of the Polish secret police. The event made a martyr of Father Popielusko and galvanized popular support in Poland for the Church as a central institution of opposition in the struggle against communist rule.

Page 59: *I think General Mielke was very short-sighted* . . . Erich Mielke presided over the Ministry for State Security for almost all of its history. Assuming control in 1957, he directed the Ministry until 1989. In 1976, he became a full member of the politburo, a development that symbolized the enhanced role and influence of the state security establishment in the East Germany of Erich Honecker. Demonstrators stormed the Ministry in early 1990, securing for public scrutiny the files that Stasi agents had compiled on six million East German citizens and bringing to light the brutally inhumane and often self-interested nature of the activities that Mielke directed. The Major seems to believe that Mielke's administration of State Security was "short-sighted" (though not necessarily morally deficient) in that its activities tended to cultivate public contempt for the Ministry. See also the note on "the job of the grandchild" for chapter 3, page 169, above.

CHAPTER FIVE

I never cared much for work just for the sake of work . . .

Page 60: *the so-called "youth initiation"* . . . See the note on "the initiation" for chapter 1, page 160, above.

Page 60: *I went to the upper high school* . . . On the "upper high school" (*Erweiterte Oberschule*), see the note for chapter 3, page 172, above.

Page 60: *I left the FDJ* . . . See the note on "the FDJ" for chapter 1, page 160, above.

Page 60: *military exercises and marksmanship classes* . . . In 1978 the GDR introduced formal military education and training into the school curriculum for all ninth and tenth graders. In 1982 a new Military Service Law expanded training programs and tightened service requirements. Classes emphasized civil defense, the duties of soldiers, the nature of possible conflicts, and the uses of different weapons and equipment. At the end of tenth grade, students participated in field exercises staged by the National People's Army or NPA (see the note on the "People's Army" for chapter 2, page 165, above). These developments spawned a growing critique of and protest against the "militarization" of East German society by religious leaders and officials in the church, which helped in turn to generate an independent peace movement in the GDR. See also the note on "Swords into Ploughshares" for chapter 4, page 174, above.

Page 60: *"You will not take the final exams here."* Although enrolled in the *Erweiterte Oberschule,* Hartmut reports that he was not allowed to complete his course of study by taking the *Abitur* or comprehensive "final exams" because of his refusal to participate in military training or do military service.

Page 61: *the paternoster elevator* ... This variety of old-fashioned elevator was widely used in continental Europe throughout the first half of the twentieth century. It was constructed as a continuous loop that required riders to step into an open compartment as it passed by. It is believed that the name "pasternoster" refers to the prayers uttered by riders before stepping into a moving compartment.

Page 62: *the Stasi guy* ... See the note on "the Stasi" for chapter 1, pages 160–61, above.

Page 64: *"We know that in everything God works for good with those who love him."* The verse is found in Romans 8:28.

Page 66: *Rolf Henrich's book* ... See the note of "Henrich" for chapter 7, page 182, below.

Page 66: *New Forum was founded* ... On 9 September 1989, some thirty activists gathered at the home of a prominent dissident to consider organizing an independent political movement. These discussions led to the creation of New Forum, an association of citizens seeking to foster public dialogue about the problems and future of East Germany that quickly evolved into a nationwide collection of activists opposed to the SED regime. New Forum defined itself, however, as simply an umbrella organization for bringing together all those protesting the existing government in order to facilitate constructive dialogue about the future of the state. At its height, it could claim some two hundred thousand supporters. See also the introduction (pages xvii–xviii).

Page 67: *the so-called "Block-Flute-CDU" this SED splinter group* ... The word *Blockflöten-CDU* puns on the fact that the CDU in East Germany was one of four satellite or "block" parties (*Blockparteien*) controlled by the ruling SED. The *Blockflöte* or "block flute" (now called a "recorder" in English) is a wind instrument similar to the flute. While each of these "block parties" typically represented itself during the campaign as standing for alternative positions and even a competing ideology, they would "all dance to the same flute (*Flöte*)," as an old German proverb puts it, after the election. See the note on "the block parties" for chapter 3, page 170, above.

Page 67: *who shouted "Hello Helmut" and later: "We are one people."* Helmut Kohl was chancellor of West Germany in 1989 and led the campaign from West Germany for unification upon the collapse of the GDR.

See the note on Kohl for chapter 8, page 184, below. The assertion *wir sind ein Volk,* or "we are one people," was a favorite chant of those demonstrators urging unification with West Germany after the opening of the Berlin Wall, when unification suddenly became a serious possibility. At an earlier stage, demonstrators had chanted *wir sind das Volk* ("we are the people") in an assertion of collective authority as they lobbied for political reform. See also the introduction (pages xix–xx).

Page 67: *with Round Tables . . .* Hartmut refers here to the structural format adopted in order to stage public dialogues on the issues of reform between the various groups engaged in the attempt to work out a new political order — representatives of the newly formed political parties and civic movements, on the one side, and of the old communist regime, on the other. Round Tables were held on a local level as well as on the national level, where sixteen meetings were convened between 7 December 1989 and 12 March 1990.

Page 68: *and smelled like in an Intershop.* See the note on "Intershops" for chapter 4, page 174, above.

Page 68: *uncovering the Stasi past . . .* See the note on "General Mielke" for chapter 4, page 175, above.

Page 71: *I take the* TAZ *rather than* Die Welt *or the* FAZ. *TAZ* stands for *die tageszeitung,* a cooperatively owned daily newspaper based in Berlin that focuses particular attention on environmental issues and has frequently backed Germany's Green Party. It has a modest circulation of just over sixty thousand. *Die Welt* and *FAZ (Frankfurter Allgemeine Zeitung)* are also daily newspapers, but with more conservative, mainstream orientations as well as much larger circulations.

CHAPTER SIX

And that's why you'd rather give in first . . .

Page 74: *She was said to work in the SED district administration.* Political power in the GDR, as in other Soviet-bloc states, was highly centralized. To facilitate centralization, the SED-led government reorganized the five newly instituted *Länder* (or "states") of East Germany, the regional centers of civil administration in the immediate aftermath of the Second World War, into fifteen new administrative units (*Bezirke*), each directly subordinate to the party's national leadership. These regional governments were organized around an elected assembly, which was headed up by a council or secretariat. They were also further subdivided into various districts (*Kreise*), both urban and rural. Both regional and district authorities, however, enjoyed very little independence, particularly in the area of policy-making. After

German unification in 1990, the earlier divisions (Brandenburg, Mecklenburg-Pomerania, Saxony, Thuringia, Saxony-Anhalt) were reinstituted as the five "new states" of an expanded Federal Republic of Germany. The city-state of Berlin is usually counted as one of the original "old states" of the FRG.

Page 74: *the changeover was a shock for many people.* On the term "changeover" (*Wende*), see the note for chapter 2, page 168, above.

Page 75: *Bernd spent his childhood in a home, in the "sailors' children's home."* Bärbel reports here that her husband, the child of sailors (*Schipper*) who navigated the inland waterways, was left in a special "children's home" (*Kinderheim*) for extended periods while his parents were at work.

Page 75: *their allotment garden.* Certain open spaces in or around urban concentrations of population were set aside for modest garden plots, or allotment gardens, where city dwellers might raise vegetables and flowers for themselves.

Page 76: *especially in the old states* . . . The "old states" to which Bärbel here refers are the original eleven West German *Länder* or states of the Federal Republic of Germany (FRG). See the note on "the SED district administration" above.

Page 77: *Now he's got an ABM job* . . . See the note on "the ABM" for chapter 2, page 169, above.

Page 77: *On October 7, 1989, when the demonstrations started in Berlin* . . . See the note concerning 7 October 1989 for chapter 3, page 170, above.

Page 77: *I got the trip through the FDJ.* See the note on "the FDJ" for chapter 1, page 160, above.

Page 77: *Later, he went to Alexanderplatz* . . . On *Alexanderplatz,* see the note for chapter 1, page 162, above.

Page 77: *his freedom was bought by the West.* See the note on "bought his freedom" for chapter 1, page 163, above.

Page 77: *because she was studying in P.* . . . . On the convention of referring to towns only by their first initial, see the note to chapter 1, page 160, above.

Page 77: *the Palucca School in Dresden* . . . The Palucca School traces its founding to 1925 as students began to flock to Gret Palucca, one of Europe's leading expressionist dancers. The school closed during the Nazi era but was revived after the Second World War. East German officials allowed Palucca to continue teaching her unique form of expressive dance along with classical ballet, which enjoyed special favor in all Soviet-bloc countries. The School's graduates became known both for technical excellence in classical ballet and for the creative expressionism of their dance.

Page 78: *telephoned the Stasi.* See notes on "the Stasi" at chapter 1, pages 160–61, above.

Page 78: *the demonstrations in Leipzig* ... The organized demonstrations that led to the collapse of the GDR grew out of Monday night vespers services at the *Nikolaikirche* in Leipzig. On 4 September 1989, participants in the Monday service staged a public march as part of their peace vigil. On Monday, 25 September, the first major demonstration took place, followed by successive "Monday demonstrations" that culminated in a tense confrontation on 9 October between some seventy thousand marchers and a police force backed up by SED militia units (*Kampfgruppen* — see the note on the "*combat group*" for chapter 10, page 190, below). Kurt Masur, the renowned conductor, whose Leipzig orchestra was making a recording of Beethoven's *Eroica* in the nearby concert hall, negotiated an agreement from local SED leaders not to resort to force as long as the demonstration remained peaceful, and a violent clash was averted. See also the introduction (pages xviii–xix).

Page 78: *With the money and everything.* See the note on "currency union" for chapter 2, page 168, above.

Page 79: *I also blame the Wessis* ... The terms *Wessis* ("westies") and *Ossis* ("easties") are mildly derogatory nicknames used in contemporary unified Germany for West Germans (those with origins in the former West Germany) and East Germans (those with origins in the former East Germany) respectively.

Page 79: *When you see on television nowadays just what happened there* ... In the wake of German unification, a host of programs and eye-witness reports appeared on television that focused on the different measures used by the GDR to control its borders, including land mines and violent dogs that were mistreated and kept very hungry. These reports also documented that almost all who sought to escape did so without a weapon, meaning that the border patrols that fired on these escapees, contrary to official GDR pronouncements, typically shot and killed unarmed individuals.

Page 81: *Many people had already been in Hungary since the summer, remember.* See the note on "the migrations" for chapter 3, page 170, above.

Page 81: *On the evening of November 9, ... the press conference with Schabowski* ... Mounting demonstrations against the SED-controlled government since late September had made clear that freedom to travel led the list of popular demands. Officials rushed to prepare legislation that would permit every citizen with a passport to obtain an exit visa at any border crossing. Since only four million East Germans had passports, this approach still promised a gradual and regulated transition to open borders. When the draft reached the Central

Committee on 9 November, it was approved "forthwith." It fell to Günter Schabowski to manage the press conference that evening announcing the impending changes. However, he had not been present at the discussion of the legislation in the Central Committee and was somewhat unclear about its meaning. Asked when the new regulations would take effect, he declared, "Immediately, without delay!" but left unspecified where and under what conditions. East Berliners began thronging to crossing points along the Wall. By 11:00 p.m., thousands had massed at the Bornholmer crossing and were calling for guards to open the gate. Facing a potential crisis with little direction from above, the guards took it upon themselves to open the gates and to allow free passage to everyone. The other crossing points soon followed suit. Within a few hours, young people were embracing each other and dancing on top of the Wall in front of television cameras that transmitted these remarkable images to an astonished world. See also the introduction (page xx).

Page 82: *We crossed at Friedrichstrasse ...* One of the major east-west thoroughfares of old Berlin, the Friedrichstrasse was cut in two by the construction of the Berlin Wall. The point at which East Berlin marked itself off from West Berlin on the Friedrichstrasse was in the very heart of the city. Checkpoint Charlie, as it was known, became the most famous of the crossing points through the Wall after a face-off there of Soviet and American tanks in October 1961, which riveted the attention of the world for a tense eighteen hours before the situation was defused.

Page 83: *how long Erich Honecker managed to stay in power.* See the note on Honecker for chapter 2, page 166, above.

Page 83: *the German-Soviet friendship.* The Society for German-Soviet Friendship (GSF) came into existence in 1949, even before the founding of the GDR, to promote knowledge of Soviet culture and society among East Germans. The GSF organized and promoted frequent student trips, language courses, and cultural exchanges with the Soviet Union.

CHAPTER SEVEN

So what's changed? Patriarchy hasn't disappeared ...

Page 85: *the one at Friedrichstrasse, the "palace of tears," as we called it ...* The train station at the intersection of Friedrichstrasse with Unter den Linden was once the city's busiest and most important hub, where mainline, suburban, and underground trains all converged. With the division of Berlin, it was left as the only place at which tracks running through the western part of the city met up with those running east. Visitors from the West could pass through customs and transfer to lines servicing East Berlin without leaving the station. As a terminus for traffic between the two halves of Berlin, however, it became the scene of many a tearful farewell. See also the note on Friedrichstrasse for chapter 6, page 180, above.

Page 86: *the wave of refugees in the summer of 1989.* . . . See the note on "the migrations" for chapter 3, page 170, above.

Page 87: *when my father listened to RIAS on medium wave.* The acronym RIAS stood for "Radio (*Rundfunk*) in the American Sector," a broadcasting station created in 1946 to serve as the mouthpiece for the U.S. military in its role as occupying power in a partitioned Berlin. The station also broadcast American music and entertainment, giving many German listeners their first taste of American pop culture. With the onset of the Cold War, RIAS came to play a key role in the ideological competition with the Soviet Union. After the formal division of Germany, broadcasts aimed increasingly at promoting an American point of view on local affairs or international events and at providing an alternative source of news and critical opinion to a population limited to the state-run media of the GDR.

Page 87: *Ulbricht bunkers.* The German *Ulbrichtbunker* was a slang construction to describe prisons used by the Ulbricht government to hold political opponents and dissidents.

Page 87: *the stories about the Stasi that everyone knows now.* See the note on "General Mielke" for chapter 4, page 175, above.

Page 87: *I didn't become a Pioneer* . . . See the note on "the Pioneers" for chapter 1, page 159, above.

Page 87: *I didn't join the FDJ, either.* See the note on "the FDJ" for chapter 1, page 160, above.

Page 87: *huge portraits of Ulbricht and Pieck and all those guys* . . . Walter Ulbricht (1893–1973) and Wilhelm Pieck (1876–1960), both longstanding members of the German Communist Party, played leading roles in the founding of the GDR in 1949. Pieck became the regime's first president and its head of state until his death in 1960. Ulbricht was appointed First Secretary (a position later renamed "General Secretary") of the SED. After the death of Pieck, he became head of state, uniting leadership of the party to the position of top government official.

Page 87: *Well, in D. he met my mother, and the rest is history.* On the convention of referring to towns only by their first initial, see the note to chapter 1, page 160, above.

Page 88: *he had once been such a Cerberus.* Cerberus is a large, terrifying three-headed dog that guards the entrance to the Underworld in classical mythology. Beate suggests that in his previous life her father was

Cerberus-like, not only in the anger and menace he could exhibit, but also in that he was capable of strong attachment and affection, that is, he seemed to have multiple heads or personalities.

Page 89: *I did vocational training and passed my final exams* . . . Beate indicates that she had completed the *Berufsschule*, at the conclusion of which she passed the comprehensive set of exams called the *Abitur* in German. On the *Abitur*, see the note on "the vocational school" for chapter 1, page 159, and on "the upper high school" for chapter 3, page 172, above.

Page 89: *"societally active," as they called it.* Opportunities for higher education in the GDR were made contingent not only on academic performance but also on ideological and civic considerations. Faithful participation in the programs and practices developed by the SED for cultivating proper socialist citizens were as important to an application for university study as an outstanding scholastic record. See the note on "issues of class" for chapter 1, page 160, above.

Page 91: *whether I'm reading* Spiegel . . . The German newsweekly *Der Spiegel* is similar in style and presentation to American newsmagazines, but its long, in-depth articles are more like those found in the *Atlantic Monthly* than in *Time* or *Newsweek*. It numbers among the most reputable media in Germany and is known for its distinctive academic writing style and its high-quality investigative journalism.

Page 91: *I met Henrich, the lawyer, read his book* The Custodial State . . . Rolf Henrich (b.1944) grew up and received his legal education in the GDR. He became a leading critic of the regime with the publication of *Der vormundschaftliche Staat: Vom Versagen des real existierenden Sozialismus* (*The Custodial State: On the Failure of Real Existing Socialism*) in April 1989. His book examines the reality of state socialism as practiced in the GDR, looks into the relation of Marxism and Christianity, and considers the future course of socialism.

Page 91: *Before the so-called changeover* . . . See the note on "the changeover" for chapter 2, page 168, above.

Page 92: *some kind of brownshirt* . . . The "brownshirts," members of the paramilitary organization known as the *Sturmabteilung* (storm division), which Hitler created early in his career with the Nazi party to maintain order at public events, were so called because of the shirts chosen as the basis of the group's uniform. Since the end of the Nazi Reich, the term "brownshirt" has become an epithet used to refer to right-wing radicals, especially those prone to acts of violence.

Page 95: *the Ossis* . . . See the note on "the Wessis" for chapter 6, page 179, above.

CHAPTER EIGHT

I always hope I won't wake up in the morning . . .

Page 96: *former "unofficial co-worker"* . . . See the note on "the job of the grandchild" for chapter 3, page 169, above.

Page 96: *I always say "*Wehrmacht.*"* The Nazis applied the word *Wehrmacht* strictly to Germany's military forces during the years of Hitler's rule (1935–45). As a consequence, it is now used only with reference to the military component of Nazi Germany, although it had previously been a generic term that could describe the armed forces of any nation. Rudi uses it out of context here to signal his ideological sympathy with the Nazis.

Page 96: *the NPA: "National People's Army."* See the note on "the National People's Army" for chapter 2, page 165, above.

Page 96: *I should apply to the radio station in C.* On the convention of referring to towns only by their first initial, see the note to chapter 1, page 160, above.

Page 97: *Listening to RIAS* . . . See the note on "when my father listened to RIAS" for chapter 7, page 181, above.

Page 97: *old receiver from the Second World War* . . . The German word used here is *Goebbelsschnautze* (literally, "Goebbels' snout"), which was a nickname for a Second-World-War vintage receiver that played on the fact that radio served as a mouthpiece for Propaganda Minister Goebbels.

Page 97: *the Stasi will never figure that one out.* See notes on "the Stasi" at chapter 1, pages 160–61, and chapter 4, page 173, above.

Page 98: *We had to learn the life stories of Ulbricht and the others.* See the note on "Ulbricht and Pieck" for chapter 7, page 181, above.

Page 98: *we got the* Bildzeitung, *the* Deutsche Soldatenzeitung, *the* Nationalzeitung, *and so on.* The *Bildzeitung* and the *Deutsche Soldatenzeitung* (German Soldiers' Magazine) are both publications connected to the right wing of postwar German politics. The former is a tabloid paper founded in 1959 by Axel Springer, who built a media empire in postwar Germany devoted to a militant foreign policy, German nationalism, and free-market economics. The latter, known as the *Nationalzeitung* since 1963, is edited and published by millionaire Gerhard Frey, who also serves as chairman of the *Deutsche Volksunion* (German People's Union), a far-right party that Frey organized in 1971.

Page 98: *the People's Police.* The People's Police, or *Volkspolizei*, was the conventional police force of the GDR. However, members of this force received military training and were regularly used like a second army for the political management of the population. In this capacity, they often worked closely with the Stasi to keep tabs on critics and opponents of the regime.

Page 99: *That was after the changeover.* See the note on "eighteen months before the changeover" (*Wende*) for chapter 2, page 168, above.

Page 100: *I'd like to give it one more try, working for the DVU.* The acronym DVU stands for *Deutsche Volksunion* (German People's Union). Officially classified as an extreme-right and openly anti-Semitic organization, it is one of only two such political parties (the other being the National Democratic Party or NPD) in postwar Germany that has managed to win seats in state parliamentary elections. It has, however, sought to avoid associating with neo-Nazi groups openly hostile to the German constitution and officially declares itself loyal to the constitutional structure of the Federal Republic. See also the note on "the *Deutsche Soldatenzeitung*" at page 183, above.

Page 100: *with Honecker, ... with Ulbricht, ... with Pieck, and now also with Kohl.* Helmut Kohl was chancellor of West Germany from 1982 to 1990. As chancellor, he led the campaign for German unification and became, as a result, the first chancellor of a unified Germany, a position he occupied until 1998, when his Christian Democratic Union (CDU) was defeated by the Social Democratic Party (SDP). On Erich Honecker, see the note for chapter 2, page 166, above. On Ulbricht and Wilhelm Pieck, see the note for chapter 7, page 181, above.

Page 101: *the SED-regime* ... On the SED, see the note for chapter 2, page 167, above.

Page 101: *Got a big percentage.* In the parliamentary system of the Federal Republic of Germany, seats in both federal and state parliaments are divided up among the contending parties in accordance with the percentage of the vote each party manages to win in the election. However, the constitution stipulates that a party must achieve a threshold of at least five percent of the vote to be allotted any representation.

Page 101: *The PDS, for example.* See the note on "a stalwart PDS man" for chapter 3, pages 172–73, above.

Page 101: *Or the Burger-Strasse.* Rudi refers here not to an actual street but to a post-unification left-wing commune movement whose adherents occupied vacant houses in cities across East Germany. After the collapse of the GDR, colonies of left-wing artists and activists took possession of dilapidated buildings in East Berlin and elsewhere (such as in C.).

Page 102: *the* Deutsche Woche. Originally the mouthpiece for the National Democratic Party of Germany (NPD) — a second party on the extreme-right of contemporary German politics that has enjoyed some success in state parliamentary elections — *Deutsche Wochenzeitung* was purchased by Gerhard Frey in 1986 and merged with its sister publication *Deutsche Nationalzeitung* to form *Nationalzeitung-Deutsche Wochenzeitung*. This composite newspaper now functions loosely as an organ of the DVU, which is formally allied with the NPD. See the note on "working for the DVU" at page 184, above.

Page 103: *I don't believe that the DVU, that Dr. Frey . . .* Gerhard Frey, founder and principal underwriter of the DVU, graduated from the University of Munich in 1956 with a doctoral degree in business law.

Page 103: *Even the Poles say so themselves.* On 1 September 1939, Hitler launched an invasion of Poland in the name of providing Germans with *Lebensraum* (room to live), repossessing territories confiscated at the end of the First World War, and restoring Germany's prewar boundaries in the east. This action precipitated the outbreak of the Second World War. At the end of the war, the former German territories remained under Polish or Russian control, while the German border with Poland was moved even further westward.

Page 104: *The Sinti and Roma . . .* "Sinti and Roma" is the official German name for the ethnic minority usually called "gypsies" in English, a group believed to have arrived in Europe from northern India in the 1400s. The Sinti, a sub-population of the Roma, now consider themselves to be a distinct minority. During the Nazi era, hundreds of thousands of the Sinti and Roma from across German-occupied Europe were systematically killed as part of the Nazi campaign to safeguard the racial purity of Germans.

Page 105: *He was in the FDJ . . .* See the note on "the FDJ" for chapter 1, page 160, and on "the FDJ Youth College" for chapter 2, page 166, above.

Page 105: *his* Sturm-und-Drang *period.* The phrase *Sturm und Drang* (storm and stress) derives from an important era in the history of eighteenth-century German literature and is identified with artistic and philosophical rebellion against the political absolutism and the repressive moral and social conventions of the day. As used here, the phrase is a metaphor for youthful rebellion in the name of creative freedom and the unfettered pursuit of one's individual genius. See also the note on Schiller's *Kabale und Liebe* for chapter 1, page 160, above.

Page 105: TAZ, *or something like that.* See the note on *TAZ*, a newspaper aimed at partisans (including participants in the home-commune movement) of different minor parties on the far left of the German political spectrum, for chapter 5, page 177, above.

Page 105: *Look at all that documentation that came out after the changeover!* See the note on "marksmen at the Wall" for chapter 2, page 165; see also the note on "General Mielke" for chapter 4, page 175, above.

Page 106: *the SED, the PDS, the KPD, the SPD, the Greens, the Alliance 90 . . .* the acronym KPD stands for *Kommunistische Partei Deutschlands* (Communist Party of Germany). SPD stands for *Sozialdemokratische Partei Deutschlands* (Social Democratic Party of Germany). One of the two major parties in the Federal Republic of Germany, it stands to the left of its major rival, the Christian Democratic Union (CDU). In recent history, the SPD has moved away from its nineteenth-century roots as a party of the working class in the direction of a neo-liberal politics, much like the British Labor Party. The Greens, or *Die Grünen,* represent the most successful political organization to grow out of the worldwide ecology-and-peace movement that sprang up in the 1970s. The Greens first won seats in West Germany's federal parliament in 1983, when they garnered 5.6 percent of the electorate. In the wake of German unification, the Greens merged with Alliance 90 (*Bündnis 90*), a coalition of East German civil rights groups, to form Alliance 90/The Greens. See also the note on the CDU and SPD for chapter 3, page 171, above.

CHAPTER NINE

Somehow or other I want to make up for the mistakes I made back then . . .

Page 107: *the haunt of the "brown comrades."* The German term here is *die braunen Gesellen,* a nickname for members of the neo-Nazi, National-Democratic Party of Germany (*Nationaldemokratische Partei Deutschlands*) or NPD. Although a presence on the political scene in Germany since the 1960s, the NPD has never achieved the five percent threshold in federal elections that would enable it to send delegates to the *Bundestag* or national parliament. See also the note on "some kind of brownshirt" for chapter 7, page 182, above.

Page 107: *a lot of Stasi guys . . .* See notes on "the Stasi" at chapter 1, pages 160–61, and chapter 4, page 173, above.

Page 107: *The famous Biermann muzzle.* See the note on "the Biermann petition" for chapter 1, page 162, above.

Page 107: *after catching up and getting a high school diploma . . .* The words "high school diploma" here translate *Abitur,* the comprehensive examinations required for entrance to university. See the note on "the vocational school" for chapter 1, page 159, and on "the upper high school" for chapter 3, page 172, above.

Page 108: *her green/purple circle of friends.* The color green is prominently identified with a progressive politics focused on ecological issues, while purple has long been associated with the women's movement and feminism. The Green-Purple List, which has fielded candidates for state parliamentary elections in the former GDR, represents a slate of delegates committed to an ecological-feminist politics.

Page 108: *my distance from the SED.* See the note on the SED for chapter 2, page 167, above.

Page 108: *the regional secretariat of the SED . . .* See the note on "SED district administration" for chapter 6, page 177, above.

Page 108: *whether the "Chekists" had discovered something or not.* Founded in the wake of the October Revolution in 1917, the Cheka was the original secret-police organization in communist Russia and forerunner of the KGB. In East Germany, the word "Chekists" was sometimes used to refer to Stasi agents, an oblique reference to the historical (if not the on-going) connection of the Stasi to their Russian counterparts. See also the note on "the 'Felix Dzierzynski' watch regiment" for chapter 2, page 165, above.

Page 108: *Trelleborg-Travemünde.* Peter refers here to a ferry route across the southern end of the Baltic Sea, between the southernmost Swedish port of Trelleborg and the (West) German city of Travemünde.

Page 109: *Before the changeover . . .* See the note on "the changeover" for chapter 2, page 168, above.

Page 111: *a mixture between SPD and Alliance 90/Greens.* Newspapers in Germany, especially those whose circulation is largely based in a certain region, tend to identify themselves with a particular brand of politics, rallying support in many cases for given candidate-lists and/or parties. See the note on "the SPD, the Greens, the Alliance 90" for chapter 8, page 186, above.

Page 111: *imitation of the German Press Agency.* The German Press Agency is the fourth largest wire service in the world. Its approach to journalism mirrors that of major wire services in the United States, like the Associated Press, which strive always to report from a neutral or nonpartisan point of view. Peter speaks disparagingly of such journalism as compared with the more politically committed and rhetorically polemical style of journalism that he favors. See also the note on *TAZ* for chapter 5, page 177, above.

Page 111: *being an Ossi . . .* See the note on "the Wessis" for chapter 6, page 179, above.

Page 112: *"you'll have a 'Wartburg' . . ."* The more expensive of the two models of cars manufactured in East German was the Wartburg, named after the famous castle overlooking the city of Eisenach, where the car was manufactured. The typical wait for the three-cylinder Wartburg was only nine years, as compared with twelve for the less expensive Trabant. See the note on the "Trabi" for chapter 1, page 164, above.

Page 113: *the invasion of Czechoslovakia* . . . See the note on "what was going on in Czechoslovakia" for chapter 4, page 173, above.

Page 113: *topics considered at that time "hostile to the state."* The German adjective used here is *staatsfeindlich*. It is part of a legal vocabulary coined by officials to legitimize the criminalization of certain kinds of speech in the interests of controlling public opinion. See also the note on "subversive agitation" for chapter 1, page 163, above.

Page 113: *"With a red book."* The communist government of China brought out *Quotations from Chairman Mao Tse-Tung* in the 1960s, which came to be known outside China as "the little red book." During the Cultural Revolution, Chinese authorities required citizens to own and to carry a copy with them at almost all times. It thus became a symbol of ideological orthodoxy and party loyalty, which is what informs Peter's playful reference to it here.

Page 113: *like in a Zille drawing* . . . Heinrich Zille (1858–1929) was a German illustrator best known for his satirical drawings of life and people in turn-of-the-century Berlin, including depictions of the cluttered and congested condition of the modern urban world.

Page 114: *"Beat-Club" was the rage at the time* . . . The West German program "Beat-Club" was the first German show to be devoted to the popular music of the beat-generation. It premiered in September 1965 and featured rock artists like Black Sabbath, Pink Floyd, and The Doors during its seven-year history.

Page 114: *Of course I was a Pioneer, in time also FDJ secretary* . . . See the note on "the Pioneers" for chapter 1, page 159; see also the note on "the FDJ" for chapter 1, page 160.

Page 114: *the FDJ celebrations in Berlin.* For an example of one such celebration, see the note on "the World Festival of Youth" for chapter 2, page 166, above.

Page 114: *my vocational training.* See the note on "the vocational school" for chapter 1, page 159, above.

Page 115: *Does the clock you watch on TV at home have strokes or dots?* The evening news broadcasts in both East and West Germany featured a ticking clock, but with "strokes" to mark its divisions in the East and "dots" in the West. Ministry of State Security officials therefore encouraged teachers to ask young children to describe, or to draw, the clock that appeared on the TV in their homes in order to determine whether the parents were watching East or West German TV news.

Page 117: *The state of Brandenburg* ... See the note on "SED district administration" for chapter 6, page 177, above.

Page 117: *Honny, open the Wall.* "Honny" was the sarcastic nickname coined for East German head of state, Erich Honecker. See the note on Honecker for chapter 2, page 166, above.

CHAPTER TEN

So how are people ever going to connect with each other?

Page 120: *when the "Riot Police" became the "National People's Army."* The occupying powers agreed at the founding of the two German states not to permit military forces to be re-established on German soil. However, as Cold War tensions heightened with the outbreak of the Korean War, the United States urged West Germany to establish armed forces. East Germany responded by transforming its *Kasernierte Volkspolizei* (Riot Police) into a full-fledged military. See the note on the "People's Army" for chapter 2, page 165, above.

Page 121: *all that Wall stuff* ... Construction of the Berlin Wall began on 13 August 1961. See the note on the "antifascist protective barrier" for chapter 2, page 165, above.

Page 121: *the waiting list for a Trabant.* See the note on "their Trabi" for chapter 1, page 164.

Page 121: *bought a Wartburg.* See the note on "you'll have a 'Wartburg'" for chapter 9, pages 187–88, above.

Page 122: *She was the first to join the collective.* See the note on "recruitment teams" for chapter 3, page 169, above.

Page 122: *an old DKW.* The acronym DKW stands for *Dampf-Kraft-Wagen,* a brand of cars and motorcycles that began as an attempt to develop a steam-powered vehicle. The company produced its most well-known cars during the 1930s. They featured two-stroke engines, front-wheel drive, and transverse mounting. Engines pioneered by DKW would become the basis of the automobile industry in the GDR.

Page 123: *a Lada, kind of like a Fiat.* The Lada, one of only three automobiles widely available in the GDR, was manufactured in the Soviet Union in factories managed by the Italian automaker Fiat.

Page 123: *I earned the name "activist" four times ... once even "best worker."* To encourage application and ambition, officials in the GDR established an elaborate system of honors and awards for workers in the nation's various industries. The title "activist of socialist work," or "activist," was conferred on workers whose performance was deemed exemplary over an extended period of time. The award took the form of a certificate, presented with a small medallion and a cash prize at a formal ceremony by the factory manager. Similarly, factories would regularly recognize a "best worker," who would be honored by having his photograph hung in the factory's hall of fame.

Page 123: *The combat group* . . . In the wake of the 1953 uprising (see the note on "June 17, 1953" for chapter 3, page 172, above), SED officials created a paramilitary organization called "Combat Groups of the Working Class," which functioned as a kind of party army to supplement and to support official military and police actions. Combat groups were organized in each of the factories, state-controlled businesses, and even large neighborhoods of the GDR. See also the note on "the demonstrations in Leipzig" for chapter 6, page 179, above.

Page 124: *That's hostility towards the state* . . . The German word is *staats-feindlich*. See the note on "hostile to the state" for chapter 9, page 188, above.

Page 124: *The changeover* . . . See the note on "the changeover" for chapter 2, page 168, above.

Page 124: *But my aunt was just not enough of an aunt — and that was that.* Günter indicates that the formal basis of his request to travel to the West was to visit an aunt who lived in West Germany.

Page 126: *so you could buy decent tools in an Intershop* . . . See the note on "Intershops" for chapter 4, page 174, above.

Page 126: *the DVU, the German People's Union.* See the note on "working for the DVU" for chapter 8, page 184, above.

Page 126: *The CDU ripped us off* . . . *The SPD doesn't help either, and don't even mention the FDP. The Greens are divided.* The FDP (Free Democratic Party) is the third largest party in the Federal Republic of Germany, behind the CDU and SPD. It came into existence shortly after the Second World War and has played a significant role in West German politics as a centrist party committed to a classical liberal and free-market ideology. Its ability to partner with both the CDU and the SPD has enabled it to participate in all but six postwar governments in the Federal Republic. See also the note on "the SPD, the Greens, the Alliance 90" for chapter 8, page 186, above.

Page 126: *The Stasi's on one side and you're on the other.* See notes on "the Stasi" at chapter 1, pages 160–61, and chapter 4, page 173, above.

Page 127: *who'd been working secretly with them, whether official or unofficial or whatever.* See the note on "the job of the grandchild" for chapter 3, page 169, above.

Page 127: *Of course, I'm not for the Republicans* . . . The Republicans (*Die Republikaner*) is a political party on the far right of the German electorate, which rose to prominence in 1989 largely on the strength of its anti-foreigner and anti-immigration stance. Its support, which has fluctuated considerably, has tended to come from protest voters who oppose the immigration or social-welfare policies of the major parties.

Page 128: *Of course, the DVU also wants to go towards "Germany, awake."* The words *Deutschland erwache* ("Germany, awake") was usually emblazoned on the Nazi flags routinely carried by so-called "storm troops," or members of the *Sturmabteilung* at mass rallies. The phrase comes from the *Sturmleid*, the "storm song" composed to inspirit and to help unify the paramilitary corps of "brownshirts" that was first organized to keep order at Hitler's beer-hall speeches and to protect him from antagonists and detractors. The first stanza reads: "Germany awake from this wicked nightmare! Give no room in your lands for the Jews. We want to fight for your resurgence! Aryan blood should not perish!" See also the note on "brownshirts" for chapter 7, page 182, above.

Page 129: *some ABM position in the district.* See the note on "the ABM" for chapter 2, page 169, above.

Page 129: *AOK insurance isn't enough in an emergency.* The acronym AOK stands for *Allgemeine Ortskrankenkasse*, the largest health insurance provider (*Krankenkasse*) in Germany. Participation in some such *Krankenkasse* is mandated by law for all citizens.

CHAPTER ELEVEN

You have to keep your mouth shut and do your job
as if it's the most fulfilling thing in your life . . .

Page 132: *I didn't think I absolutely had to go on and take the big end-of-school exams* . . . The expression "end-of-school exams" here translates the German word *Abitur*. On this term, see the note on "the vocational school" for chapter 1, page 159, and on "the upper high school" for chapter 3, page 172, above.

Page 132: *a place reserved for them as "apprentice with high-school diploma . . ."* The construction here is *Lehrstelle mit Abitur*.

Page 133: *You're Ossis.* See the note on "the Wessis" for chapter 6, page 179, above.

Page 133: *rather than a Turk.* See the note on "the Turks" for chapter 1, page 164, above.

Page 133: *labeling us as Stasi types.* See notes on "the Stasi" for chapter 1, pages 160–61, and chapter 4, page 173, above.

Page 133: *proud to be a Pioneer, of course.* See the note on "the Pioneers" for chapter 1, page 159, above.

Page 133: *the Party colleges . . .* Peter refers here to one of the regional colleges (*Parteischulen*) of the SED. See the note on "the Party University" for chapter 2, page 166, above.

Page 134: *He was in the ZK, the Central Committee of the SED.* The letters ZK stand for the German word *Zentralkomitee.* On the Central Committee, see the note on "our Politburo" for chapter 2, page 167, above.

Page 134: *the Greens in West Berlin . . .* See the note on "the Greens, the Alliance 90" for chapter 8, page 186, above.

Page 134: *no West German league games.* The *Bundesliga* (literally, "Federal League") represents the premiere level of German soccer and one of the most competitive leagues of professional soccer in the world. It consists of 18 teams that compete each season to be crowned national champion. The league was formed in 1963 to provide a structure for professional soccer in West Germany. The GDR had earlier founded its own league (*DDR-Oberliga*) of elite teams, which has now been folded into the existing structure for the organized competition of soccer clubs in the Federal Republic, but the quality of play by these teams has generally proved to be inferior to that of the *Bundesliga.*

Page 134: *Aktuelle Kamera . . .* The state-controlled daily news program of the GDR was called *Aktuelle Kamera* ("Today's Camera").

Page 135: *we had FDJ initiation.* See the note on "the FDJ" for chapter 1, page 160, above.

Page 135: *made their cadre or personal file disappear . . .* For every citizen of the GDR a "cadre file" (*Kaderakte*), a type of dossier, was created that began in elementary school and followed the individual through life. While the Stasi had access to these, the individual subjects of the files typically did not.

Page 135: *the changeover . . .* See the note on "the changeover" for chapter 2, page 168, above.

Page 136: *But what if he was an unofficial Co-worker?* See the note on "the job of the grandchild" for chapter 3, page 169, above.

Page 136: *Because I've found out what the Stasi was up to here.* See the note on "General Mielke" for chapter 4, page 175, above.

Page 137: *on November 9 . . .* See the note on "November 9" for chapter 6, page 179, above.

Page 137: *Took the commuter train to Friedrichstrasse.* On the Friedrichstrasse border crossings, see the note for chapter 6, page 180, and for chapter 7, pages 180–81, above.

Page 138: *we picked up our "welcome money" at once.* See the note on "long lines in front of the banks" for chapter 1, page 164, above.

Page 138: *My pal in East Berlin, at Bergmann-Borsig* . . . Bergmann-Borsig, a manufacturer of turbines and generators, was one of the leading heavy industries in the GDR.

Page 139: *A Wartburg.* See the note on the "Wartburg" for chapter 9, pages 187–88, above.

Page 140: *if you go to the vocational school* . . . See the note on "the vocational school" for chapter 1, page 159, above.

CHAPTER TWELVE

You can best change the world by changing yourself . . .

Page 144: *suppression of the Prague Spring* . . . See the note on "what was going on in Czechoslovakia" for chapter 4, page 173, above.

Page 144: *the exile of Wolf Biermann* . . . See the note on "the Biermann petition" for chapter 1, page 162, above.

Page 145: *he was a committed member of the LDPD.* The Liberal Democratic Party of Germany (or *Liberal-Demokratische Partei Deutschlands*) was one of the four "block parties" (see the note on "the block parties" for chapter 3, page 170, above) in the GDR that functioned as auxiliaries of the ruling SED. At its founding in 1945, however, the LDPD identified itself with a liberal-democratic politics.

Page 145: *a "construction soldier"* . . . The German word, *Bausoldat,* was coined by East German officials to describe an alternative form of military service instituted in 1964 for those who refused to bear arms. All conscientious objectors to the mandatory eighteen-month military service were subject to imprisonment. The only legal alternative was service as a "construction soldier." As a *Bausoldat,* however, one could expect to endure official harassment during one's time of service as well as discrimination in the awarding of educational or other opportunities thereafter. See the introduction (pages xii–xiii).

Page 145: *while attending the upper high school.* See the note on "the upper high school" for chapter 3, page 172, above.

Page 146: *The philosopher does not need the state, but the state needs the philosopher.* Here, Lars clearly has Plato's *Republic* in mind, where in a famous allegory the city is represented as a cave whose inhabitants are chained to the floor and compelled to look to shadows projected onto the back wall for their understanding of reality. The philosopher, by contrast, is identified by his ability to make his way out of the cave, where he beholds the outside or natural world in the light of the sun. While inhabitants of the cave are entirely dependent for their understanding of reality on the city and the shadow-images its caretakers generate, the philosopher achieves his superior understanding of reality independently of the city. Moreover, it is the philosopher's knowledge of the true nature of reality that uniquely recommends him, according to the argument of the *Republic,* for the position of king or ruler in the city.

Page 147: *Hegel's political philosophy.* Lars refers here specifically to Hegel's *Rechtsphilosophie,* or "philosophy of right." While the German word *Recht* is conventionally rendered as "law," Hegel makes clear that his treatment of *Recht* comprehends not only law or jurisprudence but also morality, ethical life, and world history. He contends that law, in the highest sense, expresses the universal morality that human history is struggling towards. The English word "right" is therefore generally preferred in translating Hegel's use of *Recht.*

Page 147: *Olof Palme's ideas on collective security* . . . Olof Palme (1927–86), a leading political figure in Sweden, where he headed up the Social Democratic Party from 1968 until his untimely death in 1986, was elected prime minister of his country three times. In 1982, he chaired an Independent Commission on Disarmament and Security Issues, which came to be known as the "Palme Commission." The report of the Commission argued that the concept of security must abandon the idea of deterrence based on stockpiles of nuclear weapons. It put forward the concept of a "collective security" based on greater international cooperation, transparency, disarmament, and demilitarization.

Page 147: *until the changeover* . . . On the term "changeover" (*Wende*), see the note for chapter 2, page 168, above.

Page 148: *I went to see Anna Seghers* . . . Anna Seghers was the penname of Netty Reiling (1900–1983), a distinguished German writer who returned from exile to settle in East Berlin after the Second World War. She received the National Prize of the German Democratic Republic for her contributions to German literature in 1951.

Page 148: *The book* The Gulag Archipelago *by Solzhenitsyn* . . . Alexander Solzhenitsyn's account of the Soviet Union's slave labor and concentration camps is a massive three-volume work that brought the atrocities of the Gulag to the world's attention. Within weeks of its original 1974 publication in Paris, Solzhenitsyn was stripped of his citizenship and exiled by Soviet authorities from his Russian homeland. The book chronicles the history of the system of forced labor camps from its inception during Lenin's rule up through the Stalinist era of the Soviet Union.

Page 148: *Bahro tried it in* The Alternative. Rudolph Bahro (1935–97) published *Die Alternative: Zur Kritik des real existierenden Sozialismus* (The Alternative: Towards a Critique of Real Existing Socialism) in 1977. An English translation appeared in 1978 under the title, *The Alternative in Eastern Europe.* His book played an influential role in the development of European Eco-Socialism. He was imprisoned in 1978 by the GDR and deported to West Germany in 1979, where he helped to found the Green Party. In *The Alternative,* Bahro argued that the failures of existing (Soviet-bloc) socialism were rooted in the persistence of social divisions in the labor structure of society and its consequent bureaucratic hierarchy. He points to an alternative socialism that will only result from the transformation of society's social divisions by a "cultural revolution" fostered by those elites in possession of what he calls "surplus consciousness."

Pages 148–49: *the generation that was over forty in 1989 and had experienced the open Wall.* Those over forty in 1989 would have been born before the founding of the GDR on 7 October 1949. They would likewise have been at least in their teens when the Berlin Wall was erected on 13 August 1961, sealing off East Germans from ready contact with West Germany.

Page 149: *a completely different German way of life from that of Prussia . . .* The Kingdom of Prussia took the lead in the original act of German unification in 1871, which fused together a number of independent, central European polities to create the *Deutsches Reich* (German Empire) and a modern German nation-state. The Prussian capital, Berlin, became the capital of the new Reich. Shaped fundamentally by the Protestant Reformation, Prussia retained its distinctively protestant character even within an imperial Germany that encompassed territories like Bavaria where Catholicism had been the dominant religious and cultural influence.

Page 149: *an article by Rolf Schneider . . .* Born to working-class parents in 1932, Rolf Schneider began his professional life as a magazine editor, only to become a leading novelist and intellectual voice in the GDR. He was among the prominent artists who signed the petition protesting the expatriation of Wolf Biermann in 1976. As a result, his endeavors as an artist and novelist were severely restricted by the state, leading him to withdraw from the official writers union in 1979. The Biermann affair, however, provided the inspiration for his 1979 novel, *November.* Many of his novels and other writings focus on political life, culture, and German identity. See also the note on "the Biermann petition" for chapter 1, page 162, above.

Page 149: *the founding articles of the SDP.* The letters SDP stood for *Sozial-demokratische Partei* (or Social-Democratic Party). Lars identifies himself as one of the founders of this party, which came into existence as an independent East German political organization in the fall of 1990 but eventually joined itself to the West German SPD. The choice to adopt SDP as the original acronym of the party emphasized the fact that it was a self-standing entity, although one that consciously sought to link itself to the German tradition of social-democratic politics stretching back to the nineteenth century, from which the West Germany SPD likewise springs. See the note on "the SPD, the Greens, the Alliance 90" for chapter 8, page 186, above.

Page 149: *infiltrated by the Stasi.* See notes on "the Stasi" at chapter 1, pages 160–61, and chapter 4, page 173, above.

Page 150: *I was on disability because of a serious operation* ... Beginning in the 1970s, various treaties and agreements between the GDR and the FRG led to a relaxing of restrictions on travel to the West for certain categories of East German citizens. These included pensioners and those who received disability payments from the state (*Invalidenrentner*) because they were unable to work. Because he fell into this latter category, Lars became eligible in 1985 to visit West Germany. At about the same time, pressure began to build on officials in the GDR to respond to Gorbachev's campaign for *perestroika* with a reform program of their own, which they tried to deflect in part by loosening restrictions on eligibility to travel to the West.

Page 150: *during conversations with Jürgen Fuchs* ... Born and educated in the GDR, Jürgen Fuchs (1950–99) became a prominent writer and dissident, before being jailed and then exiled to West Germany in 1977 for his part in protesting the expatriation of Wolf Biermann. Fuchs studied psychology at the University of Jena, and his literary endeavors reflect an abiding concern with the social-psychological dimensions of the cultural and political structures that defined the socialist order of East Germany.

Page 150: *schools became more hardline under the regime of Margot Honecker.* Margot Honecker, wife of Erich Honecker, served as Minister of National Education from 1963 until 1989. During her tenure as minister the curriculum of the schools underwent a significant "militarization," as critics put it, especially after passage of the Military Service Law in 1982. See the note on "military exercises and marksmanship classes" for chapter 5, page 175, above.

Page 151: *the Department of Internal Affairs* ... The German term here is *Abteilung Inneres.* Suspected dissidents summoned to an interview at this department typically confronted an uncertain situation, since it was never made clear whether those conducting the interview worked for the Ministry for State Security, or for the *Ministerium des Innern* (Ministry of Internal Affairs).

Page 151: *the regional church organization* ... The German word used here is *Landeskirche,* which is the name of the organizational division of the Evangelical Church in Germany (a federation of Lutheran and Reformed churches) at the regional level. As a division of authority, therefore, the *Landeskirche* oversees and governs all the individual parishes and pastors in a given administrative region. The word *Landkirche,* on the other hand, refers to an individual "country church."

Page 153: *Kurt Hager's comment about the "change of scenery" in Moscow* ... Lars here uses the term *Tapetenwechsel,* which taken literally denotes a "change of wallpaper." In a 1987 interview with the West Germany newsweekly *Der Stern,* Kurt Hager, Politburo member and "chief ideologist" of the SED, played on the meaning of this term in order to dismiss Gorbachev's campaign for reform of the Soviet system as irrelevant to the GDR: "Would you, if your neighbor redecorates (*tapezieren*) his flat, feel obliged to do the same?"

Page 153: *the legacy of the SED.* See the note on the SED for chapter 2, page 167, above.

Page 153: *Bärbel Bohley spoke about us, as did Eppelmann* ... Rainer Eppelmann, a Lutheran pastor attached to a church in East Berlin, was a leading figure in the East German peace movement that emerged in the early 1980s. He endured brief imprisonment for his part in composing the "Berlin Appeal" (1982) that helped to define the need for and aims of the movement. Bärbel Bohley was also involved in the peace movement as one of the leaders of "Women for Peace." She too was subjected to official persecution for her activities: she was arrested and held for a brief time in late 1983. See also the note on "Swords to Ploughshares" for chapter 4, page 174, above.

Page 154: *The official launch of the party took place on October 7, 1989.* On the significance of this date, see the note on "October 7" for chapter 3, page 170, above.

Page 154: *"Democratic Awakening" had tried its own launch.* On 1 October three prominent religious leaders, including Rainer Eppelmann, one of the instigators of the East German peace movement (see the note on Eppelmann for page 153, above), announced the formation of an independent political party, *Demokratischer Aufbruch* (Democratic Awakening), through which concrete objectives might be effectively pursued.

Page 154: *an unofficial informant for the Stasi for years.* The German term used here is *Inoffizieler Mitarbiter* ("unofficial co-workers"), but the attitude of the speaker is best conveyed in this case with the English word "informant." See the note on "the job of the grandchild" for chapter 3, page 169, above.

Page 154: *Sebastian Pflugbeil introduced the New Forum.* Trained as a physicist, Sebastian Pflugbeil was among the most well-known East German intellectuals involved in setting up New Forum in September 1989. Together with Olaf Georg Klein, he represented New Forum at the "Berlin Round Table" convened in December, 1989, which included a broad collection of dissident- and citizen-groups as well as officials from the city government of East Berlin. See the note on "New Forum was founded" for chapter 5, page 176, above.

Page 155: *October 9 in Leipzig* . . . See the note on "the demonstrations in Leipzig" for chapter 6, page 179, above.

Page 155: *the demonstration of November 4* . . . See the note on "November 4, 1989" for chapter 4, page 174, above.

Page 156: *the opening of the Wall in November.* See the note on "November 9" for chapter 6, pages 179–80, above.

Page 156: *the party that . . . was elected in March of 1990.* The first democratic elections in the history of the GDR were held in March 1990. The East German Christian Democratic Union (CDU), which had by then forged a partnership with the West German CDU headed up by Chancellor Helmut Kohl, captured over forty percent of the vote and a substantial plurality of the seats in the new parliament. See the note on Kohl for chapter 8, page 184, above.

Page 156: *the old block parties.* See the note on "the block parties" for chapter 3, page 170, above.

Page 156: *the discussion over the name of the party — SDP or SPD* . . . The "discussion" here concerns whether the new acronym (SPD), which all sides agreed to adopt in order to remain distinct from the successor party to the SED, would stand for *Sozialdemokratische Partei in der DDR* (Social-Democratic Party in the GDR) or *Sozialdemokratische Partei Deutschlands* (Social-Democratic Party of Germany). The latter is the name of the West German SPD. See the note on "the founding articles of the SDP" for this chapter, pages 195–96, above.

WORKS CONSULTED & CITED

Adams, Henry. *The Education of Henry Adams*. Boston: Houghton Mifflin, 1961.

Allen, Bruce. *Germany East: Dissent and Opposition*. New York: Black Rose Books, 1989.

Burant, Stephen R. *East Germany: A Country Study*. Federal Research Division, Library of Congress, 1987.

Conradt, David P. *The German Polity*. 8th ed. White Plains, NY: Longman, 2004.

Craig, Gordon A. *Germany, 1866–1900*. New York: Oxford UP, 1978.

Dalton, Russell J. *Politics in Germany*, 2nd ed. New York: HarperCollins College, 1992.

Dennis, Mike. *German Democratic Republic: Politics, Economics and Society*. London: Printer, 1988.

———. *The Rise and Fall of the GDR, 1945–1990*. White Plains, NY: Longman, 2000.

Eley, Geoff. *From Unification to Nazism: Reinterpreting the German Past*. Boston: Allen & Unwin, 1986.

Emmerich, Wolfgang. *Kleine Literatur Geschichte der DDR*. 2nd ed. Berlin: Aufbau Taschenbuch Verlag, 2000.

Havel, Václav. "Paying Back the West." *New York Review of Books* 46, no. 14 (23 September 1999): 54.

Keylor, William R. *The Twentieth Century World: An International History*. 4th ed. New York: Oxford UP, 2001.

Krisch, Henry. *The German Democratic Republic: The Search for Identity*. Boulder, CO: Westview Press, 1985.

Lane, David. *Soviet Society under Perestroika*. 2nd ed. London: Routledge, 1991.

Maier, Charles S. *Dissolution: The Crisis of Communism and the End of East Germany*. Princeton, NJ: Princeton UP, 1997.

Milosz, Czeslaw. "The Telltale Scar." Quoted in Thomas L. Pangle, *The Ennobling of Democracy: The Challenge of the Postmodern Age*, 87. Baltimore: Johns Hopkins UP, 1992.

Pollack, Detlef. "Wie ist es um die innere Einheit Deutschlands bestellt?" *Aus Politik und Zeitgeschichte* 30–31 (24 July 2006): 4–7.

Toland, John. *Adolf Hitler*. Garden City, NY: Doubleday, 1976.

Weber, Jürgen. *Germany, 1945–1990: A Parallel History*. Central European UP, 2004.

Wehler, Hans-Ulrich. *The German Empire, 1871–1918*. Dover, NH: Berg, 1985.

Wolf, Birgit. *Sprache in der DDR: Ein Wörterbuch*. Berlin: Walter de Gruyter, 2000.

Zimmerman, Hartmund, Horst Ulrich, and Michael Fehlauer. *DDR Handbuch*. Cologne: Verlag Wissenschaft und Politik, 1985.

INDEX

border guard(s), 79, 80, 81; and
    agitators, 80; and marriage problems,
    80. *See also* order to shoot
Bornholmer Strasse, 33
Boston Globe, The, xxiv
Boxhagener Strasse, 113
Brandenburg, 117, 178, 189
Brandenburger Strasse, 107
brown comrades (browns), 107
brownshirt(s), 92. *See also* Hitler;
    Sturmabteilung
Budapest, xvii, 170
Bulgaria, 134
Bundesliga. See soccer
Bundestag, 186
Burant, Stephen R., 199
Burger-Strasse, 101–2, 104, 184

capitalism, viii, 30, 47, 52, 59, 115,
    141; imperialist powers of, xii;
    Kurfürstendamm as prop for, 163
capitalist(s), 54
Carnival (*Fasching*), 10, 163
CDU (Christian Democratic Union),
    xxi, 34, 106, 126, 184, 186, 190; as
    "block party," 176; East German
    version of, 170; history of, 171;
    victory in 1990 elections, 198
Central Committee (*Zentralkomitee* or
    ZK), 134, 192. *See also* SED
Cerberus, 88, 181–82
changeover, xxi, xxv, 28, 45, 54, 74,
    83, 91, 99, 105–6, 109, 111, 114,
    124–26, 128, 131, 138, 147, 155,
    158, 173, 178, 194; explanation of,
    168. *See also* Wende
Checkpoint Charlie, 180
Chekists, 108, 187
Chernobyl, xv–xvi. *See also* Nachzeit
China, 33
Christian(s), 51, 114, 142, 145; non-,
    141
Christian Science Monitor, xxiv
church(es), 19, 91; and activism, 117;
    confirmation, 64; consistory, 32, 37;

Evangelical Church, 197; and grass-
    roots groups, 148; high school(s) 60;
    Landeskirche as administrative unit
    of, 197; local church council, 35;
    Lutheran, 153; and mass rallies, 66;
    and New Forum, 66; regional
    organization, 151; and relation to
    state in the GDR, 149, 151; repair
    of, 147; and SDP, 155; and Second
    World War, 58; and services of
    intercession, 32; and socialization,
    65; and Stasi, 51, 149; taxes, 42;
    West German, 155
Church, Catholic, 87–90; and intellec-
    tuals in Poland, 148; priest(s), 87, 90
Cistercian(s), 87–88
citizenship: as school subject, 97, 134,
    138
clocks, in TV news, 115, 188
Coca-Cola, 134
collaborator, 102. *See also* unofficial
    co-worker
collective farm(s), 35, 39, 122. *See also*
    agriculture
collective security. *See* Palme, Olof
Cologne, 108, 109, 116
combat group(s) (*Kampfgruppen*),
    xviii, 124, 179; origins of, 190
coming of age ceremony, 29. *See also*
    youth initiation
communism: East German experiment
    in, ix; Havel on, x; Polish resistance
    to, 175
communist(s), 54, 114, 118; and flag,
    42; German, viii
communist party, 48, 134. *See also* KPD
Conradt, David P., xxiii, 199
consistory. *See* church(es)
construction soldier (*Bausoldat*), 145;
    explanation of, 193; Klein as, xii–xiii
Craig, Gordon A., 199
Croat(s), 76, 133
Cultural Revolution (in China), 188
Custodial State, The, 66, 91, 182. *See
    also* Henrich, Rolf

Suddenly Everything ˙˙˙ ˙˙˙ ˙˙˙

Studies in German Literature, Linguistics, and Culture